Berlioz

Eastman Studies in Music

Ralph P. Locke, Senior Editor
Eastman School of Music

Additional Titles on Nineteenth-Century European Music

*Analyzing Wagner's Operas: Alfred Lorenz
and German Nationalist Ideology*
Stephen McClatchie

*The Musical Madhouse
(Les Grotesques de la musique)*
Hector Berlioz
Translated and edited by
Alastair Bruce
Introduction by Hugh Macdonald

Berlioz: Past, Present, Future
Edited by Peter Bloom

Berlioz's Semi-Operas: Roméo et Juliette
and La damnation de Faust
Daniel Albright

*Musicking Shakespeare: A Conflict of
Theatres*
Daniel Albright

*European Music and Musicians in New
York City, 1840–1900*
Edited by John Graziano

*Pentatonicism from the Eighteenth
Century to Debussy*
Jeremy Day-O'Connell

*French Organ Music from the Revolution
to Franck and Widor*
Edited by Lawrence Archbold
and William J. Peterson

*Schubert in the European Imagination,
Volume 1: The Romantic and Victorian Eras
Volume 2: Fin-de-Siècle Vienna*
Scott Messing

*Historical Musicology: Sources, Methods,
Interpretations*
Edited by Stephen A. Crist and
Roberta Montemorra Marvin

*Schumann's Piano Cycles and the Novels
of Jean Paul*
Erika Reiman

*Mendelssohn, Goethe, and the Walpurgis
Night: The Heathen Muse in European
Culture, 1700–1850*
John Michael Cooper

*The Substance of Things Heard: Writings
about Music*
Paul Griffiths

*Wagner and Wagnerism in Nineteenth-
Century Sweden, Finland, and the Baltic
Provinces: Reception, Enthusiasm, Cult*
Hannu Salmi

*Musical Encounters at the 1889
Paris World's Fair*
Annegret Fauser

A complete list of titles in the Eastman Studies in Music Series,
in order of publication, may be found at the end of this book.

Berlioz

Scenes from the Life and Work

EDITED BY PETER BLOOM

UNIVERSITY OF ROCHESTER PRESS

First published 2008

University of Rochester Press
668 Mt. Hope Avenue, Rochester, NY 14620, USA
www.urpress.com
and Boydell & Brewer Limited
PO Box 9, Woodbridge, Suffolk IP12 3DF, UK
www.boydellandbrewer.com

ISBN-13: 978-1-58046-209-9
ISBN-10: 1-58046-209-X

ISSN: 1071-9989

Library of Congress Cataloging-in-Publication Data

Berlioz : scenes from the life and work / edited by Peter Bloom.
        p. cm. — (Eastman studies in music, ISSN 1071-9989 ; v. 52)
    Includes bibliographical references and index.
    ISBN-13: 978-1-58046-209-9 (hardcover : alk. paper)
    ISBN-10: 1-58046-209-X
    1.   Berlioz, Hector, 1803–1869—Criticism and interpretation.   I.
Bloom, Peter.
    ML410.B5B358 2008
    780.92—dc22
    [B]

                                                          2007030946

A catalogue record for this title is available from the British Library.

This publication is printed on acid-free paper.
Printed in the United States of America.

Contents

Acknowledgments

More intense than the relief one feels on completing an enterprise of this sort is the satisfaction of acknowledging assistance. To Ralph Locke, Rochester's endlessly enthusiastic man in music, I say a thousand thanks. To my old friend Dennis Alter, presiding genius of Advanta Corporation, who has for years made grants to Smith College in support of my research, I cannot express (but hope he knows) how much I value his friendship and generosity. To Valérie Riou, associate director of Smith College in Paris, *encore merci* for holding the fort while I began to edit these papers. To my wife Catherine and children Alexandra and Caroline, thanks and *grosses bises* for patience (sort of) and understanding (sometimes) while I was with Berlioz instead of where you thought I ought to be.

For special kindnesses I am grateful to my friends Joël-Marie Fauquet, Richard Macnutt, Catherine Massip, and Cécile Reynaud; I am grateful to the brilliant outside reviewer whom Rochester had the wisdom to engage to read a first version of this text; and I am grateful to those pillars of Berlioz scholarship who are David Cairns, Katherine Kolb, and Hugh Macdonald.

My efforts have profited from many teachers, *cela va sans dire*, but here I should like to mention two in particular: John de Lancie, with whom it was my pleasure to study the oboe at the Curtis Institute of Music over forty years ago, and from whom I learned the meaning of excellence; and Jacques Barzun, with whom it has been my pleasure to correspond about Berlioz and more for almost forty years, and to whom, were it not inappropriate for the editor of a collection of essays by various hands to do so, I would gladly dedicate this book.

—P. B., fall 2007

Note to the Reader

The original texts of passages in French are included here only when they are necessary for proper comprehension or when they are not readily available in such sources as Berlioz's *Mémoires, Correspondance générale* (*CG*), and *Critique musicale* (*CM*). References to the *Mémoires* are often by chapter only, since editions vary. References to Berlioz's *feuilletons* are usually by date of publication; all *feuilletons* through 1848 may be readily found in *CM* (see the following list of abbreviations).

Pitch Notation

Abbreviations

Works of Berlioz

CG   Hector Berlioz, *Correspondance générale*
     Pierre Citron, general editor (Paris: Flammarion, 1972–2003)
CG   I   1803–1832, ed. Pierre Citron (1972)
     II   1832–1842, ed. Frédéric Robert (1975)
     III   1842–1850, ed. Pierre Citron (1978)
     IV   1851–1855, ed. Pierre Citron, Yves Gérard, and Hugh Macdonald
           (1983)
     V   1855–1859, ed. Hugh Macdonald and François Lesure (1988)
     VI   1859–1863, ed. Hugh Macdonald and François Lesure (1995)
     VII   1864–1869, ed. Hugh Macdonald (2001)
     VIII *Suppléments*, ed. Hugh Macdonald (2003)

CM   Hector Berlioz, *Critique musicale*
     (Paris: Buchet/Chastel, 1996– ; ten volumes are projected)
CM   1   1823–1834, ed. H. Robert Cohen and Yves Gérard (1996)
     2   1835–1836, ed. Yves Gérard and Marie-Hélène Coudroy-Saghaï (1998)
     3   1837–1838, ed. Yves Gérard, Marie-Hélène Coudroy-Saghaï, and Anne
         Bongrain (2001)
     4   1839–1841, ed. Anne Bongrain and Marie-Hélène Coudroy-Saghaï (2003)
     5   1842–1844, ed. Anne Bongrain and Marie-Hélène Coudroy-Saghaï (2004)
     6   1845–1848, ed. Anne Bongrain and Marie-Hélène Coudroy-Saghaï (2007)

Mémoires
     Hector Berlioz, *Mémoires*, ed. Pierre Citron (Paris: Flammarion, 1991)

Memoirs
     The Memoirs of Hector Berlioz, trans. and ed. David Cairns
     (London: Victor Gollancz Ltd., 1969; and many later editions including
     the Knopf *Everyman's Library* edition of 2002, to which page references
     here are keyed)

Les Soirées de l'orchestre (1968)
Les Grotesques de la musique (1969)
À travers chants (1971)
    Hector Berlioz, *Œuvres littéraires, Édition du centenaire*
    ed. Léon Guichard (Paris: Gründ, 1968–1971)

NBE   [*New Berlioz Edition*] Hector Berlioz, *New Edition of the Complete Works*
      Hugh Macdonald, general editor (Kassel: Bärenreiter, 1967–2006)
NBE 1a–d *Benvenuto Cellini*, ed. Hugh Macdonald (1994–2005)
     2a–c *Les Troyens*, ed. Hugh Macdonald (1969–1970)
     3 *Béatrice et Bénédict*, ed. Hugh Macdonald (1980)
     4 *Incomplete Operas*, ed. Ric Graebner and Paul Banks (2005)
     5 *Huit Scènes de Faust*, ed. Julian Rushton (1970)
     6 *Prix de Rome Works*, ed. David Gilbert (1998)
     7 *Lélio ou Le Retour à la vie*, ed. Peter Bloom (1992)
     8a–b *La Damnation de Faust*, ed. Julian Rushton (1979–1986)
     9 *Grande Messe des morts*, ed. Jürgen Kindermann (1978)
     10 *Te Deum*, ed. Denis McCaldin (1973)
     11 *L'Enfance du Christ*, ed. David Lloyd-Jones (1998)
     12a *Choral Works with Orchestra (I)*, ed. Julian Rushton (1991)
     12b *Choral Works with Orchestra (II)*, ed. David Charlton (1993)
     13 *Songs for Solo Voice and Orchestra*, ed. Ian Kemp (1975)
     14 *Choral Works with Keyboard*, ed. Ian Rumbold (1996)
     15 *Songs for One, Two, or Three Voices and Keyboard*,
        ed. Ian Rumbold (2005)
     16 *Symphonie fantastique*, ed. Nicholas Temperley (1972)
     17 *Harold en Italie*, ed. Paul Banks and Hugh Macdonald (2002)
     18 *Roméo et Juliette*, ed. D. Kern Holoman (1990)
     19 *Symphonie funèbre et triomphale*, ed. Hugh Macdonald (1967)
     20 *Overtures*, ed. Diana Bickley (2000)
     21 *Miscellaneous Works and Index*, ed. Hugh Macdonald (2005)
     22a *Arrangements of Works by Other Composers (I)*,
        ed. Joël-Marie Fauquet (2005)
     22b *Arrangements of Works by Other Composers (II)*,
        ed. Ian Rumbold (2005)
     23 *Messe solennelle*, ed. Hugh Macdonald (1994)
     24 *Grand Traité d'instrumentation et d'orchestration modernes*,
        ed. Peter Bloom (2003)
     25 D. Kern Holoman, *Catalogue of the Works of Hector Berlioz* (1987)
     26 *The Portraits of Hector Berlioz*, ed. Gunther Braam (2003)

Secondary Source

Cairns 1   David Cairns, *Berlioz* [volume 1], *The Making of an Artist 1803–1832*
(London: The Penguin Press, 1999)

Cairns 2   David Cairns, *Berlioz* [volume 2], *Servitude and Greatness 1832–1869*
(London: The Penguin Press, 1999)

Introduction

Berlioz in the Aftermath of the Bicentenary

PETER BLOOM

*Évidemment l'absurde est le vrai, car si l'absurde n'était pas le vrai, Dieu serait
cruel d'avoir mis dans le cœur de l'homme un si grand amour de l'absurde.*
—Hector Berlioz (8 June 1855)

Despite the excellent intentions of the President of the French Republic,
Berlioz's remains were not removed to the Panthéon, and despite the composer's own excoriation of the genre, the *Festival Berlioz* at La Côte-Saint-André
continued to play *arrangements*, but as Berlioz's two-hundredth birthday is succeeded by others less round in number, we continue to savor many fine performances and much good work. The international players arrogated excessive
importance neither to themselves nor to their theme: the sort of fetishizing and
retrofitting and theologizing of genius not long ago castigated in the lead article of a leading musicological journal nowhere sullied the waters.[1] Berlioz weath-
ered the storm: he remains a contender, one of the B's, one of the best.

Looking Back

Anniversaries have always encouraged performance, and this one did, too, all
around the globe. This is not the place to rehearse such worldly delights, but let
it be noted that *even in France* Berlioz's music was played, played frequently, and
played well. The Orchestre de Paris, to whose ancestor, the Société des Concerts
du Conservatoire, Berlioz gave his personal scores and parts, completed a
Berlioz cycle in 2003 that over several seasons offered almost everything we
have, including what remains of *Les Francs-Juges*, concert performances of
Benvenuto Cellini, and a *Marche pour la présentation des drapeaux* with twelve harps.
The cycle was instigated by George-François Hirsch, directeur-général of the
orchestra and *berliozien par excellence*. The same man presided over a *Comité international Hector Berlioz*, of which more below.

Another Parisian *Cellini* (now available on a Virgin Classics CD) was concerted by the Orchestre national de France and the Chœur de Radio France under the direction of John Nelson. And a spectacular Parisian *Les Troyens* (now released on a BBC Opus Arte DVD) was staged at the Théâtre du Châtelet by the Orchestre révolutionnaire et romantique under the inspired leadership of John Eliot Gardiner. Much further professional music making dotted the anniversary landscape, and so, too, did noble efforts by students from near and far. A Berlioz festival at l'Université de Paris IV (which we know as the Sorbonne) included conscientious renderings of a number of major and minor works; and on the stage at the old Conservatoire, where Berlioz first gave the *Fantastique*, D. Kern Holoman led his troops from the University of California at Davis in a program that ranged from the *Marseillaise* to the *Marche marocaine*.

Anniversaries have always encouraged scholarship, and this one was no exception. *Primae inter pares* stand two publications envisioned not long before the centenary of Berlioz's death, in 1969, and essentially brought to conclusion, *mirabile dictu*, in the year of the bicentenary of his birth: I speak of the *Correspondance générale d'Hector Berlioz*, under the general editorship of Pierre Citron, and the *New Berlioz Edition*, under the general editorship of Hugh Macdonald. Upon these mighty foundations, future Berlioz scholarship may rest assured.

The Comité international Hector Berlioz—a group of scholars, writers, artistic administrators, *Kenner*, and *Liebhaber*, who met approximately twice each year between 1997 and 2003, enjoying the superb hospitality of the Orchestre de Paris and the Bibliothèque nationale de France—initiated five international conferences. These were sponsored by Smith College, in Northampton, Massachusetts, in 2000; by the Universität Bayreuth, in 2001; by Royal Holloway and the Royal Academy of Music, in London, in 2002; by the Association nationale Hector Berlioz (and other cultural organizations), in Grenoble and La Côte-Saint-André, in 2003; and by the Bibliothèque nationale de France, in Paris, again in 2003. The papers of these conferences have been published or are in press.[2]

It was in discussions of the Comité Berlioz that the idea of a *Dictionnaire Berlioz* was nurtured and eventually brought to fruition by four members of the group.[3] The committee as a whole stirred excitement such that countless periodicals issued special Berlioz numbers, of which two deserve mention here because of their wide circulation in France: *Télérama* put out a number *hors série* of particular distinction; and *TDC* (*Textes et documents pour la classe*) introduced Berlioz to schoolchildren throughout the country.[4]

If I concentrate here on French festivities it is because many of us born elsewhere have long found it amusing to quote Gospel regarding our fellow's reception in France: "There is no prophet without honor except in his own country, and among his own relatives, and in his own house." This device, I believe, will no longer do. Jacques Barzun's exhortation—that Berlioz be viewed as a *normal* musician—has now, after well over half a century, been heard at home. One may marvel at his conspicuous uniqueness, one may have reservations about his irregular phraseology and systematic avoidance of stock phrases—"Oh! les formules! les formules! formules de chant, formules de composition, formules de mise en scène! chenilles qui dévorent la verdure de l'arbre de l'art et le feront périr si on ne parvient à les détruire!"—without assigning him to a category different from that of *musicien* or *artiste*.[5]

Knowledge of Berlioz was diffused in France by a number of exhibitions, traveling and stationary, of which the most ambitious—"Berlioz, la voix du romantisme"—was created at the Site François-Mitterrand of the Bibliothèque nationale de France. To thrilling effect, Berlioz's life and work were here generously put on display: paintings, photographs, books, scores, instruments, caricatures, newspapers, letters, account books, interviews, recordings, and more, gave voice to the great musician of the French nineteenth century.[6]

An earlier traveling exhibition, realized by Catherine Massip and Cécile Reynaud, under the auspices of the Ministère des Affaires étrangères and the Association pour la diffusion de la pensée française, revealed aspects of the life and work via some two dozen large and handsomely printed panels, of which several thousand copies were sent to various French cultural centers at home and abroad. The exhibition was associated with a small book, *Berlioz écrivain*, that includes a CD with excerpts from exceptional Berlioz recordings made by, among others, Pierre Monteux, Erich Kleiber, Serge Koussevitzky, and Charles Munch.[7]

A fine exhibition of letters and documents still preserved in the collections of the Conservatoire national supérieur de musique et de danse de Paris, the modern incarnation of Berlioz's old school, led to the production of a highly useful catalogue, *Berlioz 2003*, with valuable illustrations and bright essays by members of the administrative staff at the Conservatoire.[8] I might add that a series of lecture-concerts took place while the exhibition was on at the Conservatoire, with performances at the level one would expect at that highly competitive institution, and excerpts from Berlioz's letters that became poetry in the exquisitely nuanced recitations by the French actor Didier Sandre.

There were handsome exhibitions elsewhere as well, including at the Bibliothèque municipale de Grenoble, which put on display some of the items from its particularly rich Berlioz collections, and at the Bibliothèque-Musée de l'Opéra, in Paris, where, in the "margins" of the grand exhibition at the Site François-Mitterrand, "Hector Berlioz et l'opéra en feuilleton," nicely conceived by Pierre Vidal, excerpts from Berlioz's writings on opera were set out next to the librettos, scores, *maquettes de décor*, and *maquettes de costumes* of the works he reviewed. Brilliantly on display were portraits and engravings and lithographs of the composers, singers, dancers, and administrators whom Berlioz knew and variously admired and reviled.

The library at the Opéra is under the supervision of the Département de la Musique of the Bibliothèque nationale de France, a repository of late immeasurably enriched by the purchase of the finest private Berlioz collection ever assembled: that of Richard Macnutt. If Berlioz could praise the King of Saxony for offering to the young Richard Wagner a post with lifetime security, then perhaps I may be permitted to praise the powers that be at the Bibliothèque nationale de France for having the wisdom and foresight to purchase what will be known forever as the *Collection Macnutt.*

Scenes from the Life and Work

The twelve papers included here, evidence that the anniversary was not an adieu, are set out in six "pairs": the headings attempt to suggest the themes common to each twosome, but in fact the subjects we treat range widely and inevitably overlap.

Gracing the opening section of the book on "Aesthetics Issues" is a piece that the author completed on his ninety-eighth birthday. Jacques Barzun uses the case of Berlioz to lay open the eternal question of the nature of musical *expression* and of how it can be expressed in words. Barzun casts off the *justizzers* (citing Leonard Bernstein's "music *just is*"), brushes away the storytellers and imagists, and articulates a critique of the way we speak of our art. Frank Heidlberger, interrogating the *Te Deum* and *L'Enfance du Christ*—the one conceived before the public and private crises of the revolution of 1848 and the death in that year of the composer's father, the other compiled in the years immediately afterwards—then studies the manifold ways in which Berlioz fuses musical forms and traditions with personal reminiscences and attitudes to create these works of "artistic" or "aesthetic" religiosity.

"In Fiction and Fact" opens with Joël-Marie Fauquet's meditation on the role that utopian thinking played in Berlioz's creative imagination. After revealing startlingly that some of the original aspects of the tale *Euphonia* may not have been original at all, Fauquet, in a reading as troubling as it is lucid, goes on to show the darker side of the utopian vision that Berlioz proposes in his novella of 1844. Julian Rushton, focusing not on the "brilliant and beautiful but unworthy singer" of *Euphonia*[9] but rather upon the real singers with whom the composer actually worked, then closely studies Berlioz's particular deployment of the mezzo-soprano voice. Using a tool that gives precision to something we have heretofore been able only to feel, Rushton shows what Marguerite, Marie, Béatrice, Cassandre, and Didon have in common, and what they have that is unique.

Treating a subject with which all Berliozians have wrestled, Gérard Condé, under the rubric of "Criticizing and Criticized," comes up with some surprises as he considers the relationships between Berlioz's composing of notes and writing of words, claiming among other things that far from being a *fatalité*, as the artist alleged and as we have accepted, his career in criticism in fact *freed* him from having to compose to live. Gunter Braam, who has catalogued early Berlioz reception in Germany, then tells us how German journalists went about finding information about the French object of their critiques. In so doing he brings to light the conversation of some of the moguls of the international musical press and among other things reveals in a way we have not fully appreciated Robert Schumann's behind-the-scenes devotion to Berlioz.

In the first of two articles on the "Dramatic Symphony," Hugh Macdonald, observing a curious hiatus in what we know of the composer's creative output in the winter of 1827–1828, claims that immediately after seeing Shakespeare's play and Harriet Smithson at the Odéon on 15 September 1827, Berlioz might have written four musical "scenes" for *Romeo and Juliet*. From this display of well-informed speculation, we learn what they were like and what they became. Jean-Pierre Bartoli, whose theoretical writings on Berlioz have thankfully never portrayed Berlioz as an abnormal composer, then tackles the difficult-to-analyze love scene of *Roméo et Juliette* and finds a model for its architecture in the slow movement of Beethoven's Ninth Symphony.

On the basis of uncelebrated local newspaper accounts, Pepijn van Doesburg very closely traces the composer's first steps in the country that he and his generation took to be the Land of Music, and provides a model that others might use to trace Berlioz's subsequent steps "In Foreign Lands." Lord Aberdare (Alastair Bruce) then offers a newly detailed résumé of the composer's visits to London, which might have become Berlioz's second home, and includes the heretofore unpublished text of Berlioz's proposal for a grand Festival in the hall of the Great Exhibition that would feature the first performance of the *Te Deum*.

In my contribution to "An Artist's Life," I offer some neglected facts about the publication of the *Mémoires* and some thoughts on what variants can reveal of the *mentalité* of the author of that sometimes problematical book. David Cairns then offers a graceful look back at Berlioz's biography and autobiography, incorporating revealing autobiographical reflections of his own. If our perspectives differ, it is because such difference was and is an organizing principle of the collection as a whole. As the volume developed, its "pairs" became more complementary than contrasting. But the overarching purpose remained: the bringing together of the writings of a dozen scholars all of whom have been thinking about scenes from Berlioz's life and work for a good long time. May that purpose—neither theoretical nor political but critical and informational—be deemed sufficient.

Looking Ahead

If you follow Berlioz scholarship and reread D. Kern Holoman's 1975 essay, "The Present State of Berlioz Research," you will feel that we have come a long way.[10] The completion of Holoman's own *Catalogue of the Works of Berlioz* was twelve years in the future (who will prepare a now-needed second edition?), the conclusion of David Cairns's monumental two-volume biography was twenty-four years away. Those summas, and so much else, render it all but impossible, and perhaps unnecessary, even to attempt to describe the present state of the field. It is wide-ranging, it is fertile, it is healthy.

Apart from turning up new facts—I'll drop a little one into a note[11]—we may continue to ask the old question: What remains to be done? This brief tour began with the Panthéon. Readers of the twenty-first "evening" of *Les Soirées de l'orchestre* will remember that Berlioz—still under the spell of St. Paul's Cathedral, in London, where he heard the annual performance given by the Charity Children, six thousand five hundred strong—renewed his aspirations to create in Paris his own *musique monumentale.* "We have no St. Paul's, true; but we have the Panthéon, which affords, if not the size, at least a similar internal structure. The number of performers and listeners would be less colossal; but the edifice being also less vast, the effect might still be most unusual."[12] If Berlioz's remains cannot be translated to that grand edifice, perhaps his music can be played there from time to time, as in fact he had hoped as early as 1840 when contemplating a festival concert in the rotonda's resonant space.[13] One of the small ironies regarding the *non-panthéonisation* of Berlioz in 2003 is that during the event which apparently caused President Chirac to cancel our party— namely, the perfectly silly *panthéonisation* of Alexandre Dumas in 2002—we heard from under the dome of that deconsecrated church the famous *Tuba mirum* of a *Requiem* by Somebody we know and admire.

Berlioz's music may be too "intelligent" to achieve broad popularity, as he himself suggested.[14] But playing it regularly and well will win for him appreciation and understanding, and will prevent the critics—who of course are under no obligation to flatter the fellow or to mute what they may see as his miscalculations—from uttering the old inanities about his "faulty technique." That myth, as I have suggested above, is exploded forever. By playing Berlioz *well* I mean nothing different from playing Beethoven well, or Boulez, or Buxtehude: sounding the notes as though life itself depended on each and every one.

Reading Berlioz will always provide edification and amusement. If the future of books and articles is on the screen, as the habits of the young would suggest, let us see to it that Berlioz's are available there, too. The books are on hand— see hberlioz.com, faithfully nourished and renewed in English and French by the indefatigable Monir Tayeb and Michel Austin—but why not also the letters and the *feuilletons* and a *Holoman 2*?

Writing of the bisesquicentennial of *Mozart,* a thoughtful journalist finds that that composer "matches with uncanny precision the temper of our troubled times: our emotional uncertainty, our ability to perceive serenity fleetingly but never to attain it."[15] The very sincerity of such a pronouncement, with which one might well agree, runs the risk of ridicule—as might have come from the acid-tipped and paradox-loving pen of a Berlioz (see the epigraph above), or of a Heinrich Heine. Indeed, the qualities that Berlioz attributed to the German poet—incisiveness, humor, gravity, derisiveness, intelligence, determination, imagination—are precisely those that make Berlioz live on. "He suffered cruelly at the hands of his enemies," Berlioz wrote of Heine, in words that he might have liked to apply to himself, "but he burned them alive, one after another, in the dazzling fires of his irony."[16]

Notes

1. Paula Higgins, "The Apotheosis of Josquin des Prez and Other Mythologies of Musical Genius," *Journal of the American Musicological Society*, 57 (2005), pp. 443–510.

2. *Berlioz Past, Present, Future*, ed. Peter Bloom (Rochester, NY: University of Rochester Press, 2003); *Berlioz, Wagner und die Deutschen*, ed. Sighart Döhrung, Arnold Jacobshagen, and Gunther Braam (Cologne: Verlag Dohr, 2003); *The Musical Voyager: Berlioz in Europe*, ed. David Charlton and Katharine Ellis (Bern: Peter Lang Verlag, 2007); *Hector Berlioz: Regards sur un Dauphinois fantastique*, ed. Alban Ramaut (Saint-Étienne: Publications de l'Université de Saint-Étienne, 2006); *Berlioz: Textes et Contextes*, ed. Joël-Marie Fauquet, Catherine Massip, and Cécile Reynaud (Paris: CNRS Éditions, forthcoming).

3. *Dictionnaire Berlioz*, ed. Pierre Citron, Cécile Reynaud, Jean-Pierre Bartoli, and Peter Bloom (Paris: Fayard, 2003).

4. *Télérama Hors Série, Berlioz: L'homme-orchestre* (October 2003), with a delightful essay, "Itinéraire d'un héraut romantique," by the director of the issue, Gilles Macassar, and further contributions by Gérard Condé, Cécile Reynaud, Jean-Philippe Chimot, and Rémy Stricker (whose fine book, *Berlioz dramaturge*, also appeared from Gallimard in 2003). *TDC*, a bimonthly publication sponsored by the Bibliothèque nationale de France and the Centre national de documentation péda-gogique; the special issue of 1 February 2003 was coordinated by Cécile Reynaud.

5. "Conspicuous uniqueness" is Jacques Barzun's phrase. The quotation is found in Berlioz's article for the *Journal des débats* of 7 July 1846: "Oh, formulas, formulas! vocal formulas, compositional formulas, production formulas!—so many caterpillars that, when we fail to kill them, devour the verdure of the tree of art and put it death." I take this from *CM* 6, another foundational work of Berlioz studies still in progress. See the list of Abbreviations.

6. *Berlioz, la voix du romantisme*, the exhibit directed and the catalogue (with arti-cles by leading Berlioz scholars) edited by Catherine Massip and Cécile Reynaud (Paris: Bibiothèque nationale de France/Fayard, 2003).

7. *Berlioz écrivain*, with essays by Béatrice Didier, Cécile Reynaud, Peter Bloom, Rémy Stricker, and Gérard Condé (Paris: Ministère des Affaires étrangères/ADPF, 2001).

8. *Berlioz 2003*, ed. Anne Bongrain (Paris: Centre de recherche et d'édition du Conservatoire, 2003), with essays by Alain Poirier, Jean-Clair Vançon, Anne Bongrain, Dominique Hausfater, Marie-Hélène Coudroy-Saghaï, Bérangère de l'Épine, and Guillaume Bordry.

9. See Katherine Kolb, "The Short Stories," in *The Cambridge Companion to Berlioz*, ed. Peter Bloom (Cambridge: Cambridge University Press, 2000), p. 151.

10. D. Kern Holoman, "The Present State of Berlioz Research," *Acta Musicologica*, 47 (1975), pp. 31–67.

11. Berlioz possessed a score of Beethoven's Ninth Symphony that was offered to him, with a dedication, by Charles Gounod. In it, Berlioz made a number of

annotations: "Ange! Archange! Sublime! We are not on earth! [*sic*, in English]." Paul Claudel saw this score at the home of Édouard Herriot and wrote about it to Romain Rolland on 20 October 1941, adding that the annotations which he and Rolland had seen on Berlioz's copy of Wagner's *Tristan* "sont bien différentes!" See *Claudel/Rolland, une amitié perdue et retrouvée*, ed. Gérold Antoine and Bernard Duchatelet (Paris: Gallimard, 2005), p. 177. A copy of Beethoven's Ninth Symphony (Schott, 1826) purportedly annotated by Berlioz appears in the Gros-Delettrez Catalogue of December 2005, but this is a forgery. (The score of *Tristan* that Wagner generously offered to Berlioz, with penciled-in signs of Berlioz's disapproval, is found in the collections of the Département de la Musique of the Bibliothèque nationale de France: Rés. Vm^3 5.) Gérard Condé kindly informs me that Gounod heard an unforgettable performance of Beethoven's Ninth Symphony in Vienna, conducted by Otto Nicolai, in March 1843. He may well have purchased a copy of the full score at that time and offered it to Berlioz on some appropriate future occasion. The current location of the score is unknown.

12. *Les Soirées de l'orchestre*, p. 300. I have slightly modified the translation in Berlioz, *Evenings with the Orchestra*, ed. and trans. Jacques Barzun (Chicago: University of Chicago Press, 1992), p. 234.

13. *CG* II, p. 637.

14. "Les œuvres où *l'intelligence joue le rôle principal* sont encore, sauf de rares exceptions, celles qui sont le moins goûtées et le plus lentement appréciées" (*Journal des débats*, 5 December 1848). "Works in which *intelligence plays the principal role* are still, with rare exception, those that are the least appreciated and the slowest to be understood."

15. Nicholas Kenyon, in the *New York Times* (24 July 2005), p. AR 24.

16. "Heine a souffert de cruelles atteintes de ses ennemis, mais [il] les a successivement brûlés vifs au feu pétillant de son ironie" (*Journal des débats*, 5 January 1847).

Part One

Aesthetic Issues

Chapter One

The Music in the Music of Berlioz

JACQUES BARZUN

Music is an awful thing. What is it? Why does it do what it does?
—Tolstoy, *The Kreutzer Sonata*

Berlioz is the perfect subject for the ultimate purpose of this essay. That purpose is to ascertain the essence of music as an art and the proper way to discuss it. That there should be at this late date a need to find this out is implied in the phrasing of my title. The search for it requires that a number of prevailing ideas about music be examined and compared with those taken for granted about the other arts.

As a first example, take the recent history of Berlioz's fame. The celebration of the two hundredth anniversary in 2003 marked a turning point. He was restored to the place among the master musicians that he held in his lifetime.[1] The conferences and concerts, the publications and reviews of that year were based on half a century of studies by musicologists, conductors, and critics. A good many listeners had been prepared during that same span by excellent recordings of nearly all the works, notably the series conducted by Sir Colin Davis. A comprehensive summary of facts and interpretations in the bulky *Dictionnaire Berlioz* enshrined the achievement and showed—wonder of wonders—that at last a group of French musicians and scholars had contributed to the evidence for revision.[2] By a happy coincidence, the near-final volume of the *New Berlioz Edition*, also an international collaboration, appeared in that same year.

The point of this resume is this: What put Berlioz in his due place was the proof that his handling of melody, harmony, counterpoint, rhythm, and instrumentation was original and coherent. The myth of the ill-trained bungler with wild ideas and haphazard strokes of genius was no longer tenable. And a closer reading of his life as conductor and critic added support to the conclusion that he possessed not only genius but cool and conscious mastery of his craft. In short: "Pupil Berlioz, you have done well."

The further conclusion is that the art of music consists in the quality of the musical technique. This is the common unspoken assumption. It underlies what musicologists, biographers, and scholarly critics think is the point of their task first and last.[3]

When one doubts this identity as I do, one sees that it conceals not one but several unacceptable beliefs. By ignoring significance, it puts the art of music in a class by itself, the other arts in another. None of these is considered a display of technique alone. For example, a classical ballet is not enjoyed merely as a succession of *pliés*, *battements*, and *pas de deux*, no matter how exquisitely done. In poetry it is not grammar and rhyme scheme that determine merit; in architecture, depth of foundation and the quality of the roofing material rarely enter into the critic's judgment of a magnificent edifice. Technique is taken for granted unless deserving censure as faulty or misused. In all the arts, the attention and interest of beholder and critic alike center on the meaning expressed by the technical means, the art as against the artistry.

But one must add that some musicians and critics vehemently deny the notion of meaning in music. Indeed they carry on a campaign against it. Listen to Leonard Bernstein in one of his talks to the audience at one of his admirable Young People's Concerts: "No matter how many times people tell you stories about what music means, forget them. Stories are not what the music means at all. Music is never about anything. Music just is." And by way of reinforcement he adds that the *William Tell* Overture is only "about notes—As and Cs and even E-flats and F-sharps."[4]

In such debunking, the word "stories" is a red herring. Nobody but the tone-deaf ever believed that a piece of music could tell a story. But that denial leaves much room for meaning. The question is: Is there something in the overture that one enjoys other than the arrangement of E-flats and F-sharps but arising from it? If so, can it be sensibly talked about? When discussion is limited to analyzing that arrangement, all it shows is that Rossini knew how to compose.

If the answer is: "There is really nothing else to talk about," then music is again unique as an art in being unspeakable. Yet there is one group professionally concerned with music who do not hesitate to describe music's effect instead of devices—the effect upon themselves of the work heard that evening and the quality of its performance, also judged by its effect. These writers, the newspaper reviewers, put their impressions in words as best they can, and the audience, before reading them the next day, also verbalize their own experience, in admiration or disparagement. I shall return to the reviewer's practice when I venture to offer guidelines for creating a vocabulary for music criticism.

Although the propagandists for keeping music pure or, as they like to say, absolute, think of reviewers and the chattering audience as philistines, the fact remains that since Beethoven's time composers themselves have attached words and ideas to their instrumental works. He himself showed the way by calling his third symphony "Eroica," and he added: "Composed to celebrate the memory of a great man"—this in Italian, still in 1804 the language of musical terminology.

At first the great man had been explicitly Napoleon Bonaparte, but he had been demoted when he made himself emperor. Whoever may now be put in his place, he is generally held to be hearing in the slow movement his funeral march.

Such a linking of music with life is what the partisans of "just is" disallow. In so doing they ignore the history of music. Its beginnings were altogether for life's uses. Starting as song and dance, it served prayer and religious ritual, processions for burial and civic celebrations. In battle, music gave signals for action and courage to the wavering, rallying them as needed. In the hunt, loud horn fanfares guided and cheered the pursuers of the prey.

On these occasions the music had meaning not by convention alone, but by its mood, rhythm, tempo, and appropriate instrument. Timbre is suggestive and those other aspects compelling: try to imagine troops marching in 3/4 time; recall the difference between *reveille* and *taps*. Something in music evidently corresponds to something felt in the living listener. So important did the ancient Greeks consider the right quality of their war music that every four years their Olympic games included a contest for trumpeters.

Since then in Western culture the development of the regular forms that composers have followed shows again that certain patterns and preferences in life's activities exert influence on the art of music; these forms have not emerged as if determined alone by the characteristics of sound. It is the human mind that in most things wants symmetry, balance, variation in continuity, and return with modification to the starting point. One or more of these preferences are embodied in ABA form, rondo, canon, passacaglia, and fugue. The suite goes fast-slow-fast because a start must be rousing and a close lively, with a contrast of quiet in between.

As for the elaborate sonata form, it is clearly an echo of oratory as it was practiced for centuries. The introduction is meant to detach the audience from its concerns and point to the subject of the occasion, which appears in the exposition of themes and other elements. These are pondered and developed; the argument is then recapitulated in different terms from its original statement. A conclusion or coda is ceremonial like the beginning, more dignified and courteous than the bare "thank you" of modern speakers.

All this, by the way, is made possible in music by first tampering with nature's pitch relations within the two scales chosen from among the modes. The purpose is to create one large realm of sound within which to move freely for an ever-varying expressiveness.

That word suggests another. What of the direct imitation in music of certain familiar sounds of life? Ostensibly, Beethoven attempted it in his Sixth Symphony, which he named "Pastoral" to prepare the listener's mind for its effects. The bird, the brook, the storm, and thunder are supposed to affect us— How? Are we to think of their counterparts, visualize them and marvel at the composer's skill as a nature painter? A good ear demurs. The notes of the bird's song may be accurately rendered, but their true liquid quality is not. The brook is even less convincing—too regular and even more remote from liquidity. The thunder seems the nearest approximation, though the underlying "grumble" is missing. Again, in the moot *William Tell* Overture some suppose that they hear the oarsmen rowing across the lake, part of the William Tell adventure. But granted that rhythm in music can match life's exactly, no musical use of it reveals its cause.[5] And Beethoven tersely denied the intention simply to copy: "mehr Ausdruck der Empfindung als Malerei"—the symphony was "expression rather than painting."

The art of music then—since technique is not its equivalent—resides in expressing—but What? Beethoven answers: Sentiment, or as is more usually said in English, Emotion. Berlioz stated more fully the conclusion that composers who can think all accept: "The author knows perfectly well that music can never replace speaking or drawing. He never entertained the absurd notion of trying to express *moral qualities* or *abstract ideas* but wishes rather to express energy and feeling."[6]

In his score of *Egmont*, Beethoven wrote next to a passage: "The entry of the trumpets indicates the victory of Liberty for the Fatherland," and at the head of the last movement of his last String Quartet, he wrote the mysterious "Muss es sein?" followed, over the Allegro, by "Es muss sein!" This has been interpreted as Necessity. These two connections seem possible but remote. What they confirm is Beethoven's faith in music's expressive power.

The inevitable association of music with feelings is emphatically demonstrated by a fact the purists ignore, no doubt because it is so familiar. Open a score at random and look at the expression marks: *andante, adagio, affetuoso, tremolo*; and again the terms for common devices—*appoggiatura, portamento, pizzicato*. All are based on alikeness to things felt or done in ordinary life. The case of *affetuoso* is telling in a curious way. It directs the performer to play tenderly, yet some composers have chosen to extend it to call for a tempo between *andante* and *adagio*.

It is no use arguing that music doesn't walk, tremble, or sound at ease, nor does a note in an *appoggiatura* lean against another. In Tom Wotton's scholarly *Dictionary of Foreign Musical Terms*, the hundreds of entries show the limitless variety of impressions that composers have wanted their work to make.[7] Phrases in English, German, and French relate the passage they affect to the feelings it is to arouse in the listener. Some indeed seem too subtle to execute: *narquois* (sly) or *Geschwind, doch nicht zu sehr, und mit Entschlossenheit* (fast, but not too much, and with decisiveness). Composers could not do without these directions to players, and the list would be still longer if the shouts of conductors during rehearsal were recorded. Later, in performance, they are translated into continued gestures paralleling the musical flow and inviting the listener as it were to go through a unique physical and emotional journey.

All the foregoing points are obvious once stated. But they have been obscured—indeed, blotted out—in the minds of critics, as in Mr. Bernstein's, by their familiarity. The purists thought they were bringing back music to its original condition—a product of nature complete in itself and without ties to anything else in the world. This vision attracts some musicians in part by seeming to get rid of a difficulty: how to decide what an expressive passage denotes. For is it not absurd to say that music *expresses* and stop there, never naming the thing expressed, as one expects after a transitive verb?

It may be answered that everybody finds a wedding march expressing happiness and joy, and a funeral march sadness and loss. No doubt, but is it not the repeated use of a piece on these occasions that makes everybody say so? Change the setting and the joyful music will express the pride and respect shown by the citizenry when Queen Elizabeth enters Oxford with her retinue; and the funeral march will suit the Retreat of the Ten Thousand slowed by the desert sands.

We are forced to conclude that the number of situations that music can, if not express in detail, still be *plausibly associated with*, is quite large. No better proof is needed than the composer's habit of transferring a piece written for one project to another, often one of very different bearing. Berlioz provides an example in his first symphony. Part of the third movement, entitled "Scène aux champs," comes from the second section of the Gloria of the Mass he wrote in 1824. Moussorgsky's masterly opera *Boris Godunov* is a patchwork of earlier fragments. When Liszt completed the symphonic poem we know as *Les Préludes* he took that name from a poem by Lamartine, because the original label, *Les Quatre Éléments*, a poem by Joseph Autran, like the poet, had become obscure. The subjects of the two poems are quite unlike, but Liszt thought his music fitting for either.

Despite all these limitations and confusions, the hearing of any piece impresses so many unique musical details on our mind that it seems to "mean" only one thing. The English critic Edmund Gurney solved the puzzle with finality when he condemned "the prosaic fallacy that the essence of music is vague namable expressiveness, instead of definite unnamable expressiveness."[8]

Recognizing this truth compels us to look within and find out precisely what music does to our senses besides that of hearing. I suggest the term *visceral response*. Like emotion it is an inner event but without a name, and its variations in character and intensity correspond to the rise and fall of expressiveness in the music. Why is it not an emotion—or sentiment, as Beethoven called it? Because it does not cause us real pain, horror, pleasure, anger, but their artistic equivalents. Besides, it is only at certain moments in the stream of sound and in certain works that we are tempted to give a name to that visceral effect. In Bach's Chaconne for unaccompanied violin, for instance, we get the clear sense of a highly dramatic recital, but feel no impulse to associate it with any drama, actual or imaginary.

Reflecting on this question of naming those visceral impressions leads to asking why the subject of musical meaning has become a matter of debate only since Beethoven's time. This is tantamount to asking why he began labeling as he did. The answer is: it was then that a radical change took place in instrumental music, hence in the way it was regarded. He was the prime contributor to that change. Earlier, music had been at once the special province of people trained to produce or enjoy it without deep reflection; and for everybody else, it was a source of casual entertainment. One is shocked to learn that much of Haydn's finest work was dinner music for his patron's family and guests at Esterházy.

True, in Haydn and in Mozart are outstanding elements of what was to transform the character and conception of music, making it "important" on a par with the other arts, an interpreter of life, a spiritual force, a subject of serious talk by the general public and of daily report in the news, and for composers a challenge to "creativity," meaning perpetual originality. The worship of art by the Romanticists, contemporary with Beethoven, encouraged this redefinition. And at the same time, machine industry contributed to the increased power of instruments. By the first quarter of the nineteenth century, the woodwinds had been made secure in intonation by keys, the brass by valves, and some extended in range by slides. The tuba replaced the ophicleide and "factors" such as Adolphe Sax designed new instruments. Performers could now be asked to play passages formerly risky or impossible, while timbre gained new prominence.

Finally, the regular distribution of strings, wood, and brass for balance in orchestras, some enlarged up to more than a hundred players, made it one instrument, akin to the organ for variety of effect.[9] This size made music go public, so to speak, since it needed a large hall and large revenues after its long residence in small groups in church and private houses. Goethe in old age gives us an idea of the previous attitude of cultivated people toward music. In a letter to the composer Carl Zelter, who was his music mentor, he confides his relish for string quartets: "You listen to four sensible persons conversing, you profit from their discourse, and you get to know the individual character of the instruments."[10] And in a collection of maxims, he declares: "The holiness of church music, the gaiety and lightness of popular music are the two things on which true music turns. If music is too complicated, it confuses the listener; if it is too weak, it is dull; and if it is applied to didactic or descriptive poems and such, it becomes cold."[11]

Other changes in music had social consequences. Each program offered to the general public at the concert hall comes on one or two days only,[12] unlike the opera, which in season plays six days a week and twice on Saturday—it is entertainment. Striving for "significance," the new music ruled out composing by the yard with ready-made formulas. Beethoven wrote nine symphonies and sixteen string quartets. Boccherini in the latter half of the eighteenth century turned out over thirty symphonies, more than one hundred string quartets, more than one hundred twenty-five quintets, and much else.

Beethoven's enriched instrumental music bewildered most listeners, especially when he and other composers began to modify sonata form and other patterns for the sake of expressiveness. E. T. A. Hoffmann called the new genre "opera without words," but even opera-goers were disoriented. Their musical pleasure came from the feats of virtuoso tenors and sopranos, seldom from how well the music of the aria expressed the meaning of the words. They cared so little that the regular devotees were said never to have seen the first act of any opera. It was fashionable to come only when the vocal fireworks were expected.

The eighteenth-century opera moreover had become a vehicle for two principal voices who addressed each other and their two subordinates and neglected stage action. The drama was conveyed by musical formulas called "the affections"—all features that concentrated interest on performance. In view of these limitations, the early nineteenth-century defenders of Beethoven had the novel idea of publishing commentaries on his and other works of the kind that Berlioz called *le genre instrumental expressif.* They pointed out its capacity for "cosmic significance" when handled by a "heaven-storming" mind such as Beethoven's, and for each symphony, these critics—Hoffmann, Moscheles, Schumann, and others—made up incidents, situations, stories to direct the listener's imagination. Thus the first four notes of Beethoven's Fifth Symphony might suggest "Fate knocking at the door."

Some of these images became clichés and are still quoted. Their authors did not take them literally, but the public did and thereby set off the unending debate about "program music." This phantom stands behind the Bernstein warning to the young and, earlier, it gave rise to the absurd notion that Berlioz and Liszt had invented a new genre under that name.

The hook on which this superstition hangs is the scenario that Berlioz wrote for the first performances of his first symphony, the *Fantastique,* in 1830. He had the skit distributed *in the program* as an aid to the listeners, just as the Germans were doing for Beethoven. From its occasional rehashing by reviewers nowadays, we learn that Berlioz imagined "five episodes in the life of an artist," to accompany the large-scale work. What each episode provides is not a description of each movement, but an occasion for it, thus directing the attention along one line as the surroundings of the leading theme express five different musical moods.

These "occasions" account for the presence of a waltz and a march and suggest the temper of the other three movements. For the patchwork sequel *Lélio,* Berlioz used another device—a speaker who introduces each piece. Knowing that music cannot tell a story, he did not pretend that his did. It is therefore a waste of time to inveigh against what cannot be done.

When the *Fantastique* was well known, by mid-century, Berlioz dropped the program, saying that the titles of the five movements sufficed, as indeed they did, for by that time the public had become used to orchestral works bearing a title. Against this development, due not alone to Beethoven interpreters or to Berlioz and Liszt, but to all the composers of the nineteenth century, the proponents of "absolute music" argue that serious works ought not to be "literary" or have a subject. The origin of this doctrine is worth a brief digression, because it arose out of a curious—and ambiguous—idea about music put forth by a man of letters.

Absolute music was a term unheard until near the end of the nineteenth century, when it drew its force from some English critics of painting. They declared that representation in painting and sculpture had had their day; now the pure essence of these arts—nothing but color, line, and form—was to be their superior future. This prediction came true, as we all know—the square outlined against a colored background, the grouping and balance of irregular colored patches, the sculpture that is but a shape have monopolized production and attention.

Behind the critics' dictum was the curious principle I referred to. It came much earlier, from the English writer Walter Pater. In his collection of essays on the history of the Renaissance he said: "Art, then, is thus always striving to be independent of the mere intelligence, to become a matter of pure perception, to get rid of its responsibilities to its subject or material." Poetry and painting, he added, are examples of art in which "form and matter in their union or identity, present one single effect to the 'imaginative reason.' [. . .] It is the art of music that most completely realizes this artistic ideal, this perfect identification of matter and form [. . .] and to it, therefore [. . .] all the arts may be supposed constantly to tend and aspire."[13]

The words "pure" and the release from duty to anything external have an inherent appeal to those who look to the arts for "perfection." By contrast, "subject," "purpose," "program" are felt to cater to vulgar tastes. Even so, in the sense of plan dictated by occasion, religious or social, program has had a long and honorable history. It is told in detail by Frederick Niecks in his stout volume *Programme Music*.[14] He distinguishes six periods in its development, beginning with works by such sixteenth-century masters as Jannequin, Palestrina, and Orlando di Lasso. The sixth ends with Brahms, even though he signed a declaration disapproving and disowning the use of programs.[15]

Well before Brahms's day, nearly all composers had been giving evocative titles to their works. Brahms himself would have us distinguish by fitness to occasion between his *Academic* and his *Tragic* Overture or why label them? The playing of an opera overture at concerts soon after Gluck's reform of the genre gave the model and impetus to this naming. Next, overtures were composed to stand alone, without title except for *Grande Ouverture caractéristique*, this adjective implying a subject.

It was a short step further to label that character. After a trip to Scotland, Mendelssohn wrote the compact masterpiece *Fingal's Cave* Overture, also known as *The Hebrides* Overture (as if to show the flexibility of music's expressiveness—one hollow rock or a group of islands). The opening theme may suggest the lapping of the waters on one or all these tourist spots that inspired a musical mind; the listener is free to label his own impressions.

Much later, Debussy's *La Mer* had a similar starting point, but one may regret the subtitle of "From Dawn to Noon" for the first movement. For as with "Fate at the door" there is and can be no follow through.[16] Usually the first theme of a piece, especially of one named after a character, tries for distinctiveness, and that is enough to mark the mood of the piece as a whole. Rhythm and tempo, note value and intervals, together with instrumentation, differentiate the character of Strauss's *Salome* from that of *Till Eulenspiegel,* and this in turn from the wanderings of the denizen of woods and caves in Debussy's *Prélude à l'Après-midi d'un faune.*

The whole nineteenth- and early twentieth-century orchestral repertory is a mass of works bearing a tag chosen by the composer to recall a place or a book or some other circumstance, ceremonial or commonplace, that sparked his desire to write. His listeners are not expected to do more than *associate* the music with the title-subject, just as when hearing a famous aria one recalls its place in the drama, even when one hardly makes out the words.[17] This practice in all its varieties unites composer and listener in the conviction that a link exists between music and life, though it is obvious that music cannot describe or narrate. But while critics have wasted breath assuring everybody that programs are wicked, none has given thought to the workings of the mind when it perceives the fitness of a piece of music or even of a single phrase to a moment of living experience.

If my suggestion of *visceral response* is acceptable as describing the nature of this inner event, which is not an emotion and, as Gurney stated, is not nameable, then what is needed in order to discuss the art of music in its own terms is to create these terms. Granted that art and technique are fused in any work of merit, analyzing the technique does not tell us anything of that merit in the work in which fusion has occurred. The same effect can be produced by different means; many a masterpiece shows passages of clumsy technique,[18] and is obviously ranked high on other grounds than technical perfection.

Before offering a sample or two of a vocabulary that might serve for discourse about the music in the music of Berlioz, it is helpful to go back for contrast to the daily reviewers, who give every concert they hear interpretations that readers apparently find enlightening. Clearly, listeners regard music as a form of discourse and they are not satisfied with mere tags or a mention of moods. The new insatiable appetite for Mahler has provided many illustrations of such detailed commentary on whole symphonies, and here is an example from Mr. Anthony Tommasini, the most qualified and perceptive, as well as the best writer of the *New York Times* critics, describing the Mahler Sixth in A Minor:

> But the tragedy is defiant, not pitiable [. . .]. [A] hero marches willfully into the morass of life, fiercely determined, yet prone to bouts of wistfulness and depression. By the end he is struck down by hammer blows of fate. [The first movement is] a crazily insistent march [to which the conductor brought] a jumpy, jerky surface quality that kept you off guard. [The] reflective second theme [. . .] seemed like an unearthly chorale drifting in from afar [. . .]. In the impassioned theme that Mahler named for his wife, [the conductor drew] burnished sound and impetuous lyricism [. . .]. He brought a strange beauty to the development section of this long movement, which is

like the hero's vision of some now impossible bucolic life, full of amorphous harmonies, mystical harps, and rustic cow bows [*sic*].

The middle movements are a Scherzo and an Andante [. . .]. After the restlessness
of the first movement, the pensive soulful Andante was a welcome balm. This in turn
gave more freshness to the Scherzo—a bitter parody of the first movement's march.

The epic finale had breadth and urgency. As the hero forges ahead with mindless
determination, the first hammer blow (made by a percussionist pummeling a great
wooden box with a fearsome-looking, felt-covered wooden hammer) knocks him loopy.
Crazed and wild-eyed, he tries to go on, or so it seems from the frantic outbursts of
counterpoint that are scattered in the orchestra. But the second hammer blow levels
the hero and the bucolic music comes back, this time, as performed here, in some
unhinged, dissipating state. Imagine a "Star Wars" character being slowly vaporized.[19]

This re-rendering of a long and complex work is impressive by its fullness and
strength of imagination. Over fifty adjectives and images packed into several
terse paragraphs turn into visions the visceral responses the symphony evoked
from a trained listener. A final sentence adds that the conductor's "cool" prevented the work from seeming "melodramatic"—an ultimate epithet that com-
pletes the fusion of life and literature into one source of pleasurable edification.

It will be said that no other critic's report is likely to coincide with this one in
its choice of terms.[20] That is so and it is the basis of the argument that true music
is nothing but self-sufficient E-flats and F-sharps. The critic Roger Fry, a main
expounder of autonomous art, found that he had to call for more, and more
precise, terms to use in the criticism of painting. Obviously, as soon as lifelike-
ness and other plain qualities (to say nothing of anecdote depiction) were ruled
out, there was nothing to say. Fry knew that the French painters' studios had
developed over the years a fuller vocabulary than the English; they spoke of *gri-
saille, méplat*, and *nuance*.[21] *Nuance* has become English, but to this day reviewers
of exhibitions are reduced to fantasizing freely, even less plausibly than the
reporters on music. In a large canvas full of whorls of white paint on a light background, a reviewer found "intimations of innocence." With such judgments
there can be no demurrer, no discussion, and the term Criticism loses all meaning. One must add that poetry today is in the same limbo and some avant-garde
works of fiction too—a dead end.

In the presence of music anyone who wants to communicate a judgment is
balked not only by the lack of terms but also by the difficulty of pointing to the
role in the work of whatever caused the particular visceral response. Before I
propose some possible means to those ends, a passage from Pater on the work
of a traditional painter may serve as a guide, not to say model. The critique is of
Botticelli's Madonnas.

At first [. . .] you may have thought there was something in them mean and abject even,
for the abstract lines of the face have little nobleness, and the color is wan. For with

Botticelli she too, though she holds in her hands the "Desire of all Nations," is one of those who are neither for Jehovah nor for His enemies; and her choice is in her face. The white light on it is cast up hard and cheerless from below, as when snow lies upon the ground and the children look up with surprise at the strange whiteness of the ceiling.[22]

Two technical details, and the rest are effects and comparisons, all pinned down to the spots where they belong. In the first review of Mahler the "hammer blows" came close to being one equivalent, alone among the list of unanchored and sometimes dubious events, such as vaporizing the hero.

The base for precise reference in music is solid enough—air waves are as material as steel, but they move fast and catching the portion that "expresses" takes practice. One might have thought that over the years the frequent performance of the standard operas, reviewed by the same newspaper writers, would have established some firm connections between musical effects and the words and situations they accompany. This has not happened. Operatic words tend to be *in*expressive and are rarely heard beyond the first two or three by which famous arias are known. Another obstacle is that the relation of words to the sensations of life is far from clear-cut. We call "anger" quite a number of distinct feelings—there is hot or cold anger, vocal or suppressed, weary from sameness of the cause, touched with surprise or contempt or even with amusement (if the cause is a child's prank).[23]

All these considerations set limits to our purpose: a vocabulary for music criticism must point to portions of the work by terms agreed upon that name recognizable types of human expression. Once the effect is assigned to a passage or even a single chord, the critic is free to add a nuance of his choice—*his* visceral response, which one may dispute, but at least both judges are talking about the same "object."

For this solid core, what kind of words is suitable? A rereading of the first Mahler review contained possible indications: *insistent, restlessness, bucolic, parody* (as against the narrowly personal *determined* and *unhinged*) could all lead to the right sort of indicative label. It should be neutral, not a motive assumed to be at work. If well chosen and likely to seem apt, such words could become conventional, and since conventions develop out of trial and error, I venture to make up a sample of vocabulary, using once again the music of Berlioz as their locus.

In tribute to Mr. Tommasini, I choose his "restlessness" and testing it for form and essence, I extract from it the impersonal *agitation*, and gain assurance from the established expression marks *agitato con passione* and *agitato con piance* (with passion and from grief). This sample rose spontaneously from the music itself: agitation is the character of the first thirty-five bars of *Harold en Italie*. It is cut off grandly for the entrance of the hero's theme on the viola. Without conscious search on my part, *agitation* brought to mind another opening, the Introduction to the dramatic symphony *Roméo et Juliette* (bars 1–65) and, in a third distinct mood, the passage in *La Damnation de Faust*, after the opening of Part III, where (at scene xi) Marguerite in her chamber is strangely apprehensive before Faust's unexpected arrival and seduction. These three agitations might be qualified respectively as: brooding or impatient; angry or combative; and restless with anxiety. Supposing the root term validated by usage, it would then appear in a review or critique with the writer's individual response added by an adjective or comment as to fitness, originality, or other judgment on the art displayed, not on the means used to achieve it.

We have touched our goal, but I offer one more potential term of reference to illustrate how such a word can serve to state the difference between an artistic element that is unique to a composer from one that is merely distinctive. Uniqueness defies comparison. In an excellent book on *The Berlioz Style*, Mr. Brian Primmer rightly shows that the creation and use of melody singles out Berlioz from his notable contemporaries, obsessed by the expressive power of harmony. Behind Berlioz's melodic style was the psalmody of Gregorian chant, the polyphony of the fifteenth-century Flemish school, and Gluck's doctrine of opera as drama throughout.[24]

These influences, heightened, modified, and fused by genius, changed melody from being simply an attractive tune or else thematic material to be subdued to formal and harmonic uses to a major element of structure. Often combined with another melody and varied by inventive rhythm, melody is the unique element that has entranced the devotees of Berlioz's music—and bewildered the public and other musicians for over one hundred fifty years.

Playing such a role throughout his works, Berlioz's melodies need terms to indicate their different characters. The conspicuous one is length.[25] Its extent led some critics to complain that he had no melody, others that one never knew "where it was going," and still others were surprised that, although successive sections had an uneven count of bars, the whole was "in balance just the same." These are clues for our purpose. A given melodic passage in Berlioz might be called *lyric* when its balance is clear, its bearing complete and perhaps repeated—*stanza form*, so to speak. When it goes on unpredictably, it is *prose* melody, or better, *discourse*.

To make use of these pointers: in the *Scène d'amour* of *Roméo et Juliette*, the opening flute and string chords are interrupted early by a measure of silence, so marked by Berlioz, to establish calm after the rowdiness that ends the Capulets' party. A sense of space and darkness is conveyed by the distant voices of some revelers departing from the ball. That they sing its rhythm not quite right could testify to their less than sober condition. Next come moments of agitation, fragmented, and the emphatic accents so divided that they bring to mind the lovers, alike uncertain, excited. The declaration of love when it comes (in A Major, bars 146–155) is lyric, of course. It is repeated (in C Major, bars 172–181), then followed by an interlude of discourse—prose, though not prosaic—which you are free to interpret according to your own imagination. The lyric returns at the end, punctuated by gestures that deserve the appellation of *menace* or *foreboding*. I prefer the first as the more neutral, and therefore more widely applicable.

The discourse portion of this scene has an eloquence that warrants a couple of examples of similar rhetoric, where we have words—or a title—to help us make sure we are not wrong calling discourse the extended type of Berliozian melody, which replaces standard recitative.

One such example is the monologue at the opening of Part II of *La Damnation de Faust*, "Sans regrets j'ai quitté les riantes campagnes." Its fifty-two bars at times accompany the words, at times comment apart from them. It is a reverie of unstable moods that heightens tenfold the dramatic shock of the Easter chorus when it arrives suddenly in *piano*, with regular meter and new tempo. Again, for a wordless sample, none is more beautiful than the middle movement of the *Symphonie funèbre et triomphale*, where we have Berlioz's own appellation of *Oraison funèbre*. Its use of the trombone as discourser was to be expected, since the instrument's capacity for *portamento* creates an impression of speech. It does so again in the Introduction to *Roméo et Juliette*, where the Prince seems to intervene, at bar 78, in the agitation mentioned earlier and may be supposed to call for coolness and peace. A third occasion where a lyric section is interrupted by discourse is the Narrator's melody for the Holy Family's rest in the desert in the Deuxième Partie of *L'Enfance du Christ*, particularly at "Puis, s'étant assis sous l'ombrage" (bars 123ff.).

I do not flatter myself that I have achieved the purpose I set myself, solved the problem of how to talk about music as an art. But even if mine is a failed attempt, I think I *have* succeeded in showing that to treat exclusively of E-flats and F-sharps, like the reviewers' plausible fables that match here and there the flow of sound, is to escape the critic's duty. Since, as all but a few admit, music is expressive, leaving that conviction incomplete is intellectually irresponsible. Composers give the lie to the absolutists when they give titles to their works. It is not their business, it is ours as judges and appreciators to devise the means of assessing merit and giving reasons for our judgment. May musicologists and scholarly critics do their duty and endow us with the terms to match our responses to the music in the music of any composer.

Notes

1. Peter Cornelius voiced the consensus in Germany by joining him to Bach and Beethoven as "the three B's." See Cornelius, *Ausgewählte Schriften und Briefe*, ed. Paul Egert (Berlin: B. Hahnefeld, 1938), pp. 134–135. Much later, when the reaction against romanticism swept Europe and classical calm was looked for in the arts, Hans von Bülow chose Brahms to make up the trio in place of Berlioz.

2. *Dictionnaire Berlioz*, ed. Pierre Citron, Cécile Reynaud, Jean-Pierre Bartoli, and Peter Bloom (Paris: Fayard, 2003).

3. For example, in a review of a trio concert, Mr. Bernard Holland commends the group for its "scrupulous attention to European musical grammar" and he shows how "harmonic change stretches time and orders phrases." The idea is stressed in the headline, "Grammar, Vocabulary and Other Musical Lessons" (*New York Times*, 11 October 2005). The concert hall turns out to be a branch of the conservatory.

4. The texts of Bernstein's lectures (this one on "What Does Music Mean?"), widely quoted, may be found on a Kultur Video DVD and on the internet at http://www.leonardbernstein.com/youth.html.

5. Comparable attempts have been few and equally in need of explicit labels. The best known are Rimsky's "Flight of the Bumble-Bee" and Honegger's *Pacific 231*, the designation of a type of steam locomotive, given by the number of paired wheels.

6. Of the *Symphonie fantastique*, Berlioz wrote: "L'auteur sait fort bien que la musique ne saurait remplacer la parole, ni l'art du dessin; il n'a jamais eu l'absurde prétention d'exprimer des *abstractions* ou des *qualités morales* mais des passions et des sentiments" (*NBE* 16, p. 170).

7. Tom Wotton, *A Dictionary of Foreign Musical Terms and Handbook of Orchestral Instruments* (Leipzig: Breitkopf & Härtel, 1907).

8. Edmund Gurney, "Wagner and Wagnerism," in *Topics of the Time*, No. 6 (New York: G. P. Putnam's Sons, 1883), p. 190.

9. Usually three quarters strings to one quarter woodwind and brass, each of these singly or in pairs, with the exception of bassoons, of which the French orchestra used four to the German two. A further consequence was the publication of books that taught the art of using these sources of timbre in combination. Berlioz's work, issued in 1844 after serial publication, was entitled *Traité d'instrumentation et d'orchestration modernes* to show that the sound of the modern orchestra is not the result of a single formula.

10. Goethe, letter of 9 November 1829. See *Goethes Briefe*, IV, ed. Karl Robert Mandelkow (Hamburg: Wegner, 1967), p. 349. Zelter was the man to whom Goethe showed the *Huit Scènes de Faust* that Berlioz, aged twenty-eight, had sent him, and who pronounced them gibberish.

11. Goethe, *Sprüche in Prosa*, trans. W. B. Rönnfeldt as *Criticisms, Reflections, and Maxims* (London: Scott, 1892), p. 144.

12. Even the Gewandhaus, used as a concert hall in Leipzig, had to open its doors to the general public. While it served only subscribers to quartet series and the like, it offered only five seats to random customers.

13. Walter Pater, "The School of Giorgione," in *The Renaissance* (London: Macmillan, 1935), pp. 127–128.

14. Frederick Niecks, *Programme Music* (London: Novello, 1907). Liszt argued in favor of "programs" and kept on writing them for his "symphonic poems," no doubt thinking that a new form required fuller guidance than the title of the work and its parts, as in his *Tasso*, which is subtitled *Lamento e Trionfo*. He explained that one of a program's purposes is to "guard the listener against a wrong poetical interpretation and to direct his attention to the poetical idea of the whole, or to a particular part of it" (quoted by Roger Scruton, "Programme Music," in *The New Grove Dictionary of Music and Musicians*, 2nd ed., ed. Stanley Sadie [London: Macmillan, 2001], vol. 20, p. 396).

15. The declaration, published in 1860 in the *Berliner Musik-Zeitung Echo* and signed by Brahms along with Joseph Joachim, Julius Grimm, and Bernhard Scholz, was directed against Liszt and the "new German school"—the term coined in 1859

THE MUSIC IN THE MUSIC OF BERLIOZ 25

by Franz Brendel, editor of the *Neue Zeitschrift für Music,* to refer to the music, heavily influenced by Beethoven, of Berlioz, Liszt, and Wagner. So chaotic is usage on the subject of "programs" that one finds writers denying Beethoven's priority in composing "program music" and citing Bach as precursor, because of his *Capriccio on the Departure of His Most Beloved Brother* (BWV 992) with its various subtitles. See "Beethoven" in the second and third editions of *Grove's Dictionary of Music.*

16. If Fate knew her business, she would keep pounding on the same four notes, not play around with changes of pitch and value. Still, the mood of menace is not contradicted by the rest of the movement, which is enough. The addition to *La Mer* opens the way to such jibes as Erik Satie's, that he liked particularly the passage around half past eleven.

17. The English drama critic James Agate, who was a good musician and a concert- and opera-goer, reports his belated discovery "that *Ombra mai fu* was addressed to a tree, which robbed it of half its charm." See Agate, *Ego 8* (London: Harrap, 1948), p. 145.

18. For a series of examples, see Harvey Grace, *The Organ Works of Bach* (London: Novello, 1922). Among other strictures he says of the Prelude and Fugue in C, Book VII: "It opens with one of the worst pedal solos ever written—bar after bar of C-Major arpeggios. Things improve when the manuals get going, but it is all very primitive." And in the reverse direction, on a Passacaglia and Fugue: "Despite a few weak passages, this is a far finer work than is generally realized," quoted by W. J. Turner in "The Great Sebastian," in *Musical Meanderings* (New York: Dutton, [1928]), pp. 27, 29.

19. *New York Times* (24 June 2005).

20. Compare Mr. Bernard Holland's review of the same work in the same paper five months later (15 November 2005).

21. Roger Fry, *Vision and Design* (London: Chatto and Windus, 1920); and idem, "Words Wanted in Connexion with Art," *Society for Pure English,* tract number 31 (Oxford: Clarendon Press, 1928), pp. 330–332. See also Clive Bell, *Since Cézanne* (London: Chatto and Windus, 1922).

22. Walter Pater, "Sandro Botticelli," in *The Renaissance,* p. 53.

23. Need I add that this inadequacy of literal speech is one reason for the existence of the arts? By re-presenting our experience in a variety of ways they enlarge our understanding of life.

24. Brian Primmer, *The Berlioz Style* (London: Oxford, 1973), esp. chapter 2.

25. Just once, Berlioz permitted himself to compare his art with that of his contemporaries. In the *Post-Scriptum* to his posthumous *Mémoires* he refers to "petites drôleries"—the "funny little things"—that they call melodies, specifying that to him the word meant a musical element of greater magnitude than a theme or a closed form.

Chapter Two

"Artistic Religiosity": Berlioz Between the Te Deum and L'Enfance du Christ

FRANK HEIDLBERGER

The road which lies before me, however long,
cannot be very different from that which I have traveled.
I shall find the same stony, uneven ways, the same ruts and deep pot-holes,
with here and there a stream or the cool peace of a grove,
or some sublime rock towering up,
where I shall laboriously climb to dry myself in the evening sun
from the chill rain endured all day in the plains.
　　　　　　　—Berlioz, *Memoirs*, chapter LIX (18 October 1854)

One week after the first performance of his *trilogie sacrée*, *L'Enfance du Christ*, on 10 December 1854, Berlioz wrote confidentially to Franz Liszt: "So I have become a good little boy, human, clear, melodic; I am finally writing music like everybody else—the common voice now proclaims! Farewell—the sensation caused by this conversion is growing. Let us allow it to continue to do so."[1]

This remarkable statement invites a close investigation of the composer's identity in the later years of his life and career. It is not without sarcasm that he declares himself a "bon enfant" who finally knows how to please the public with melodious tunes. On the surface, the simple irony of the comment refers to the extraordinary success of the shepherds' farewell in Part II of the sacred trilogy. This chorus evokes some vaguely "ancient" musical epoch by means of an apparently effortless and naive compositional style that no one, certainly not the critics, expected from the likes of Berlioz. *L'Adieu des bergers à la Sainte Famille*, the embryo of what became a large-scale composition, had initially appeared in concert as a separate piece purportedly composed by a seventeenth-century *maître de chapelle*.[2] It delighted the public with its simple melodic phrasing and seemingly traditional harmonic progressions;[3] it might have reminded Parisian listeners of

Christmas carols and put them in a nostalgic frame of mind as they imagined a "hopelessly cozy" Holy Family.[4] By following the Christmas story, audiences could associate their own experiences and cultural identities with the characters and feelings presented in the new work. Indeed, it appears that it was much easier for Parisian listeners to cope with Joseph, the shepherds, and even Herod, than it was for them to deal with Byron, Romeo, or Faust. Even Heinrich Heine admitted in his own ironical way that Berlioz had "plucked a nosegay of the most exquisite blooms of melody," and that *L'Enfance du Christ* was "a masterpiece of simplicity."[5] In other words Berlioz's often disturbing musical passions were now seen as tamed and reduced to an illustrative style that could do no harm. In the eyes of the public, this work, as Berlioz put it, alluding to Handel's ever-popular oratorio, became his *Messiah*: "They say that I have corrected my ways," he wrote with caustic humor to the Princess Sayn-Wittgenstein, "that I have changed *my manner of doing things* . . . and other such stupidities."[6] Nonetheless, despite Berlioz's light-hearted reference to the new composition as his "petite *sainteté*," there is nothing light about the place of *L'Enfance du Christ* in Berlioz's œuvre: indeed it provides a weighty challenge to our understanding of the principal contours of Berlioz's profile as composer and artist.

The creative history of the *Te Deum* goes back at least to the mid-eighteen-forties.[7] In terms of compositional intention, its roots are found even earlier, in the soils of the dawn of Berlioz's compositional career and of the *Messe solennelle* of 1824. There we find an expression of the spirit of glory in the monumental *Resurrexit* with its central line "Et iterum venturus est cum Gloria"—"And He shall come again with glory." It is this ritual component of musical expression (as well as a specific musical borrowing) that links his early Mass with his last liturgical work. The occasion of the latter's performance, in 1855, was not a patriotic celebration of victory, but an international industrial fair. Instead of glorifying the nation and the new emperor, as Berlioz had hoped, it was used to exalt the wonders of the industrial revolution at a time of great conflict and change in European politics, economics, and society.

L'Enfance du Christ and the *Te Deum* are Berlioz's last two major works on religious subjects. More importantly, they are representatives of the composer's state of mind in what might be called his post-1848 condition—a condition marked less by musico-stylistic changes than by self-evaluation or "introspection," as Peter Bloom has it, and by what David Cairns more precisely terms "the call of the past."[8] What is particular in Berlioz's artistic biography in the years around and after 1848? What do his contemporary works reveal of his attitudes regarding history and the present, art and politics, musical expression and passion? Is there a "code" in these works that in some way links both of them to Berlioz's remembrance of his past and to his acute awareness of the turbulence of the musical present? Recent scholars have spoken of his approach to life and art as one of "autobiographical construction," claiming that his musical works are founded upon an ongoing process of self-reflection and imagination that models autobiographical scenes, or poetic inspirations, into musical actions.[9] Such a contention is not new, but as Jacques Barzun has lately pointed out, the challenge still remains in Berlioz studies to achieve "an exposition of the total 'aesthetic,' to use a word Berlioz detested."[10] The challenge remains, as I prefer to put it, to analyze Berlioz's creativity as a multidimensional process of "self-creation" in poetic and musical patterns based upon his own perception of a "romantic" aesthetics that he found variously ambiguous, contradictory, and disturbing.

"Artistic Religiosity" and the Idea of Genius

Berlioz refers to the *Te Deum* and *L'Enfance du Christ* in the *Post-Scriptum* of the *Mémoires*, written in 1856, not long after the first performances of both compositions.[11] There he summarizes his artistic credo with these two key works functioning as archetypes of his style and aesthetics. From a certain perspective they do indeed concisely represent Berlioz's musical ideology by synthesizing the dialectics of his musical language and expression. Both engage narrative subjects that the composer, now over fifty, had been dealing with since his early twenties: religion and religiosity as matters of a secular artistic philosophy. It is not devout religiosity that motivates his notion of subjective musical expression, but rather the ritualistic and spiritual power of religious ideas.

The *Te Deum* and *L'Enfance du Christ* were composed without commission and without promise of immediate performance. Their musical styles are as different as their genres: the liturgical work is based on a text long used in France to represent the correlation of religion and royal power;[12] the fictional narrative (an imagined scenario of ancient orientalism) is historically related to the events around the birth of Christ as related in the New Testament. Despite such contrast the works are related. Indeed, following the genealogy that Berlioz invented for the *Te Deum*—a "brother" to the *Requiem*,[13] one may also say that *L'Enfance du Christ* is a "second cousin" to the *Te Deum*, for both put forth religion as a source not of spirituality but of ritual—ritual that includes epic grandeur, nightmarish delusion, melancholic contemplation, and pastoral imagery. These were long the central colors of Berlioz's expressive palette. They may be seen to develop an artistic (or "aesthetic") religiosity with ramifications that may not be obvious at first sight, but that become clear when one reads Berlioz's language as that of an artist acutely attuned to the romantic era's secularized "religion of art": "Romanticism was its expression for two generations of artists," Jacques Barzun writes, "who did not need any catechism to be ardent worshippers."[14] Barzun might have more forcefully underlined Berlioz's conspicuous status as a musician-writer who created a relationship between the arts more ardent than those created by almost all others of his generation. From this point of view Berlioz's critical writings may be understood as the catechetical exposition of his own subjective readings of the arts, based upon his critical perception of "genius."

Early in that *Post-Scriptum* Berlioz speaks to his fervent admiration of the great masters: this becomes his exclusive and sole acceptable means of judgment. Beethoven, Weber, Gluck, and Spontini forge his idea of the genius who follows no given rules and no given laws, the genius who defines "good" and "bad" exclusively by his own creative powers. Here, the aesthetic judgment of the "quality" of the work of art merges with a moral principle: that certain individuals have the *right* to establish their own laws rather than the *obligation* to follow the laws established by some external authority. This explains Berlioz's antipathy to the authority of the Conservatoire personified by its indefatigable director, Luigi Cherubini.[15] Of particular significance is the wording of the entire passage, which takes the form of a creed: Berlioz poses as an "incrédule en musique"—a non-believer, an infidel, a heretic—who believes only in the "religion" of Beethoven and the other gods of music. He intensifies the moral aspect of his pseudo-catechetical statement by insisting on judging a work solely upon the effects produced by certain combinations of sounds: "l'effet produit par certaines combinaisons devant seul les faire condamner ou absoudre."[16] This sort of quest for a balance between condemnation and absolution seems to motivate Berlioz as composer, critic, lover, and "believer."

It is obvious that Berlioz's assertion—in form as well as in content—harks back to his early enthusiasm for Victor Hugo's encomium to the freedom of genius, proffered in the *Préface* to *Les Orientales* of 1829, which the composer cites in one of his first important articles:

> Romantic composers [. . .] have inscribed upon their banner the words "free inspiration." They outlaw nothing and employ in their work everything proper to the domain of music. Their motto comes from Victor Hugo: "Art has absolutely nothing to do with handcuffs, limits, and gags; it says to the man of genius *go forth* and releases him into the garden of poetry, where no fruit is forbidden."[17]

The statement, endorsing as it does the freedom of the subjective mind endowed with creative brilliance, may be read as making a transition from the realm of aesthetics to the realm of political morality, inasmuch as the genius's rejection of authority and acceptance of only his own rules can imply his sanctioning of anarchy. Berlioz's "Napoleonism" must be seen in this light, as well as his admiration of other heroes or anti-heroes, such as Hérode in *L'Enfance du Christ*. The anarchical undercurrent of his thinking becomes obvious in his apparent praise of absolute power, particularly in the eighteen-forties, in such works as the *Symphonie funèbre et triomphale*, the *Hymne à la France*,[18] the short story *Euphonia* (where the main character, Xilef, performs a mass execution in response to the infidelity of his lover),[19] and the *Te Deum*, with its re-interpretation of the last judgment. In the *Te Deum* Berlioz moves the line "Judex crederis esse venturus" to the end in order to accentuate the authority of judgment as a final existential power that allows for no compromise in life and in art. The musical structure of this movement reflects this absoluteness in meaning by its grandiose musical dimensions, leading Berlioz to dub it "unquestionably the most imposing of all the works I have produced."[20] The *Judex crederis* is the final statement of a steady musical and poetic narrative process that reiterates the theological and teleological significance of the last judgment. The same process is found in the early *Messe solennelle*, with its *Resurrexit* that became an independent work and then a central part of the *Requiem*, as well as in his operatic project, *Le Dernier Jour du monde*.[21]

For Berlioz the last judgment seems to signify the highest imaginable instance of resolute power that rules the world and determines its history. Berlioz applies this symbol primarily to his dreams of political power. During his stay in Florence, precisely when drafting *Le Dernier Jour du monde*, and in an outburst of frustration that led him to exclaim that he no longer believed in anything at all ("moi je ne crois plus à rien"), he expresses his admiration for Napoleon with almost maniacal passion:

> Oh, Napoleon, Napoleon! Genius! Power! Force! Will! . . . Why, with your iron hand, did you not crush yet more swarms of human vermin! Oh, Colossus, with your feet of bronze, how with the slightest step would you flatten all their pretty little patriotic and philanthropic designs. Ridiculous riffraff![22]

It is the "genius" who, in Berlioz's variously romanticized reiterations of this statement, acts with similar ruthlessness in the realms of art and culture. In a letter to Victor Hugo dated 10 December 1831 (only seven months after the letter to Ferrand), he again uses the notion of the "ruthlessness" of the power of genius:

> Oh, you are a genius, a powerful being, a colossus who is at once tender, pitiless, elegant, monstrous, hoarse, melodious, volcanic, gentle, and *contemptuous*. The last-mentioned quality of genius is surely the least common of all; it was manifest by neither Shakespeare nor Molière. Among the *immortals*, only Beethoven took the just measure of the human insects that surrounded him: next to him I see only you.[23]

Here Berlioz presents a series of paired antonyms—*tendre/impitoyable; élégant/monstrueux; rauque/mélodieux; volcanique/caressant*—with only *méprisant* standing on its own, underlined, and singularly representative of the full force of the pitiless power of "les grands." Here the idea of the last judgment is secularized, as the authority of God is replaced by the authority of Genius. With Napoleon in mind, as well as Beethoven or Hugo, or his own father and himself, Berlioz creates a narrative that concerns a visionary, subjective, *political* authority; he constructs his own God by converting the idea of the last judgment into a metaphor of the ritual execution of power. Each of these ideal figures or "models" created his own world and his own rules, whether in life or in art, less by evolutionary development than by revolutionary change—change motivated by more than art and aesthetics, as the origins of the *Te Deum* show. Because, although finalized when the composer was still reacting to the events of 1848, the *Te Deum* itself finds its initial impulses in Berlioz's longstanding admiration for Napoleon, which we have observed, as well in his feelings of respect for the authority of his father, who died in July of 1848.

This results in a paradox: Berlioz's interpretation of the last judgment is of a secular sort, but his veneration of Napoleon is almost religious. The young composer learned of Napoleon I as, among other things, a patron of the arts who supported such an "official" composer as his teacher, Jean-François Lesueur, and who earned the admiration of both his father and his uncle, Félix Marmion, who long served in Napoleon's army. It was through the expression of a Napoleonic patriotism that Berlioz tried to justify his musical career to his father. In May 1832, traveling through northern Italy towards home, "le cœur plein de souvenirs napoléoniens," he considered the idea of a *Symphonie militaire* in two movements, "Adieux du haut des Alpes aux braves tombés dans les champs d'Italie" and "Entrée triomphale des vainqueurs à Paris," that would idealize Napoleon's return from the victorious Italian military campaign.[24] He revisited the idea in 1846, mentioning in a letter to his father of 10 October a choral symphony for three thousand players and singers entitled *Le Retour de l'armée d'Italie*.[25] With these projects, he would transform political consciousness into a melancholic recollection of an earlier, now-lamented heroism, imagining Napoleon's victorious return from Italy as a nostalgic musical scene that might restore the lost *gloire* of the nation—an idea his father might finally endorse as a project appropriate to his son's musical career as French citizen and patriot. This was surly not his sole reason for pursuing such a venture, but the juxtapositioning of his creative vision with his father's worldview is indeed a subtext of his career through 1848, as I shall suggest below.

Jacques Barzun notes that Berlioz "declared himself an atheist" later in his life, thus espousing a nihilistic approach to the world: "He had come to the very modern Existentialist conviction that the universe is blind, cold, and senseless. He saw death and dissolution as the goal of existence."[26] I do not fully subscribe to this radical conclusion, since Berlioz at least believed in his own presence (overcoming the suicidal temptations of his earlier years that would indeed fit the existentialist narrative), and in the ruling power of genius over his own world. Such a subjective and even utopian view of history, as opposed to the Hegelian, ultrarational notion of historical consciousness, thus renders him a "romantic" artist in a very particular sense of the term. The revolutions of 1830 and 1848 failed to establish the artistic world of Berlioz's dreams. His desolate situation after the revolution of 1848, and the pessimism and isolation we find described in the *Préface* to the *Mémoires*, represent his persistent, subjective view of the world.

Excursus—The "Colossal Nightingale"

Berlioz's ideology is revealed as well in other contemporary narratives. Heinrich Heine offered a metaphorical approach to Berlioz's music in his famous essay in *Lutetia*, which Berlioz quotes in the *Post-Scriptum* of the *Mémoires*.[27] Heine's likening of the composer to a "rossignol colossal"—to a "colossal nightingale; a lark the size of an eagle"—is a fair reaction to the *Requiem*, for example, when reduced solely to its monumental components.[28] But it must be remembered that Heine's essay was originally written for the opening of the 1844 concert season and specifically in anticipation of the *Concert spirituel* that Berlioz would direct at the Opéra-Comique on 6 April of that year. On that occasion the only movement of the *Requiem* to be performed was an arrangement of the *Sanctus*. Otherwise the program seems to have featured Berlioz's overtures *Le Roi Lear* and *Le Carnaval romain*, Teresa's cavatina from *Benvenuto Cellini*, the cantata *Le Cinq Mai*, and selections from Beethoven, Meyerbeer, Palestrina, and Gluck.[29] The main points of Heine's essay must thus be seen from a "metachronic" perspective, as pertaining generally to Berlioz's style and not to any particular movement or work.

Heine's intertextual approach, with its references to music, architecture, and painting, tells as much about Heine as it does about Berlioz. The German poet transforms the traditional metaphor of the nightingale as a symbol of natural simplicity and beauty into a symbol of the immeasurability of music. This nightingale is not to be found in some Arcadian sanctuary of pleasure and cheerfulness, but in the darkness of some antediluvian, prehistoric, humanly incomprehensible era. (Heine further compares Berlioz's music to the "passion" of the Assyrian-Babylonian-Egyptian architectural period, mentioning Niniveh, the Mesopotamian city on the banks of the Tigris, whose archeological discovery in 1842 caused a sensation in fashionable salons across the European continent.)

With these metaphors and allusions, exhibiting a double perspective of history and continuity (ancient Oriental culture being at once distant from and the fountainhead of modern Western culture), Heine manifests a cultural consciousness that replaces the Hegelian concept of objective rationalism with the idea of cultural subjectivity.[30] Rejecting the seemingly linear development of culture and art as a process of reason and inner spiritual logic, Heine (in his review of the Paris salon of 1831) declares his opposition to classicism, to the authority of tradition, and to much of "current art," which appears to him as "still rooted in the decrepit *ancien régime*." He further seeks a "new time period that bears a new art which will be consonant with itself and even its new technical approach." Heine comprehends the present as an interim period characterized by "self-drunken subjectivity" ("selbsttrunkene Subjektivität"), which he nonetheless prefers to the lifeless "spectre of the old art."[31] It is not surprising that the spirit of these remarks—set down shortly after Heine's arrival in post-1830-revolutionary Paris—should reflect those of the same period from the pen of

Victor Hugo, likewise a champion of artistic revolution. Heine could hope for such a revolution only in the emancipated atmosphere of the French capital, not in the authoritarian environment of the Prussian Empire.

The revolutions of 1830 and 1848 thus provide meaningful boundaries for the decisive period of subjectivism in art, an interim period that is easily misinterpreted if its primary foreground phenomenon is portrayed only as "romanticism." Berlioz, for Heine, is the paradigmatic figure of this interim period, overcoming in his work the balance and proportion that would characterize a classical era. Heine's further likening of Berlioz to the English painter John Martin clarifies and accentuates this visionary idea. He finds it appropriate to compare the "mad Englishman" to the French composer because his paintings incorporate like tendencies to rupture balance, shape, and form by means of gestures both violent and immense. In his comparison of musical and visual elements Heine makes reference to Berlioz's lack of melody, the equivalent in painting of a "lack of color." A painting such as John Martin's *Great Day of His Wrath* (1851–1853) could perhaps be seen to confirm Heine's analogy, with its depiction of a savage natural catastrophe in which the bodies of the damned appear lost at the edges of the darkly crimson scene overwhelmed by clouds, waves, and fire.[32]

By protesting that Heine misinterpreted his concept of melody, as Berlioz does in the *Post-Scriptum* of the *Mémoires*, he reveals his own misreading of Heine's statement—which is a poetic rendering of a positive quality rather than a negative criticism of a single structural issue. Heine offers a critical assessment in language that goes far beyond that of the "Rossinistes" and others who accused Berlioz of lacking melodic skill; in fact he uses "lack of melody" as a metaphor for the new art, and for the "drunken subjectivity" of the "new genius." The poetic character of Heine's text emerges from its fierce rejection of the principles of the outdated monster of "classical" art: seeking "no melody . . . little beauty and absolutely no heart" is exactly what the new art expects from the ruthless or "contemptuous" genius, to use the word Berlioz applied to Hugo, of which Heine would have approved.

Berlioz's Musical Identity after 1848

Berlioz opens the *Post-Scriptum* with an affirmation of his stylistic coherence and stability, saying that he would have written the lately well-received *Enfance du Christ* in precisely the same manner twenty years earlier, that is was the subject to hand and not some new stylistic "development" that engendered the new work's musical language. Indeed, it is not surprising that Berlioz should reject the notion of "development" since even his earliest important compositions contain structural features that reappear—further explored, further refined—in later works. Berlioz not only made great use of self-borrowings (sections of the *Messe solennelle,* for example, were reused in the *Symphonie fantastique,* in the *Requiem,* in *Benvenuto Cellini,* and even in the *Te Deum*) but also maintained consistency of expression as a structural and aesthetic matter. Certain musical procedures are thus markers of Berlioz's personal compositional technique, while others demonstrate his desire occasionally to associate his music with distinct traditions, as Ralph Locke has noted in the case of the pastoral melancholy of the *Christe eleison* of the *Messe solennelle,* with its explicit references to pastoral scenes in Handel's *Messiah* and in Gossec's Christmas oratorio *La Nativité.*[33] However, Berlioz's vocabulary changes in accordance with the requirements of a particular work. That vocabulary—specific musical "topoi," often derived from autobiographical experience or from association with literature, poetry, or even natural science—may be viewed as following essentially two major tracks: the dramatized epic of the last judgment, and the symphonic "poetry" of the "romantic hero." These tracks—the first represented by the *Messe solennelle* and its separable *Resurrexit,* the *Requiem,* and the *Te Deum;* the second represented by the *Symphonie fantastique, Lélio,* and the following "dramatic symphonies" up to and including *La Damnation de Faust*—are of course not entirely discrete. The hybrid genres of *Roméo et Juliette* and *La Damnation de Faust* (which is even more heterogeneous, with its pseudo-religious scenes and symbols), merge the vocabularies of the two tracks by rendering the components of their plots as interpretations of the "ritual" subjectivity of love and damnation.

L'Enfance du Christ fits comfortably into neither of the two categories. Its diverse parts, composed and performed separately between 1850 and 1854, follow neither the track of dramatic or epic expression nor the track of romantic or religious passion. Its vocabulary generates a unique musical narrative that surprised the public and the critics alike. Adolphe Adam, among those startled by the work, prefers to speak not of Berlioz's "new style" but of a "new attitude" that has been brought to bear upon Berlioz: "It has been said, incorrectly, I think, that in this work Berlioz has changed his approach. I strongly believe that it is rather we who have changed our approach as concerns our feelings and our appreciation."[34]

Analyzing the principal musical strategies of *L'Enfance du Christ,* one readily finds references to Berlioz's earlier works. The dualistic and sometimes conflicting representations of "passion" and "melancholy" are particularly felt in Hérode's dream scene and in the scenes with the Holy Family—scenes prefigured as early as the Easter Hymn of *Huit Scènes de Faust,* itself a model, as Julian Rushton has suggested, for "Berlioz's intimate style of sacred music."[35] Another component of this stylistic sphere is the *Méditation réligieuse,* where Berlioz merges religious contemplation with the forlorn romantic melancholy that he found in the verses of his favorite romantic poet, Thomas Moore. That work may have been in Berlioz's mind as he conceived the meditative endings of sections of *L'Enfance du Christ,* all three related by their declamation, in *pianissimo,* of "Hosanna," "Alleluia," and "Amen," and by their special effects of instrumentation and space.[36]

Berlioz constructs the "past" in *L'Enfance du Christ* primarily by replacing common practice voice leading with modal inflections and progressions that are in fact more associative than authentic. In a letter to John Ella he describes the melodic style of the overture to Part II, for example, as being "in F-sharp Minor without the leading tone, a mode no longer *à la mode* that resembles plainchant and that the specialists will tell you is a derivative of some Phrygian or Dorian or Mixolydian mode from ancient Greece, which fact is of absolutely no consequence except that it lends to the music the melancholic and somewhat simplistic quality of a popular old lament."[37] The reference to the "melancholic" and "simplistic" or "folk-like" character ("mélancolique et un peu niais") of this melodic invention, with the omission of the leading tone, is the significant element of the description. Berlioz doesn't care at all about the correct definition of the mode, only about the appropriateness of simplicity and innocence as signifiers for the following scene. He refers to the simplicity of Greek antiquity as of a sort that does not undergo change or development.

Berlioz likewise uses a Phrygian inflection in the Hérode scene, scene ii, of Part I (see exx. 2.1a–c). Here the half-step A♭–G♮ appears both as part of the main motive in the Andante misterioso of the dream aria, "O misère des rois" (bars 38–39 and throughout; ex. 2.1b), as well as at the final cadence, with its plagal progression from iv to i in "G Minor" (bars 125–126; ex. 2.1c) in the bass. The pseudo-Phrygian mode is introduced at the very end of the aria's instrumental introduction (ex. 2.1a): a descending scale, from E♭ to G with a penultimate A♭, brings to a conclusion the nervous ostinato that characterizes Hérode's state of mind as he begins what Berlioz calls the "insomnia aria."[38] This modality is not consistently maintained. At "régner et ne pas vivre!" (bars 41–43; ex. 2.1b), for example, the vocal range is from E♭ to C♮, E♭ is the *finalis*, and A♭ the fourth, thus suggesting E-flat Major as the tonal center. The harmonization of this passage, however, refers to A♭ and preserves harmonic and melodic ambiguity, enhanced by the distinctive sounds of the low strings and trombones. The scene is completely focused on Hérode, who is charged with the burden of royal authority and forced to decide matters of life and death— a sinister "hero" in a tense psychological situation. Above and beyond the desire to create an ancient middle-eastern atmosphere, it is the need to portray the psychic tension of the protagonist and to foreshadow the catastrophe of his decision to murder the children that leads Berlioz to apply to the scene this kind of modal coloration.[39]

References to the past achieved by the use of modality to generate harmonic incertitude are likewise present in the *Te Deum*. After the opening progression from G to E♭, in the *Te ergo quaesumus*, for example (see ex. 2.2), we hear a Phrygian progression from A♭ to G (bars 3–4) that is indeed harmonically ambiguous. Something of the "mystical and emotional unrest" that Berlioz experienced from hearing the music at his first communion (as he notes in chapter I

(a)

(b)

(c)

Example 2.1. *L'Enfance du Christ*, Hérode's aria. (a) mm. 35–37; (b) mm. 38–43; (c) mm. 123–126.

of the *Mémoires*) may be heard in this *Te ergo quaesumus*, whose opening lines are rendered increasingly complex by irregular phrasing and chromatic inflection. This movement is not only a retrospective-sounding composition, it is in fact almost entirely based on the *Agnus Dei* of the early *Messe solennelle*, here reused in a compatible religious context.[40] This must be seen not merely as a recycling of earlier musical material, but as the uncovering of a concealed layer of the past linked to a present reflection of an individual identity. The surface of the *Te ergo quaesumus* may be said to express a "present" founded on a recollection that links the composer to his past; the use of memory in this way leads to musical expression of a timeless sort.

Example 2.2. *Te Deum, Te ergo quaesumus*, mm. 1–11.

The description of Berlioz's first communion was written in 1848, during the period of the composition or revision of the *Te Deum*: "I thought I saw the gates of heaven, a heaven of love and of pure delight, a heaven more pure and a thousand times more beautiful than the one so often described to me. How magnificent is the power of true expression! How incomparably beautiful is melody that comes from the heart!" As is well known, Berlioz then discovered that this moving religious melody was nothing other than an arrangement of the aria "Quand le bien-aimé reviendra" from the *opéra comique* by Dalayrac, *Nina, ou la folle par amour*. He would long associate religious experience with the truthful expression of that simple melody, that "chef-d'œuvre dans son extrême simplicité."[41] Indeed, the aria almost becomes a poetic leitmotif in the *Mémoires*: he mentions it again in chapter V in an arrangement for the ballet as played on the English horn by Gustave Vogt: "Whatever the talents of the singer who created to role of Nina, I find it hard to believe that this melody found in her interpretation an expression as truthful and touching as that of Vogt."[42]

These allusions to the past are significant because they provide the subtext of musical procedures in the *Te Deum* that cannot otherwise be fully explained. This retrospective dimension is also revealed by the static character of certain procedures of harmonic and rhythmic ostinato and "collision." The "Salvum fac populum" of the final movement of the *Te Deum* (bars 57ff.), for example, eventually "collides" with the opening *Judex crederis* section, when the 9/8 *Judex crederis* frame is superimposed upon the "Salvum" music, which is in 3/4. These juxtapositionings provide not only musical contrasts but also manifestations of the struggle of two states of consciousness linked to Berlioz's own past and present. In addition, the use of ostinato itself must be seen in the context of musical "stasis." We first find this procedure in the regular reiteration of the main theme of the *Marche de pèlerins* of *Harold en Italie*, which is repeatedly interrupted by the "kneeling" of the congregation as indicated by the bell-like sounds of the flute, oboe, and harp (bars 26, 36, 46, etc.). Here the ostinato serves an illustration of an imaginary scene. Similarly, the ostinato played by the strings in the *Course à l'abîme* of *La Damnation de Faust* quite obviously represents galloping horses, but it may also be interpreted as a metaphor for the strictness of the subjective path of fate that leads inevitably, no matter what the obstacle, to damnation.[43] In the *Te Deum* Berlioz introduces an ostinato-like repetition—using the main motive with its fivefold reiteration of the note B♭ before the move to C♭ (see ex. 2.3a)— that serves not as an illustrative device but as a symbol: the text, "Judex crederis esse venturus," links the ostinato to the steadiness of fate. The ostinato-like repetition of the D-flat-Major violin motive that accompanies the "benedicamus" and "laudamus" sections of the "Salvum fac populum" episode (see ex. 2.3b) again seems to evoke the intensity of Catholic devotion (as Berlioz himself might have once experienced it). The total design of the last movement of the *Te Deum* may thus be interpreted as one of immense contradiction and conflict,

(a)

(b)

Example 2.3. *Te Deum, Judex crederis.* (a) mm. 8–10; (b) mm. 77–80.

represented by strictly defined parameters of ambiguity (obvious in the harmonic progression at the beginning of the movement) and stasis (ostinato). The contradiction and conflict are different from those of *L'Enfance du Christ*—the polarity in that work occurring between the melancholy of the shepherds' scene, on the one hand, and Hérode's "distressing dream of genocide" on the other[44]—but not unrelated.

Autobiographical (Re-)considerations

Surveying the decade from 1845 to 1855, framed by the composition of *La Damnation de Faust* and the first performance of the *Te Deum*, we encounter various contradictions and conflicts in Berlioz's life: professional failures in Paris; grand successes elsewhere in Europe; a period of exile in London before and during the revolution of February 1848; the death of the composer's father; the death of his sister Nanci; the illness and death of Harriet Smithson; the marriage to Marie Récio.[45]

Such events would naturally lead Berlioz to reconsider his ambitions as an artist and his strategies as a composer. His psychological patterns would be altered, his musical language would bear different semantics. Melancholic reminiscence seems no longer to function as the catalyst of poetic construction, as it does, for example, in *Harold en Italie*. It is now *autobiographical reflection* which assumes that role, and it is the process of autobiographical reflection that marks Berlioz's new, post-1848 state of consciousness. The renderings of his early years in the opening chapters of the *Mémoires*, with their emphasis upon religious experience and upon the quite different characters of his parents, seem to reveal more about Berlioz's current psychological state than about his psyche as a boy in La Côte-Saint-André.

The single event that may have precipitated this sort of self-awareness was the death of his father, which occurred on 28 July 1848, and which led, the composer tells us, to a "state of utter dejection." "It seems to me that my life no longer has a purpose," he wrote to his sister Adèle. "In everything I have tried to do until now I was instinctively inclined to think of my father, motivated by a desire to have him approve of my efforts and by a hope that he would be proud of them. And now . . ."[46]

Losing his father meant losing a major source of creative energy, for the intellectual and free-thinking man who had educated his son in classical literature and who had urged him to follow his footsteps as a physician was nothing if not that. Indeed, a good portion of the *Mémoires* tells of Berlioz's struggle, essentially without success, to convince his father of the rightness of his decision to dedicate his life to music. The importance of such father-son conflict cannot be underestimated: "the nineteenth-century bourgeois family, especially in France, made much of the children's obligations to their parents, especially—as when the choice of a profession was under discussion—to their father," as Peter Gay has written. "To disobey strong recommendations was an act almost of impiety."[47] Imperial authority—we have noted that Berlioz was careful to tell his father about the heroic work by which he intended to memorialize Napoleon in 1846—is the political side of the coin whose other side bears the stamp of patriarchal authority. After the death of his father, Berlioz returned to the idea of Napoleonic authority as both a retrospective element and as an element of a vision, sometimes realistic, sometimes utopian, of a future Empire of the Arts. The *Te Deum,* inspired by Berlioz's nostalgia for Napoleon in the early eighteen-forties and perhaps designed as a realization of earlier Napoleonic projects, was the first work that Berlioz brought to completion after the loss of his father: that fact allows us to read it as a symbolic reference to the very idea of authority, both private and political, and renders all the more understandable and poignant the depth of the composer's disappointment that his father never heard, or praised, a performance of this or any other of his monumental compositions. In these circumstances, his father's death may be seen as having had the psychological effect of a "damnation de Berlioz."

If we see the *Te Deum* as reflecting the authority of power—incarnate in Berlioz's father and represented in his psychic universe by the historical figure of Napoleon—then we may see *L'Enfance du Christ,* and particularly its pastoral centerpiece, as reflecting the converse: the contemplativeness and devotion of religious faith as embodied (imperfectly) in the naive Catholicism of his mother, with whom Berlioz's relations always remained problematical and unresolved. Madame Berlioz had condemned her son for his musical ambitions, as he so vividly recounts in chapter X of the *Mémoires*: "My mother was therefore convinced that by devoting myself to musical composition (which exists nowhere, for the French, outside of the theater) I was setting out upon a road that led to disgrace in this world and to damnation in the next."

With an acute sense of the dramatic intensity of this scene, Berlioz continues to recount his conversation with his mother, who calls her son *vous* rather than *tu* and who in the end denounces him: "You are no longer my son! I curse you!" We do not know a great deal more about Berlioz's relationship with his mother. After his five-month stay in La Côte-Saint-André in 1832, during which period relations with her were cordial and not without understanding,[48] he never again returned home during his mother's lifetime. His mother's death in 1838 is nowhere mentioned in the *Mémoires.*

From a psychological perspective, the second part of *L'Enfance du Christ* may thus be seen to represent the feminine, melancholic aspect of Berlioz's view of religion. The foreground of the work delivers the biblical story, while the background evokes Berlioz's own religious experiences, realized musically by allusions to the carols he would have heard as a boy in the provinces. Berlioz's actual attitude to the melancholy of the shepherds' scene, however, is not one of religious sublimity or devotion, but rather one of irony, as we know from the hoax he concocted around the *maître de chapelle imaginaire*, the would-be seventeenth-century composer of this music. In *L'Enfance du Christ* we have, on one level, an idealized presentation of a pastoral tale from the Bible, and, on another level, the work of a composer who seems to be reflecting upon what it is to tell that tale. Remembrance of religious acts and emotions is the medium that relates these two dimensions of artistic religiosity.

Notes

This article emerged from various presentations at the University of Würzburg (2003), the University of British Columbia, Vancouver (2004), the Universities of Mainz and Zürich (2005), and the University of the Saarland (2006). I am grateful to colleagues, students, and friends at these institutions, and to the editor of the present volume, all of whose questions, comments, and criticism provided invaluable assistance as I reconsidered and revised the text.

For the sake of clarity, I note that the most important works discussed here are *La Damnation de Faust*, composed in 1845–1846 and first performed on 6 December 1846; the *Te Deum*, essentially composed in 1848–1849, revised in 1852, and first performed on 30 April 1855; *L'Enfance du Christ*, first performed in its entirety on 10 December 1854; and *La Fuite en Égypte* (which became the *Deuxième Partie* of *L'Enfance du Christ*), first performed in its entirety on 2 December 1853. *L'Adieu des bergers* and *Le Repos de la Sainte Famille* (sections 2 and 3 of *La Fuite en Égypte*) were first performed, respectively, on 12 November 1850 and 3 May 1853.

1. *CG* IV, p. 647 (16 December 1854): "Ainsi, je suis devenu bon enfant, humain, clair, mélodique, je fais enfin de la musique comme tout le monde, voilà qui est bien convenu. Adieu, la sensation causée par cette conversion augmente. Laissons-la augmenter."

2. Berlioz first told this story in a letter of 15 May 1852 (*CG* IV, pp. 156–159); he reprinted it in *Les Grotesques de la musique*, pp. 185–189. The score of *La Fuite en Égypte*, printed in 1852, included the subtitle *Fragment d'un mystère en style ancien*.

3. In fact the mediant relationship expressed at the beginning of the fourth phrase became common only in the nineteenth century.

4. Julian Rushton, *The Music of Berlioz* (Oxford: Oxford University Press, 2001), p. 324.

5. Heine as quoted in the *Post-Scriptum* of Berlioz's *Mémoires*.

6. *CG* IV, p. 645.

7. Berlioz mentions a completed *Te Deum* in the "Labitte Catalogue" of 1846, but correspondence proves that the composition was not finished before 1849. See *NBE* 10, p. viii; and Rushton, *The Music of Berlioz*, pp. 55ff.

8. Peter Bloom, *The Life of Berlioz* (Cambridge: Cambridge University Press, 1998), pp. 117ff.; *Cairns* 2, pp. 428ff.

9. See, for example, Klaus Heinrich Kohrs, *Hector Berlioz: Autobiographie als Kunstentwurf* (Frankfurt am Main: Stroemfeld Verlag, 2003), "Vorwort," and p. 31.

10. Jacques Barzun, "Fourteen Points about Berlioz and the Public, or Why There Is Still a Berlioz Problem," in *Berlioz: Past, Present, Future*, ed. Peter Bloom (Rochester, NY: University of Rochester Press, 2003), pp. 193–201, here, p. 200.

11. This postscript appears as a letter to a biographer ("M." [Eugène de Mirecourt]) dated 25 May 1858. The year 1858 is a misprint for 1856: Mirecourt's biography of Berlioz appeared in August of that year.

12. Cf. Ralph P. Locke, "The Religious Works," in *The Cambridge Companion to Berlioz*, ed. Peter Bloom (Cambridge: Cambridge University Press, 2000), pp. 36–107, here, p. 98: "[T]here was a longstanding Bourbon tradition of performing a *Te Deum* on the occasion of a military victory."

13. "Oui le Requiem a un frère [. . .]" (*CG* V, p. 77)—a letter sent to Franz Liszt on 30 April 1855, the day of the first performance of the *Te Deum*. Berlioz used a similar metaphor when he spoke of the *Lacrimosa* of the *Requiem* and the *Judex crederis* of the *Te Deum* as "first cousins" (*Cairns* 2, p. 431).

14. Barzun, "Berlioz as Man and Thinker," in *The Cambridge Companion to Berlioz*, pp. 11–19, here, p. 13.

15. See, for instance, *Mémoires*, chapter IX.

16. *Mémoires, Post-Scriptum*: "Je suis un incrédule en musique, ou, pour mieux dire, je suis de la religion de Beethoven, de Weber, de Gluck, de Spontini, qui croient, professent et prouvent pas leurs œuvres que tout est bon ou que tout est mauvais; l'effet produit par certaines combinaisons devant seul les faire condamner ou absoudre." Cairns's translation of the first phrase as "I am a free-thinker in music" diminishes the pseudo-religious subtext of this passage, while the German translation by Elly Ellès (1903–1905), often reprinted, accentuates the religious overtones: "Ich bin ein Atheist in der Musik. . . ." See Berlioz, *Memoiren*, ed. Wolf Rosenberg (Munich: Rogner & Bernhard, 1979), p. 477.

17. Berlioz, "Aperçu sur la musique classique et la musique romantique," *Le Correspondant* (22 October 1830): "Les compositeurs romantiques [. . .] ont écrit sur leur bannière: 'Inspiration libre.' Ils ne prohibent rien, tout se qui peut être du domaine musical est par eux employé. Cette phrase de Victor Hugo est leur devise: 'L'art n'a que faire de menottes, de lisières et de bâillons, il dit à l'homme de génie, *va* et le lâche dans ce grand jardin de poésie où il n'y a pas de fruit défendu.'" Berlioz slightly alters Hugo's original text: "L'art n'a que faire des lisières, des menottes, des bâillons; il vous dit: Va! et vous lâche dans ce grand jardin de poésie, où il n'y a pas de fruit défendu."

18. This work was first published in 1844 at a time that may have seen the first plans for what became the *Te Deum*. One may also mention *L'Impériale*, written in 1854, which links empirical power with praise of God, as does the *Te Deum*, as yet unperformed.

19. Katherine Kolb has brilliantly pointed out the political and social importance of "fidelity" in the structure of *Euphonia*: "Fidelity is the very foundation of the Euphonian creed: the musicians are bound—trained—to love, honor and obey the great composers whose works they perform. Their greatest god is Gluck—not Beethoven, as one might expect—because Gluck represents the famous reformer of Italian musical 'promiscuity' in the name of fidelity to the text" (Kolb, "Plots and Politics: Berlioz's Tales of Sound and Fury," in *Berlioz: Past, Present, Future*, pp. 76–89, here, p. 84).

20. Berlioz, *Mémoires, Post-Scriptum*.

21. On 3 July 1831 Berlioz explained to Humbert Ferrand his plan for a large-scale work in which a despotic dictator rules with injustice and cruelty until a prophet announces to him that he is about to face the last judgment: "The prophet would censure him for his crimes and announce to him the end of the world and the

last judgment. The angry despot would have the prophet thrown into prison, and, returning to his sacrilegiously voluptuous pleasures, would be surprised in the middle of his revelries by the terrifying trumpets of the resurrection; and, in the finale of this musical drama, we would witness the dead rising from their graves, the living shrieking with unbridled horror, the whole word staggering, and the angels thundering in the clouds" (*CG* I, pp. 467–468).

22. *CG* I, pp. 424–425 (12 April 1831).

23. *CG* I, p. 507.

24. See D. Kern Holoman, "The Berlioz Sketchbook Recovered," *19th-Century Music*, 7 (1984), pp. 282–317, here, p. 291. See also Wolfgang Dömling, *Hector Berlioz und seine Zeit* (Laaber: Laaber Verlag, 1986), p. 195, for a detailed description of these plans and their development.

25. *CG* III, p. 368.

26. Barzun, "Berlioz as Man and Thinker," p. 18.

27. See Heinrich Heine, "Musikalische Saison von 1844, Erster Bericht" (Paris, 25 April 844), in *Lutetia—Berichte über Politik, Kunst und Volksleben* (1854), published in French, one year before Heine's death, as *Lutèce* (Paris: Michel Lévy, 1855). A modern critical edition is Heinrich Heine, *Historisch-Kritische Gesamtausgabe*, vol. 14/1 (Hamburg: Hoffman und Campe, 1990), pp. 127–145.

28. See Rushton, *The Music of Berlioz*, p. 210: "The 'Lacrimosa' is the best justification for Heine's metaphor, to which the composer took exception, of Berlioz as a 'colossal nightingale, a lark in the size of an eagle.' "

29. See *CG* III, p. 172.

30. See Udo Köster, *Literatur und Gesellschaft in Deutschland, 1830–1848: Die Dichtung am Ende einer Kunstperiode* (Berlin: Kohlhammer Verlag, 1984), p. 144.

31. Heinrich Heine, "Gemäldeausstellung von 1831," in Heine, *Historish-Kritische Gesamtausgabe*, vol. 12/1 (Hamburg: Hoffmann und Campe, 1980), p. 47.

32. Martin's painting, in the Tate Gallery, London, may be seen at http://www.tate.org.uk/servlet/ ViewWork?workid=9310&roomid=1384, accessed 15 March 2006.

33. See Locke, "The Religious Works," p. 101.

34. Quoted in *CG* IV, p. 650.

35. Rushton, *The Music of Berlioz*, p. 61.

36. At the end of the Part I of *L'Enfance du Christ*, the door to the offstage room from which the chorus of angels has been singing is to be closed, thus providing a *sourdine vocale*. At the end of Part II the chorus of angels, accompanied with spare instrumentation, is to be placed even farther offstage. At the end of Part III the *chœur mystique* and the chorus of angels (still offstage) sing the Andantino mistico without accompaniment, fading to nothing on the final "Amen."

37. *CG* IV, p. 158 (18 May 1852). Berlioz writes "mixtolydien." It is not clear whether the misspelling is intentional. In the reprint of this letter in *Les Grotesques de la musique*, p. 187, it is just "lydien."

38. Letter to Hans von Bülow of 28 July 1854 (*CG* IV, p. 559). In the same letter Berlioz sets down what we know as a rising Phrygian scale, admitting that he does not know its proper Greek name but noting that it creates harmonies and cadences appropriate to the situation.

39. One may compare this modal procedure to that of "Le Roi de Thulé" in *La Damnation de Faust*, a "chanson gothique" that evokes historical antiquity via a pseudo-Lydian (or raised) fourth, proceeding from F up to C via B♮, with the curious

instrumentation of the solo viola, but here in the context of a naive girl singing "Once upon a time." See Rushton, *The Music of Berlioz*, pp. 175–176.

40. See *NBE* 23, p. 11. David Cairns suggests that the "Salvum fac populum" section of the *Judex crederis* was likewise inspired by Berlioz's first communion experience (*Cairns 2*, p. 428).

41. *Journal des débats* (1 January 1852).

42. This issue and its significance for Berlioz's understanding of instrumental music are further discussed in Kohrs, *Berlioz*, pp. 172–177.

43. At the Salzburg Festival in 1999, the ostinato served as a symbol for the relentlessness of the machines of the industrial era.

44. The phrase is used by Manfred Angerer in "Exotik und Historismus in *L'Enfance du Christ* von Hector Berlioz," in *Festschrift Othmar Wessely zum 60. Geburtstag*, ed. Angerer et al. (Tutzing: Schneider, 1982), pp. 1–10, here p. 7.

45. Comprehensive chronologies of Berlioz's life may be found in Dömling, *Berlioz und seine Zeit*, in *The Cambridge Companion to Berlioz*, and, most detailed, in Pierre Citron, *Calendrier Berlioz* [*Cahiers Berlioz*, 2] (La Côte-Saint-André: Association nationale Hector Berlioz, 2000).

46. *CG* III, p. 572 (21 August 1848).

47. Peter Gay, "Berlioz's Berlioz," in *Berlioz: Past, Present, Future*, pp. 3–15, here, p. 6.

48. See *Cairns 1*, p. 548.

Part Two

In Fiction and Fact

Chapter Three

Euphonia *and the Utopia* *of the Orchestra as Society*

Joël-Marie Fauquet

Tyranny and anarchy are never far asunder.
—Jeremy Bentham

Centropolis, a city in the Republic of Benthamia, is built on the Isthmus of Guatemala. A universal capital, it is home to the Assembly of Nations. Festivals of interplanetary dimension are given here in an outdoor amphitheater. Not only has Nature greatly favored this space for the projection of the voice, but so, too, have the arts.

> On one side we find a sharp wall of rock composed of superposed layers of prismatic basalt, rising to a height of some fifty feet; on the other side, a small, almost perfectly semicircular hill that leads gently down to the base of the rock, taking more or less the form of the ordinary amphitheater. Indeed, it was necessary to add only a small amount of earth in order to achieve a perfect likeness of such a structure.[1]

All solemn performances here are preceded by a religious ceremony whose beginning is marked by the firing of a hundred canons, thunderously leading the assembled masses, kneeling, to intone the Universal Hymn: one hundred thousand voices—and not a single sour note.

> The people of Bentham are so musically practiced that the ensemble of their four-part choral performance leaves nothing to be desired. In order to maintain proper rhythm among such a tremendous number of performers, in such a large area, a great flag placed high on the rocks—not far from a colossal statue of Jeremy Bentham, and manipulated with total regularity and precision by a series of levers controlled by the President of the Musical Institutions of the Republic—ensures that the beat is seen and felt even by those situated very far away. The harmoniousness of the hymn is all the more assured in that all the singers, having themselves long before chosen the lines best suited to their vocal ranges, have memorized their parts. True, the result of such freedom of choice is that the inner voices are somewhat neglected. But on the other

hand—and this is essential—the soprano and bass lines are sung with more than ample vigor, and, in addition, all voices are supported by an orchestra of ten thousand artists and amateurs, who give and maintain the pitch. Furthermore, without in any way denigrating the emotional power of the harmony, it has to be said that the stanza which produces the most astonishing effect is the one sung entirely in unison. To me, there is simply nothing under the heavens more capable of enchantment, of filling my breast with pride, of thrilling me to the point of tears, of electrifying me to the point of dizziness, than the unison singing of one hundred thousand voices.[2]

Was Félix Bodin aware of the orchestration of *La Marseillaise* that Berlioz set down in 1830? Was Berlioz aware of *Le Roman de l'avenir*—"the novel of the future"—that Bodin would publish four years later? Is it pure coincidence that Rotceh, the composer and prefect of wind instruments in the musical city of Euphonia (in Berlioz's tale of that name), directs a performance in the metropolitan amphitheater of a hymn by Gluck, with six thousand voices accompanied by "a hundred families of clarinets and saxophones, a hundred others of flutes, four hundred cellos, and three hundred harps," all as practiced as the singers and players of Bentham?[3] Is it possible that Berlioz remembered the mechanically controlled flag that beat time for the Benthamians when he imagined his own electric metronome capable of keeping together variously massed musicians? And was he thinking of Bentham's President of the Musical Institutions of the Republic when he developed his own concept of the orchestra conductor as an all-powerful master reigning over an empire of sound?

Fabio Mummio, the Anglophile hero of *Le Roman de l'avenir*, speaks for those who have never had occasion to attend a grand *festival* or *musical meeting*. Listeners, he notes,

should not be placed at ground level in order fully to appreciate such musical effects; they should rather be positioned at a height of approximately eight hundred fifty feet. Thus, hovering over this vast and magnificent scene are more than fifteen hundred hot-air balloons, filled with the most elegant women of Centropolis's high society, the thousands of colors of their garb creating an extraordinary and brilliant rainbow. At that height, the sounds of the hundred thousand voices and instruments seem to the ear to be blended together as one; they are beyond description, like a vast and ineffably fine harmonic mist.[4]

From this it becomes clear that *how* one listens is what in a way creates musical space—a notion over which the twentieth century's avant-garde has spilt a great deal of ink. But let us not get ahead of ourselves. Mummio's vision reminds us of the distance between the theater orchestras of the eighteenth century, whose players were called "symphonistes" or "concertistes," and the orchestra described here as composed of families of instruments. Recognized as a community of musicians whose combined efforts would lead to the glory of one—the composer—the orchestra may be seen as a symbolic projection of a utopian society in which the means of production, put in place by an industrial culture, are idealized.

If, in large measure thanks to Berlioz, that orchestra rapidly acquires the status of a unique and singular musical instrument played by one extraordinary musician, namely, the conductor, it is first and foremost because the composition they perform creates the musical "space" in which the players, united by a shared ideal of perfection, form a collective—a collective that is at once egalitarian and hierarchical. Like all utopian communities under the aegis of a figure of authority, the orchestra submits to one dominant individual who, with the baton as the symbol of his status, affirms his power and organizes the work.

History and Memory

A number of contemporary texts bring to light the close connection between the social and musical realms, not the least important of which is the brief historical résumé found in Georges Kastner's *Cours d'instrumentation considéré sous les rapports poétiques et philosophiques de l'art à l'usage des jeunes compositeurs*, which implicitly and closely associates the progress of orchestration and the progress of civilization itself. (When Kastner mentions the performance in Vienna in 1811 of a Handel oratorio, by an ensemble of five hundred ninety musicians, for example, he imagines the city "invaded by harmony."[5]) But it is of course à propos of Berlioz that various commentators have pointedly evoked the notion of a utopia and of the role such a notion might have played in some of the works he realized or imagined, such as the oratorio *Le Dernier Jour du monde*, conceived in late 1830. In order usefully to treat this question, it seems to me that we must first examine Berlioz's own personal and particular linking of history and memory.

It is readily apparent that Berlioz is the "god" of his own genesis. That is to say, for him, in the beginning, there was not simply history, but *his* history. Berlioz the artist was as it were born fully armed with his earliest emotions, and with them a nascent world of sound. The work of art for him is the completion of a process of crystallization that grows in accordance with the life cycle itself: a first emotional shock—a "secousse," as he calls it—which corresponds to an awakening in the world of nature, and which serves as the impulse to further creativity. Those who trigger the shock for him—Virgil, Shakespeare, Gluck—are more than his poetic protectors, they are the very fathers of his musical destiny. In relation to his own history, Berlioz takes it upon himself to accomplish, beyond history, a dutiful act of memory. Aeneas becomes a man of action when, in a dream, he receives from the ghosts of the gods Priam and Hector (at the beginning of Act V of the opera *Les Troyens*) the order to complete his mission: "Il faut vivre et partir"; "Il faut vaincre et fonder." Berlioz himself received such orders from Virgil, Shakespeare, and Gluck. The entirety of his œuvre will be propagated by the genetic resonance of their voices. Berlioz remains so faithful to his progenitors that he comes to believe that only he can conceive the text of his Virgilian operatic epic. He is his own poet at the same time that he is the composer of the history of Aeneas, that is to say, in a sense, the composer of the history of himself.

Berlioz is thus a creator in accordance with the dictates of his memory. As a composer, he seeks out "lost" sonorities, the sonorities that first made him aware that he existed and that he experienced sensation via music. He is the resonating memory of his own history, for whom history otherwise does not exist. He demonstrates his consciousness of this fact when he writes that the theory of ancestors and descendents in art "is, for me, a palpable and offensive absurdity. [. . .] Time, period, nationality, age—all of that means nothing to me." As assiduous a reader of Michaud's *Biographie universelle* at sixty-three as he was at fifteen, Berlioz condemns so many biographers' contradictions about "those poor little rascals whom they call great men," and concludes, significantly, that "history, like so many other received ideas, is a hoax."[6] It is his opposition to the idea of history as the legitimate foundation of civilization that, for Berlioz, opens the way to utopia.

Berlioz's historical notions are accompanied by a heightened and despondent awareness of the fleetingness of time, of ageing, of decline. Having rendered into artistic forms so many images that originated in his memory, having relived them and revivified them by means of the kinesics of music itself, Berlioz, in old age, plagued with boredom, indifference, and bitterness, found his imagination depleted of the musical impulses that had long shielded him from the scourge of Nothingness. His mission accomplished, he is condemned, suffocating, to a quotidian existence, with no hope for the future. He reveals himself to be extremely vulnerable to the weight of times past. The realities of the very history he didn't trust in effect condemn him to death. One could almost say that Berlioz dies as a victim of the revenge that history wreaked upon his personal story, which he had early on transformed into a creative utopia.

The Imaginary Mirage

Several of Berlioz's works, because of their subject or their form, seem to be the products of a utopian stream of thought. One, for example, is the very mediocre *Chant des chemins de fer*, of 1846, which represents a resuscitation, however unlikely, of the passing interest he demonstrated in 1831 for the socialist doctrines of the Saint-Simonians.[7] Another work bearing the stamp of utopianism is *Le Temple universel*, for two male choirs who juxtapose, then superimpose, words in both English and French. True, this bilingual "duet for two peoples," as Berlioz calls it, conforms to the universalist intentions of those who prepared the World Exhibition in London, which was to take place in 1861. But in fact Berlioz's devotion to utopian thought has deeper roots. All things considered, the work that best reveals them is *Les Troyens*, whose action would finally lead to the dawn of a new city and a new civilization. Here the past of the destroyed city of Troy is brought to life in the present and prosperous city of Carthage, which Aeneas then abandons in order to accomplish the mission of the foundation of a new capital, Rome, destined eventually to dominate the universe.

We must nonetheless carefully distinguish between what emanates from the imagination and what belongs properly speaking to the domain of the utopian. For if utopian ideas cannot come into being without the imagination, it does not follow that all products of the imagination are utopian.[8] Now, Berlioz is more than anything else "possessed" by his imagination. This is what is responsible for his singular status in the minds of contemporary critics, if one is to believe Pierre Boulez, for example, who notes of Berlioz that "a large part of his work remained in the realm of the imaginary [. . .]":

> He has as much imagination as he does practical sense. One of the constants of his character is precisely this admixture of the real and the fantastical—the realism capable of being as meticulous as the fantastic is extravagant. [. . .] The spectacle of which Berlioz always dreamed is a spectacle of himself, projected into an imaginary world, into a future dimension nourished by an extraordinary and now extinct past.[9]

As a practitioner of the *genre instrumental expressif*, Berlioz quite lucidly measures the gulf between the real and the imaginary, and the impenetrable obstacle this gulf presents to the creator. When he attends the celebration of the feast of Corpus Christi in Rome, his traveling companions provoke his enthusiasm by promising that he is going to hear a *coro immenso*. "I was already thinking of the musical pomp of the religious ceremonies of the Temple of Solomon, my imagination burned hotter and hotter, I went so far as to allow myself to hope for something comparable to the extravagance of Ancient Egypt. . . . Imagination be damned! You do nothing but make of our lives an interminable mirage!"[10]

Somewhat later, Berlioz evokes the disillusionment that is the lot of a musician "with love of art in his heart" when he is condemned to live in Rome. "He will experience constant torture as he sees his poetic illusions crushed, one by one, and constant agony as he watches the grand musical edifice composed in his imagination come tumbling down amidst so many disheartening and depressing realities."[11]

In the *Traité d'instrumentation*, realism and fantasy sometimes combine on another level that seems utopian: while establishing the basis of a poetics of sound inseparable from the work of the imagination, Berlioz nonetheless constructs a rational hierarchy of instrumental forces and possibilities. The orchestra becomes an instrument unto itself because and only because it is an ideal "society" in which the work of each member is properly encouraged and appreciated.[12] In this regard, in 1903, the year of the centenary of "our" Berlioz (that is, the Gallic Berlioz, the counterweight to the Teutonic Wagner), the nascent Musicians' Union (the *Syndicat des musiciens*), whose spokesman was Alfred Bruneau, was overflowing with gratitude: "Thank you [, dear Berlioz,] for having put an end to the belittlement of our labors, as was common in times past, and for causing our onerous daily travail to be honored and even revered. Thank you for having transformed musicians into artists!"[13] Always a controversial figure, Berlioz meets with unanimity on at least this particular point: he is the incarnation of the modern orchestra. The members of this orchestra are his "colleagues" and his "friends." If Berlioz is an artistic benefactor, and he is, then he must also be a social benefactor. It is in this way that the role of the musician is revealed as being "political" in the literal sense of the word.

Lélio and the Genesis of the Orchestra as Hero

As I have suggested elsewhere,[14] the five parts of the *Symphonie fantastique*, above and beyond the literary and emotional program that supports them, comprise five different species of movement: the first, "Rêveries, Passions," and the last, "Songe d'une nuit de sabbat," suggest interior mental spaces, or, as Henri Michaux would put it, "l'espace du dedans";[15] the second, "Un bal," third, "Scène aux champs," and fourth, "Marche au supplice," suggest external social spaces—the salon, the site of social relations par excellence; the country, the site of isolation of the self; and the city, the site, in the age of romanticism, of the social order's most menacing exertions upon the individual. The last movement paints the disintegration of the self of the artist (poisoned by opium in the preceding nightmare of the march) as he rejects the social order and descends into hell. The *Fantastique*, subtitled *Épisode de la vie d'un artiste*, represents, on the psychological and structural level, on the wings of a transcendent and entirely original score, the gradual immolation of the self in a progressive and violent combustion of orchestral timbres. The "mélologue" *Le Retour à la vie*, later restyled "monodrame lyrique" (and *Lélio ou Le Retour à la vie*), forms the sequel to the symphony, whose action it reverses: this is the story of the reconquering of the hero by himself, of his symbolic reinsertion into society via the intermediacy of nature, a process in which the orchestra serves as both image and instrument. The protagonists of this heterogeneous and unclassifiable work are separated into two groups: the real and the fictive. Lélio, "real," is a composer and a friend of Horatio; Horatio, "fictive," is a poet and Lélio's "double." Lélio's motto is "vivre [. . .] pour mon art et pour l'amitié"—"to live, for my art, and for friendship." This ambiguity between the real and the imaginary, which generates the illusion of life itself, is a characteristic of Berlioz's œuvre that will gradually give rise to his idealistic vision of the orchestra. After the *Ballade du pêcheur*, the opening number of the *monodrame*, Lélio reflects inwardly: "What in the world can it be, this singular faculty that substitutes the imagined for the real? What is it, this ideal orchestra, which sings inside of me?"

In *Lélio* the resurrection and mental reconstruction of the hero are accomplished in the context of a recognition of the orchestra as the artist's sole viable social space—the space, that is, that welcomes the work of art in the best possible conditions. *Le Retour à la vie*, the "return to life," presents an ideal society, the orchestra, in "real" space. That orchestra rehearses a new work—a *Fantaisie sur La Tempête* after Shakespeare—marked by the strikingly innovative sonority of the piano as an orchestral instrument; and this allows the hero, emerging from the throes of passion, to find himself, to live, and once again to create. With *Lélio*, then, Berlioz posits that art puts the life of the artist on the line; that the artist lives in order to create (and not the opposite). To express this notion, he prepares a text that implicitly traces the birth of the orchestra; by conceiving a gradual progression from the pale void of death to the variegated colors of life, Berlioz literally becomes the all-powerful genitor of that orchestra. The choice of *La Tempête* compels an analogy, for the "magician who troubles and calms the elements at will," as Berlioz describes Shakespeare's Prospero, is to the fictive space of the imaginary world what the composer-conductor is to the "real" space of life. This ambivalence continues when Lélio, amplifying the description of the work he has conceived, imagines "choruses of airy spirits capriciously scattered among the orchestra." And then the idea of society-as-orchestra becomes distinctly more precise: "My many students are now coming in," the narrator says, which leads him to express the hope that the "ardor" of this youthful orchestra will perhaps revitalize his own.[16]

After this mental projection of the work, we find the description of what will permit its actual, spatial realization. Here is it particularly important to note that the hero becomes the conductor—and the conductor becomes the hero. He is literally the *maître d'œuvre*, the "foreman" of the enterprise, as fiction meets reality. Lélio's comments and instructions lead to the creation of a story-within-a-story that is much clarified by the stage directions, which indicate precisely where the chorus is to be placed in order for the newly sketched work, the *Fantaisie sur La Tempête*, to be properly performed. Like Prospero, Berlioz as conductor gives orders in a threatening manner; "[il] commande en menaçant." And the orchestra-society sounds as though we are hearing it for the first time. The extraordinary presence of the piano may well be symbolic: the instrument for which orchestral scores are traditionally "reduced" is now incorporated into the larger ensemble; a former rival has now surrendered and agreed to serve as a prism for the reflection and transmission of a rainbow of sound.

Lélio-Berlioz is thus the personage who exercises verbal authority over the spatial organization of the society of sounds and timbres that is represented by the orchestra. If he insists upon being seen by all members of the chorus, it is not only because there must be a proper coordination of the voices with the projection of sound, but also because the projection of the sonorous "edifice" itself must be in perfect equilibrium. At this stage, the orchestra appears as the symbolic depiction of an ideal society whose "citizens," harmoniously ordered, work devoutly for the sake of art. This is the sole society that corresponds to the hero's aspirations, the sole society in which the hero can live and (which is to say the same thing) create. "Good. Everything is ready. Let us begin!" These are the last words he pronounces before the music takes over the recitation.

To resume, it is not that space is imposed upon the orchestra, it is rather that the orchestra in effect creates space. In accordance with this principle, Berlioz believes, as he posits in the *Traité d'instrumentation*, that one must acquire the art of training orchestras that are suited to giving faithful performances of compositions of "all forms and dimensions."[17] In other words, the orchestra must be situated in a manner suitable to the sonorous space created by the musical composition itself.

The Berlioz whom the unionized musicians of 1903 were saluting, through the voice of Bruneau, was the inventor of the orchestra seen as the sum total of its individual members; a human whole, as it were; a society offering certain privileges, but also certain duties. If this humanitarian vision of the orchestra was somewhat exaggerated at the time because of the nationalistic or patriotic tendencies of those who wished to honor the great man, it must not cause us to forget that Berlioz himself, as both technician and "player" of the orchestra, was devoted to the rather mechanistic notion of an "army of executants" whom he saw as an amalgamation of "machines become intelligent," and whose work he likened to the actions of a gigantic keyboard played by the conductor under the composer's supervision.[18] Such a mid-nineteenth-century conception may be said to arise at a chronological intersection of past and future, at a point of transition between the "instrument-machine" dear to Diderot in the eighteenth century and the orchestra conceived, in the twentieth century, as a totally mechanized industrial community.

The Musical Utopia of *Euphonia*

It is not with notes but with words that Berlioz will construct his utopia. In 1844 he invents an imaginary city whose inhabitants are all of them workers in the tyrannical field of music. Whatever the *ville musicale* of Euphonia may owe to Félix Bodin's Centropolis, it is no doubt equally indebted, for some of its features, to Tyrama, the capital city painted by Étienne Cabet in his novel of 1840, *Voyage en Icarie*, where music plays a similarly central role. Appearing four years before *Euphonia*, this book offers a highly detailed utopian project in which the socialist doctrine, transplanted for its realization to America, eventually meets with a failure that is detrimental to the colonists who attempt the venture. In Icaria, as in Euphonia, music is made by and for the entire population; music, vocal and instrumental, is the mark of excellence of an egalitarian society in which goods are not sold but rather shared and exchanged. Everyone studies music from childhood; everyone comes passionately to love it. "Here, all people—men, women, the very young, the very old—are now musicians, although in the past our musicians were almost exclusively foreigners. You cannot imagine the happy consequences of this musical revolution!" Although he arrives from a country in which choral singing is widely cultivated, Lord William

Carisdall, a guest in the Icarian Republic, is no less surprised by the collective and intense qualities of its music making:

> All children without exception learn vocal music, all know how to sing, all learn to play an instrument. In addition, wherever you go, you hear music and singing—at home, at public meetings, at church and at the workshop, when you take a walk, when you go to the theater. You encounter groups of musicians of all kinds, sitting in delightful salons designed expressly for music, and, beyond that, numerous concerts given by machines that replace the musicians and that imitate them so well as to seem to be the real thing.
>
> "Almost all signals are given by the trumpet, although it is to the sound of the horn that our thousands of public transportation vehicles depart and take flight. Don't you find their fanfares charming?"
>
> . "Charming indeed."
>
> "And wait until you hear the music for our national holidays, sung by choruses fifty or a hundred thousand strong."[19]

After the French Revolution, those who used to think Mass now thought Hymn, as Berlioz was himself well aware. The man who orchestrated *La Marseillaise* destined for "all those who have a voice, a heart, and blood in their veins!" could not have forgotten—especially if he had read the *Voyage en Icarie*, as seems likely[20]—the emotions felt by Cabet's narrator when he hears the national anthem of Icaria:

> Valmor had already begun to sing, all the children joined in as a choir; and the fathers, who were engaged in chess, and the mothers, who were busy at another table, stopped playing their games in order to turn towards the singers. Finally everyone, carried away by the same enthusiasm, lent their voices to the singing of the patriotic hymn. And I surprised myself by joining the chorus at the third stanza, something that caused a good deal of laughter and a good deal of applause.[21]

Obligatory musical instruction begun at an early age; mechanization of musical activities; musical signs and signals; a communal fervor for choral singing—all of these things are to be found, programmed and systematized, in *Euphonia, ou la ville musicale*, Berlioz's "novel of the future" (set in 2344), which describes a veritable musical dictatorship situated in the heart of Germany. The town is a kind of "vast conservatory" where the practice of music is subject to the laws of a military government—the only government recognized as efficacious: "Hence the perfect order which obtains in study and the marvelous results that ensue for art." All Euphonians are exclusively occupied with playing, singing, making instruments, or engraving and printing music. In addition, as in Françis Bacon's *New Atlantis* (1624), which first appeared in French as *La Nouvelle Atlantide* in 1702,[22] "some give their time to acoustical research and to the study of that branch of physics which relates to the production of sound."

Art is the sole object of all Euphonia's solemn festivities. A proper utopian, Berlioz traces the map of the city in accordance with categories of musical employment, just as, in the *Traité d'instrumentation*, he arranges the pyramid of the orchestra-society as a series of instrumental *families*. "Each type of voice and instrument has a street bearing its name; the street is inhabited only by that section of the population which practices that particular voice or instrument. There are streets of sopranos, of basses, of tenors, of contraltos, of violins, of horns, of flutes, of harps, and so on." Here, as in the Republics of Bentham and Icaria— but of course Euphonia is not a Republic—gigantism is the measure of the collectivity and the object of its festivities, which fill an enormous roofless enclosure that can house ten thousand musicians and twenty thousand listeners. In the Icarian Republic the trumpet and horn tell the population when to work, when to rest, when to have fun. In Euphonia, those instruments are replaced by a steam-driven organ invented (long before 2344) by Adolphe Sax as a substitute for the church bells of ancient times. The flag used to coordinate the singing masses of Centropolis becomes in Euphonia a telegraph poll, which, with as much nuance as anyone could desire, reproduces for the performers the gestures of the prefects who direct the rehearsals.

The Ear as Musical Space

But the truly utopian musical space of Euphonia, in the most creative sense of the word, is the ear of Berlioz himself. The "cité de la musique" is born of that ear's extraordinary sensitivity to beauty of sound, accuracy of intonation and tempo, dynamic gradation, and expressive accent, all of which must be practiced incessantly in order to reflect with exactitude the intentions of the composer. In addition, if Euphonians are required to render themselves worthy of the art they serve, those who come to hear them are likewise obliged to render themselves worthy of what they hear: "The Minister of Fine Arts selects from the population of the several cities of Germany the twenty thousand privileged listeners who are permitted to attend these festivals. The choice is always determined by the greater or lesser intelligence and musical culture of those individuals." The totalitarian character of the utopian ideology here becomes transparently obvious. It is confirmed by the attitude, common to the regimes which inspire such utopia, that consists in denying any and all contradiction. In the present case we might ask, for example, *where* the privileged few selected by the powers that be can acquire the distinctive qualities that gain them admission to Euphonian festivities, if not, among other things, by attending those festivities in the first place.

Let there be no mistake. *Euphonia, ou la ville musicale* is a serious fantasy, and, on close inspection, a rather frightening one at that. It replies to the question posed by Lélio: "What is this ideal orchestra that sings from deep inside myself?" But it satisfies in a drastic way the final injunction issued by that same Lélio to his assembled instrumental and choral forces: "Good. Everything is ready. Begin!" The order, which is nothing if not severe, represents a severity that appears as a *sine qua non* of music.

The "Description of Euphonia" forms a section of the novella distinct from the rest of the tale; it is similar to a medallion in a painting, or to an island in the sea. This description is not at all arbitrary: it formulates a technical and aesthetic program that is fixed and inviolate. Euphonians have but one goal: to attain a perfect musical appreciation decreed in authoritarian fashion, under the bright star of Gluck, to be the sole appreciation possible. "The rare capacity to appreciate varieties of expression, whether in a composer's work or in its performance, ranks above all others in the minds of the Euphonians." Woe to him whose abilities fail to meet the required standard, woe to him whose works fail to produce the accepted varieties of expression, for that poor soul is "inexorably banished from the city, however eminent his talent, however exceptional his voice, unless he consents to accept some inferior employment, such as the preparation of catgut for strings or the tanning of skins for kettledrums." Is this not an ominous prefiguring of the degrading and punitive measures of which the totalitarian regimes of the twentieth century give us far too many examples?

And that is not all. Berlioz's almost maniacal musical demands in the realm of musical technique—and he assuredly deserves credit for having been the first in France to introduce genuine professionalism into orchestral practice—lead him to establish a division of labor that, as the sociologists have taught us, tends to alienate the workers. As the principle of the division of labor is applied, "the worker becomes less strong, less broad-minded, less independent. Art progresses, artisans regress. [. . .] It thus happens that as industrial science continues to lower the class of workmen, it raises the class of masters."[23] Tocqueville's words serve well to define the new relationship established between conductor and musician, because a system of division of labor is applied to Euphonia's industry of sound: "In addition to the principal master who directs the main study of the instrument, there is one who teaches exclusively the pizzicato, another the use of the harmonics, still another the staccato, and so on. [. . .] Hence the wonderful degrees of *piano* which in Europe the Euphonians alone know how to produce."

The constraining aspects of this sort of specialization—similar to those of the industrial system of mass production as proposed and developed in Berlioz's time—are more than compensated by the advantages it offers. And yet we cannot sufficiently emphasize how much the establishment of a meritocracy, and the ostentatious character of the ballyhoo that accompanied it, tended in industrialized countries (including those with republican forms of government) to mask the inhumane existence it imposed upon its workers. In Euphonia, where everyone sacrifices his existence to music, "prizes have been established for agility, precision, and even for beauty and fitness of tone."

It remains to ask what attitude Euphonians are permitted to adopt when subjected to the effects of the music they produce. This aspect of individual physical engagement with music in the context of a utopian community is hardly unimportant, especially when a relentless discipline theoretically offers liberty to the collectivity, while a dictatorial authority maintains jurisdiction over the liberty of the individual.

In contrast to what prevails in Euphonia, Icarians do not only sing and play. Their musical activities are largely based on the dance. "The ball is always organized as a drama or a ballet in which everyone has a role." For the many balls that take place at weddings, at country gatherings, and elsewhere, there are not enough musicians in Icaria to go around. That is why the accompanying orchestras there are almost always artificial, mechanical, and invisible.

Euphonians, by contrast, seem never to dance. They rest while listening in order to discover how better to perform. When one knows of Berlioz's interest in the dance, and of the brilliance of those moments in his works that suggest choreographic inspiration, one is astonished to see, in *Euphonia,* how little understanding he shows of the corporal expressivity that grows naturally from the musical gesture.

Any marking of the rhythm by bodily movements while singing is strictly forbidden to the choral singers. They are also trained in silence, a silence so absolute and profound that if three thousand Euphonian choristers were assembled in the amphitheater or in any other resonant place, one could still hear the buzzing of an insect [. . .]. They are so highly practiced that even after a long silence during which they may have counted hundreds of rests, they have been known to attack a chord *en masse* without a single singer missing his entrance.

What Lélio-Berlioz asks for is carried out in Euphonia with a technical prowess that leaves nothing to chance. Thus, for example, "a tuning fork attached to every desk enables the instrumentalists to tune noiselessly before and during the performance," while a mechanical device quite similar to the electric metronome later conceived by the Belgian inventor Joannes Verbrugghe (whom Berlioz will encounter in Brussels in 1855), "is actuated by the conductor without being visible to the public, [and] indicates to the eye of each performer, and quite close to him, the beats of each measure. It also denotes precisely the several degrees of *piano* or *forte.*" The work at rehearsals is carefully planned in advance. The orchestral rehearsals take place section by section under the severe supervision of the prefects. Then the orchestra rehearses as a group, and finally the chorus and orchestra rehearse together. At that point the "author," the supreme master, appears and takes control of "this huge intelligent instrument." In this way, Berlioz concludes, the master can then say with perfect truth that "he is *playing the orchestra.*"

From all of this we see that in Euphonia there reigns an official art, and there is admitted only one way to cultivate and appreciate it. The existence of "chairs of musical philosophy" should create no illusions, even if "the most learned men of the time serve to spread among the Euphonians sound ideas as to the purpose and importance of art," "the laws on which it is based," and "accurate historical notions of the revolutions it has undergone." Because it is the task of one of these masters to organize an event that is surprising, to say the least, and which reminds us of the close family relationship between Berlioz's fiction and the utopian spirit in its most totalitarian form: I refer to the peculiar institution of concerts of *bad music*—Berlioz underlines the phrase *concerts de mauvaise musique*—"which Euphonians attend at certain periods of the year in order to hear the monstrosities admired for centuries throughout Europe." This sort of exhibition makes us think of the concerts of *Entartete Musik*, or degenerate music, by which the Third Reich, stigmatizing the modernist excesses produced and appreciated by those of supposedly abhorrent races, essentially the Jew and the Black, hoped to block certain paths to the future. But in Euphonia, what happens is precisely the opposite. The wise men of art intend to settle music's accounts with the past and to demonstrate to their fellow citizens that older works are by no means automatically worthy of admiration, especially those whose principles are not in accord with the current aesthetic norms of the *ville musicale*. Nevertheless, if the objectives are different, the intentions are the same, because in both cases creativity is subject to authoritarian power.

The significance of Euphonia is amplified when the description of the city is placed in the context of the larger novella, which reveals Berlioz as a true pioneer in the literature of anticipation, or science fiction. Because the text is in fact a narrative of multiple revenge accomplished by the various characters whom the author puts on the stage: revenge against a woman, in the guise of the pianist Camille Moke; revenge against Italian music; revenge against mediocre orchestras; and revenge against bad music, which leads to misfortune—to the final crime, carried out by a horrendous instrument about which we shall say a word below. *Euphonia*, like all good stories, may be read on several levels; it offers the reader more than a few surprises.[24] Suffice it to say here that the fiction, with its autobiographical undertones, its action motivated by an exceptional artist, portrays with remarkable clarity the orchestra as an autonomous community that is socialized by music.

The Revenge of the Orchestra-Piano

To represent the entire world of sound by means of a single instrument and simultaneously to communicate every possible wish of the composer—such is the dream that Balzac's Gambara attempts to realize precisely when the various socialist utopias are trying to establish harmonious living conditions for all actors on the stage of the new industrial world.[25] Note that neither of the two instruments particularly emblematic of industrial manufacture—the organ, not yet symphonic, and the piano, assimilator of all musics but in forms severely reduced—can claim to put forth the sum total of all means of musical expression with the efficaciousness of the "panharmonicon" constructed by Gambara. In fact the panharmonicon owes its utopian character both to its singular mechanism and to the composer-performer's desire to enter into a kind of extraordinary, hypothetical space that is appropriate to this anything but ordinary instrument.[26]

The sound machine invented by Gambara finds an equivalent in the gigantic instrument that Berlioz imagines in *Euphonia* and that brings about the tale's tragic dénouement. The description of the *ville musicale*, to broaden the context of what has been said so far, is the project of reform that Rotceh sends to Xilef (the composer who is Euphonia's prefect of voices and string instruments) in order that Xilef may then forward it to the Academy of Palermo. Berlioz proceeds in the manner of a proper utopian: he intends to replace a musical reality that he takes to be corrupt with a harmonious city imprecisely situated somewhere in Germany, the land of "true" music, a city conceived solely for the purpose of supporting the cause of that great art whose pinnacle is represented by Gluck. Such an effort is motivated by the author's aversion to Italian music, and by his conviction that a reign of art at once great and true can be instituted only by means of a drastic disciplinary reform of all the forces and institutions required for the production and performance of music. In contrast to the sad spectacle offered in Italy by so many poorly constituted orchestras, by so many uncultured singers and conductors, and by the emptiness of so many works that only corrupt the taste of the musical public, we are thus offered the musical city of Euphonia, whose inhabitants are compelled by the police to devote themselves totally to music in order to be able impeccably to perform it.

What is more, the framework of the novel makes use of certain autobiographical facts more or less transposed for the occasion, such as the artistic and personal betrayal by the singer Ellimac (an obvious inversion of Camille), who has broken off relations with Xilef. Ellimac has decided to travel to the *ville musicale* in order to take part, under the pseudonym of Nadira, in the festival in honor of Gluck that will be directed by Rotceh (Hector), composer and prefect of wind instruments, as we have seen. At first Rotceh refuses to collaborate with Nadira because of his aversion to Italian music. But he eventually changes his mind when he hears her sublime interpretation of an aria from Gluck's *Alceste*. Indeed Rotceh's admiration for Nadira is then transformed into love, which she returns. Xilef, meanwhile, to whom Ellimac had earlier said she was leaving for America, abandons his posts in Euphonia and goes off in a vain search to track her down. Back in Euphonia, he attends a garden party given by Nadira and Rotceh at their villa. On seeing his former mistress in the happy company of his friend, he is perfectly willing to adopt a stoical resignation, but when he realizes that the woman is in fact openly deceiving Rotceh, Xilef deplores this second betrayal and determines to take revenge upon her both for himself and for his friend.

The instrument of vengeance, as Berlioz conceives it, is a monster in all senses of the word. It consists of an amalgamation of the piano and the orchestra of a sort that the author, we suppose, takes to be a perversion of nature. First, for acoustical reasons: the piano is rarely the object of Berlioz's unadulterated affection, except under the fingers of a Chopin, primarily because performers tend to abuse the pedal, which creates "intolerable" harmonic dissonance, as he writes in the *Traité d'instrumentation*.[27] Second, for sentimental reasons: Camille Moke, the attractive young pianist, was also guilty of betrayal when, in 1831, she rejected Berlioz (already known as a kind of "orchestra-man") and married Pleyel. Third, and finally, for symbolic reasons: the opposition that provokes the rupture of the amorous relations between two of the main characters reveals an artistic rivalry between two entities—the piano, an instrument that can play anything but that can become an orchestra only by means of a fundamentally reduced orchestral score; and the orchestra, an amalgamation of instruments that is nonetheless viewed by Berlioz as irreducible and thus as one. As a result, the "orchestra-piano" that Xilef advises Rotceh to offer to Nadira cannot help but be dangerous to all those who are seduced by it. Along with the "orchestra-piano"—this is the ultimate nicety of the fiction—Rotceh will also offer Nadira the round steel pavilion or summer house specifically constructed to accommodate the listeners to this unnatural keyboard crossbreed. Once again, through a utopian prism, Berlioz lays down the principle that the space appropriate to music is a function of the instrument that plays the music, and not the reverse.

The "orchestra-piano" in the story is constructed by a "celebrated mechanical genius" from the utopian city of Euphonia. The instrument resembles "a huge piano whose variegated sound was so powerful that under the fingers of a single virtuoso it could hold its own with an orchestra of two hundred players." Rotceh, entirely unaware of Xilef's sinister intentions, is to hear the instrument for the first time on the occasion of Nadira's birthday, in the presence of her closest friends, all invited to the inaugural ball. On the appointed day, Nadira welcomes the guests, among them all of her *eighteen* lovers. While Rotceh improvises irresistible dance tunes on the new giant piano, Xilef presses a special button on the outer wall of the steel pavilion. As the vertiginous music continues on, the walls of the pavilion begin inexorably to roll in upon themselves, first suffocating the dancers and finally crushing them to death. Rotceh, in despair at having lost Nadira, goes stark-raving mad. He dies some twenty-four hours after Xilef, who, on observing that justice has been done, has inhaled the vapors from a flask of cyanide and thus immediately done himself in.

One may well smile on reading such a preposterous but, alas, premonitory description of so many atrocities—of the horrible, systematic work accomplished by a monstrous machine that comes to a halt only when it is finally "worn out over the unresisting mass of bloody clay." The tragedy, surrealistic though it may be, raises an ethical question that the twentieth century, by inventing weapons of mass destruction, was unable to resolve: Who is the truly guilty party, the person who *uses* such a weapon, or the person who *creates* it? In Berlioz's story, the person responsible for the massacre is clearly Xilef. But there is also the prior existence of the "celebrated mechanical genius whose inventions aroused universal wonder" among the Euphonians. How could it be otherwise in a utopian city where the individual must, no matter how great the sacrifice, acquiesce to whatever seems to represent progress for all?

It is by no means clear, in the final analysis, what becomes of Euphonia in the aftermath of the catastrophe that deprives the city of its two leading musicians. Contrary to what one might think, the event seems not to forecast the decline and fall of this *ville harmonieuse*, for in a certain sense the moral of the story is also utopian. The tragedy provoked by the monster-piano plunges the city into silence, a silence—accompanying the funeral procession of the two friends, both victims of the same woman—that graces the occasion with an eloquence equal to that of the most beautiful music one can imagine.

(Translated by Peter Bloom)

Notes

1. Félix Bodin, *Le Roman de l'avenir* (Paris: Lecointe et Pougin, 1834), p. 163.

2. Ibid., pp. 167–170.

3. *Rotceh* is the anagram of *Hector* that we find in the original version of *Euphonia ou la ville musicale*, Berlioz's novella that first appeared in a series of eight installments in the *Revue et Gazette musicale* in 1844 (18 and 25 February; 3, 17, and 24 March; 28 April; 2 June; 28 July). In the revised version of the story, published in *Les Soirées de l'orchestre* in 1852, *Rotceh* becomes *Shetland*, an anagram of *Stendhal*.

[Quotations from *Euphonia* in the French text of this article are from the original version as printed in *CM* 5. English translations here are taken, with slight alteration, from Berlioz, *Evenings with the Orchestra*, ed. and trans. Jacques Barzun, with a foreword by Peter Bloom (Chicago: University of Chicago Press, 1999). —*Ed.*]

4. Félix Bodin, *Le Roman de l'avenir*, p. 163.

5. See Kastner, *Cours d'instrumentation* (Paris: Meissonnier et Heugel, 1839); and Joël-Marie Fauquet, "L'Innovation instrumentale devant l'Académie (1803–1851)," in *Musique et Médiations*, ed. Hugues Dufourt and Fauquet (Paris: Klincksieck, 1994), pp. 197–250, here p. 220.

6. *CG* VII, pp. 437–438 (to Carolyne Sayn-Wittgenstein, 13 July 1866): "L'histoire est une duperie [. . .]."

7. The most important document in this regard is Berlioz's letter to Charles Duveyrier of 28 July 1831 (*CG* I, pp. 476–477). See Ralph P. Locke, "Autour de la lettre à Duveyrier: Berlioz et les Saint-Simoniens," *Revue de musicologie*, 63 (1977), pp. 55–77, and 64 (1978), p. 287.

8. The notion of a utopia is furthermore not necessarily an additional sign of the originality that is usually attributed to artists of genius. Thus, for example, the imaginative principles of musical narration that Berlioz employs to create the forms of his works have nothing particularly utopian about them in the sense of the word we

employ here. Cf. Christian Wasselin, "Concert, théâtre et utopie de la forme chez Berlioz," *Revue de la Bibliothèque nationale de France* (October 1999), pp. 42–48.

9. Boulez, "L'Imaginaire chez Berlioz," in *Points de repère* (Paris: Bourgois/Seuil, 1981), p. 233 and passim.

10. *Revue européenne* (15 March 1832); *CM* I, pp. 75–76.

11. *Le Rénovateur* (13 April 1834); *CM* I, p. 211.

12. It is useful to remember here that the name of the orchestra Berlioz knew best—the *Société* des Concerts du Conservatoire—was not chosen arbitrarily.

13. See Joël-Marie Fauquet, "Les Débuts du syndicalisme musical en France," in *La Musique: Du théorique et politique*, ed. Hugues Dufourt and Fauquet (Paris: Klincksieck, 1991), pp. 219–259, at p. 231: "O Berlioz [. . .] Merci d'avoir supprimé les basses besognes qui nous accablaient jadis et d'avoir rendu attrayant et sacré notre long travail quotidien! Merci d'avoir changé les musiciens en artistes!"

14. In particular in the *Guide du musée de la musique* (Paris: Musée de la musique/RMN, 1997), p. 24.

15. Henri Michaux (1899–1984), the Belgian-born writer, poet, and painter whose work is often associated with that of the French surrealists. A collection of his writings, *L'Espace du dedans*, appeared in Paris, from Gallimard, in 1944.

16. The quotations are from the libretto of *Lélio*, found in *NBE* 7.

17. *NBE* 24, p. 480.

18. Ibid.

19. Étienne Cabet, *Voyage en Icarie* [1840], 2nd ed. (Paris: J. Mallet, 1842), p. 81.

20. Berlioz mentions Cabet in a letter of 8 May 1849 (*CG* III, p. 633).

21. Cabet, *Voyage en Icarie*, p. 48.

22. Berlioz might have known the work from the *Œuvres philosophiques, morales et politiques de François Bacon* (Paris: A. Desrez, 1836).

23. Alexis de Tocqueville, *De la Démocratie en Amérique*, vol. 2, section 2, chapter 20.

24. See, for example, the reading of *Euphonia* found in Katherine Kolb, "The Short Stories," in *The Cambridge Companion to Berlioz*, ed. Peter Bloom (Cambridge: Cambridge University Press, 2000), pp. 146–156, here, pp. 150–153.

25. Balzac's short story *Gambara*, widely available in modern edition, first appeared in the *Revue et Gazette musicale* on 23 and 30 July, 6, 13, and 20 August 1837.

26. In his story, Balzac transforms the panharmonicon into a utopian instrument, but such an instrument did in fact exist. Around 1803, the German inventor Johann Nepomuk Maelzel, whose name is of course associated with the perfection of the metronome, constructed an instrument composed of air-driven organ pipes and percussion devices that was capable of imitating the sounds of an entire orchestra. Maelzel displayed the panharmonicon in various European capitals, Paris among them. It was for this behemoth that Beethoven composed *Wellington's Victory or the Battle of Vittoria*, Op. 91, first performed in Vienna in 1813.

27. *NBE* 24, p. 138.

Chapter Four

Berlioz and the Mezzo-Soprano

JULIAN RUSHTON

I like an aria to fit a singer as perfectly as a well-made suit of clothes.
—Wolfgang Amadè Mozart

We have nothing from Berlioz as memorable as Mozart's sartorial metaphor.[1] The French composer recognized, no less than other opera composers, that singers were vital to the success of his vocal works. There is no reason to suppose that Berlioz looked on singers, or could afford to look on them, as mere adjuncts to his compositional plans, whose abilities, less open to new technical demands than instrumentalists', could be bent to his creative will. Indeed, singers may be counted among his friends as well as among the objects of his bile and the butts of his humor. Berlioz is even one of the select group of composers who married singers, including Hasse, Mozart, Rossini, Johann Strauss the younger, Verdi, and Richard Strauss.

Although Berlioz's works, unlike Mozart's and Verdi's, were rarely first performed by pre-selected singers, the matter of suiting the voice to the role concerned him closely: "The art of writing for individual voices is in fact conditioned by a thousand different factors which are hard to define but which must always be borne in mind; they vary with the individual singer."[2] This section of the *Traité d'instrumentation* is necessarily concerned with voice-types, as it deals with choral rather than solo voices. But when a composer writes for a particular singer, he attends not to the vocal category but to that individual's qualities at that time in her career. Over the years, as her voice changes, the same singer may perform roles assigned to different voice-types. Furthermore leading singers in a revival are allocated principal roles conceived for someone else. In these circumstances, roles have often been modified. In the nineteenth century this led less to the composition of new arias (as earlier happened in Handel and Mozart) and more to transposition, adjustment, and alterations of detail. This is not necessarily a harmful practice, and it continues to the present day, despite establishment of a canon and the still powerful concept of *Werktreue*, or fidelity to the text.

By his own account Berlioz as a young operagoer was an obstreperous adherent of such fidelity, pillorying performers and arrangers who departed from the sacred texts of Gluck, Beethoven, and Weber.[3] But as a composer and arranger, it is clear that he was not implacably opposed to changes in musical texts, including his own. Berlioz never forgot the powerful impression made on him by Caroline Branchu in the title role of Gluck's *Alceste*, her dramatic delivery compensating for the liberty she took in transposing certain sections down. Branchu is nevertheless classified "soprano," not "mezzo-soprano."[4] She was nearing the end of her career when Berlioz heard her, and when she was understandably distressed by the rise of the "diapason," or standard pitch.[5] Berlioz combined extracts from the French and Italian versions of *Alceste* in his own concerts, and in 1861 he collaborated with Pauline Viardot, who also transposed some sections down.[6] Within *La Damnation de Faust*, he incorporated alternatives for the role of Méphistophélès, and for one performance he sanctioned lower notes to exploit the talent of Nicolas-Prosper Levasseur.[7] Quite possibly much more of this kind of thing went on without leaving any documentary trace.

Unlike composers regularly working in the theater, Berlioz could not always determine who would take part in his first performances. If he conceived *Les Troyens* with Viardot in mind, the delay in producing it led to the role of Didon being taken by Anne Charton-Demeur. Viardot is designated "mezzo-soprano" in works of reference, but is also referred to as a "contralto."[8] Could a singer who required downward transpositions in *Alceste* have sung Didon? As will be seen below, the answer, perhaps counterintuitively, is Yes. Charton-Demeur was also the first Béatrice in Berlioz's last opera; and this fact epitomizes the problem of associating roles with voice-types rather than with individual singers. The role of Didon is assigned to "mezzo-soprano" by the *New Berlioz Edition*, and Béatrice to "soprano," yet both were performed to Berlioz's evident satisfaction by this same singer.

It is nowadays customary to identify voice-types for dramatic roles (see table 4.1A), and Berlioz sometimes prescribed them for songs (see table 4.1B). The broadly established female voice-types distinguished by range—soprano, mezzo-soprano, and contralto—were those Berlioz himself recognized.[9] But "mezzo-contralto," a term unused today, was applied in the nineteenth century to Rosine Stoltz and to Pauline Viardot's sister, Maria Malibran; it is "a particular style of voice with affinities with both the mezzo-soprano and the contralto [. . .] Singers to whom it is applied [were] noted for their wide range and weight of tone."[10] But there is no consistent agreement about where to draw the line between these types, of which "mezzo-soprano" is the most ambiguous both as a voice-type and as a descriptive term. Furthermore, mezzo-soprano appears to have changed its meaning between Berlioz's time and ours. This article attempts to establish a coherent understanding of the term in relation to the music of Berlioz.

Table 4.1. Mezzo-Soprano Music by Berlioz
A. Female roles in dramatic works

Date	Title, Role, or Section	Voice type (*NBE*)	Singer(s) (W = Weimar)
1828	*Herminie*	soprano	Dabadie Prix de Rome trial performance only
1829	*Huit Scènes de Faust* "Le Roi de Thulé"; *Romance*	soprano	"Le Roi de Thulé" in G Not performed
"	*Cléopâtre*	soprano	Lavri Prix de Rome trial performance only
1838	*Benvenuto Cellini:* Teresa	soprano	Dorus-Gras; Milde (W)
"	*Benvenuto Cellini:* Ascanio	soprano	Stoltz; Wolf (W)
ca. 1842	*La Nonne sanglante:* Agnès	soprano?	Not performed
1846	*La Damnation de Faust:* Marguerite	mezzo-soprano	Duflot-Maillard; Milde (W)
1854	*L'Enfance du Christ:* Marie	soprano	Meillet; Genast (W)
1856– 1858	*Les Troyens:* Cassandre	mezzo-soprano	Not performed
"	*Les Troyens:* Ascagne	soprano	Estagel
"	*Les Troyens:* Didon	mezzo-soprano	Charton-Demeur
"	*Les Troyens:* Anna	contralto	Dubois
1862	*Béatrice et Bénédict:* Héro	soprano	Monrose
"	*Béatrice et Bénédict:* Béatrice	soprano	Charton-Demeur; Milde (W)
"	*Béatrice et Bénédict:* Ursule	mezzo-soprano	Faivre, Amélie (1863)

B. Other vocal works suited to mezzo-soprano

Date	Identification	Designation	Performers known to have sung
1830	*La Belle Voyageuse*	1830 "jeune paysan" 1849 "chant"	Récio
"	*L'Origine de la harpe*	soprano ou tenor (1830; 1849; "chant")	
1832	*La Captive* (piano)	*NBE* 15, versions 1–4 in E: "chant" or "soprano"; version 5 in D, contralto or mezzo-soprano	Berlioz, others (1832)

Table 4.1. (*continued*)

Date	Identification	Designation	Performers known to have sung
1848	*La Captive* (orchestra)	contralto or mezzo-soprano	In E, Viardot (1848); in D, Widemann, Stoltz, others
1833	*Le Jeune Pâtre breton*	Version 2 tenor or soprano	Récio
1834	*Je crois en vous*	mezzo-soprano	
1839	*Roméo et Juliette* "Premiers Transports"	contralto	Widemann Several later performers
1840–1841	*Les Nuits d'été* (piano)	mezzo-soprano or tenor except No. 5 (tenor only)	
"	*Les Nuits d'été* (orchestra) *Villanelle, Absence, L'Île inconnue*	mezzo-soprano or tenor	*Absence*: orchestrated for Récio; all three songs dedicated to female singers
"	*Le Spectre de la rose*	contralto	In B rather than D
"	*Sur les lagunes*	baritone or contralto or mezzo-soprano	In F Minor rather than G Minor; male dedicatee
1842	*La Mort d'Ophélie*	soprano or tenor	Solo version
1843	*La Belle Isabeau,* Gertrude	mezzo-soprano	
1845?	*Zaïde*	soprano	Treffz
1850?	*Le Matin*	mezzo-soprano or tenor	
1850?	*Petit Oiseau*	tenor, baritone, or mezzo-soprano	

The "Mezzo-Soprano"

One reason for Berlioz's predilection for the female voice type lower than that of the conventional prima donna is expressed in the *Traité d'instrumentation*: "The voices of mezzo-sopranos (second sopranos) and contraltos are usually more homogeneous [than sopranos] and more even, and so much easier to write for."[11] In his surviving works there are only two roles for full soprano, both comparatively ingenuous characters: Teresa in *Benvenuto Cellini* and Héro in *Béatrice et Bénédict*. A number of other roles, including Ascanio in *Benvenuto Cellini* and Béatrice herself, are designated "soprano" but were in fact sung by performers associated with mezzo-soprano roles. Neither ascends much above the treble staff. The more complex characters—Marguerite, Marie, Cassandre, Didon, Béatrice—have all been taken by mezzo-sopranos, and to these may be added two trouser roles, curiously with variants of the same name, Ascanio and Ascanius (Ascagne) in *Les Troyens*.[12] Table 4.1A accordingly includes where possible the names of the first singers.

The term "mezzo-soprano" is widely used in modern times for singers who might, fifty years ago, have been called "contralto," and for whom the term "mezzo-contralto" might usefully be revived. In the *Traité d'instrumentation* "mezzo-contralto" is not used, and "mezzo-soprano" occurs only in passing, as cognate with "second soprano." Berlioz mentions the contralto as a distinct voice-type, while lamenting its rarity in France. Yet although his terminology took time to settle, he used "mezzo-soprano" relatively often when he suggested appropriate voice-types for his songs. The early songs are usually marked for "voix" or "chant," but the *Canon libre à la quinte* (published in 1823), mixing modern and obsolescent terminology, is for "contralto" and "basse-taille." The contralto's range is c′–a″, however, a range which decidedly suggests a soprano (or mezzo-soprano). There is no reason to suppose that Berlioz had particular singers in mind for these early songs, and given his later understanding of "contralto," this seems to be an aberration.[13]

Berlioz indicates voice-types from 1830, with the publication of *Neuf Mélodies*, later called *Irlande*. He specifies "contralto" for the lower voice of *Hélène*, and in the duet version of *Sara la baigneuse* (ca. 1850), where the contralto lies conspicuously lower than the soprano. Elsewhere in *Irlande*, and in *mélodies* of later years, Berlioz may have had a mezzo-soprano in mind. *La Belle Voyageuse* was performed by Marie Récio, the mezzo-soprano whom Berlioz later married.[14] In the original edition, the voice part is for "jeune paysan."[15] This would not preclude a male singer—the three songs explicitly for tenor in this collection use the same clef—but the vocal style is very different from the tenor songs, and in dramatic works a young peasant singing a naive ballad would probably be a trouser-role, like those of the apprentice in *Benvenuto Cellini* and the peasant boy in *Tannhäuser*. The bucolic love-song *Le Jeune Pâtre breton* is usually assigned to a tenor, but it was also sung by Récio.[16]

In *Les Nuits d'été* Berlioz marked the title-page and most of the individual songs "mezzo-soprano or tenor." The tenor style, even in *Au cimetière* (the single song assigned to tenor only), is different from that of *Irlande*, where all three tenor songs—like the contemporary *Le Pêcheur*—are considerably higher in tessitura than any songs assigned to "mezzo-soprano or tenor." In the latter, by range alone, the tenor could be a light baritone. In writing for baritone in the orchestral version of *Sur les lagunes*, Berlioz requires a strong f′; *Villanelle* and *Absence* rise only a semitone higher. Given, again, that *Absence* was orchestrated for Récio, whereas two songs were transposed down to accommodate a contralto, we may derive some understanding of Berlioz's conception of the mezzo-soprano from this cycle.

There is an important difference between songs and dramatic roles; the latter make more use of the higher notes in the range, extending to b♭″ or even b″. It may be that Berlioz's operatic preference for the lower female voice is due to his memory of Branchu: he heard her not only in Gluck's *Alceste* and in *Iphigénie en Tauride*, but also in Salieri's *Les Danaïdes* and Spontini's *La Vestale*. None of these roles, even with the modern diapason, lies very high. Berlioz was perhaps less impressed by the operatic prima donna in Grand Opéra than by roles apparently for second soprano, such as Isolier in Rossini's *Le Comte Ory*, whose vocal style contrasts with that of the countess, and Alice in Meyerbeer's *Robert le diable*, a peasant but a substantially more dramatic role than that of Robert's noble bride. Such roles, or extracts from them, were sung by both Marie Récio and the celebrated Rosine Stoltz.

Music for Stoltz

Berlioz began composing *Benvenuto Cellini* as an *opéra comique*, and thus without considering singers at the Paris Opéra.[17] The first Ascanio, Rosine Stoltz (1815–1903), joined the Opéra a year before the première of *Benvenuto Cellini*, and thus after much of the music was composed.[18] As a person of influence—she was the mistress of the director, Léon Pillet—she could command an enlargement of her role. Thus while Ascanio's first aria, "Cette somme t'est due," was probably composed before the role was cast, the second, "Mais qu'ai-je donc?" was written expressly for Stoltz. It was one of the best-received numbers; throughout the contemporary reviews, Stoltz's lively performance is widely praised, as it was by Berlioz himself.[19]

Early in her career, Stoltz undertook soprano roles. Before arriving in Paris she sang Alice in *Robert*, whose range extends to c‴, and she made her début at the Opéra in August 1837 as Rachel in Halévy's *La Juive*, a role generally less high but dramatically no less exacting. With Ascanio (as perhaps with Isolier, another trouser-role), her acting ability contributed to her success. Berlioz gave an intriguingly mixed account of her début in *La Juive*. Her voice is "fine and lovely, very ample, very sonorous in the middle register, a little harsh on certain high notes, less lovely in the lower register where her range is somewhat restricted, but overall expressive and powerful. This is a true Grand Opera soprano." He praised her diction and acting, but made a number of recommendations concerning vocal support and how she should practice, advice made palatable by calling her "too much an artist" for it to be needed.[20]

Curiously, both D. Kern Holoman and the *New Berlioz Edition* label Ascanio "soprano" in the original version of *Benvenuto Cellini*, but "mezzo-soprano" in the Weimar version.[21] In fact the role lies higher in Weimar, though by an insignificant amount. In the first aria, a slight lowering of tessitura took place before the first Paris performance, presumably to allow Stoltz a more grateful approach, vocally

Example 4.1. *Benvenuto Cellini*, Act I, the climactic bars of Ascanio's first Air, in the Paris 1, Paris 2, and Weimar versions.

and musically, to her highest note, b″ (see ex. 4.1). Other tiny changes raise the tessitura by a minute amount for the Weimar singer (see tables 4.2A and 4.2B).

In table 4.2, I employ a measurement of tessitura called "Pitch Center of Gravity" (PCG). This averages the pitches sung against their duration. Each pitch is allocated a number from 1 (g) to 30 (c‴), which is multiplied by its total duration. The sum of these figures is divided by the duration of the sung role, and the result is the PCG. For sopranos it will normally be in the region 19–21, corresponding to the pitches c♯″–d♯″; for mezzo-sopranos, a tone or a minor third lower (16–18: b♭′–c″); for contraltos about a tone lower still. This measurement has the advantage of being indifferent to key, and distinct from a simple measurement of range. A full soprano role uses more high notes and thus has a higher tessitura than a mezzo-soprano role, even when their ranges are the same. An occasional high or low note only slightly affects the PCG, without diluting its findings. But if all that is measured is range—considering for

Table 4.2. Range and Tessitura of Berlioz's Mezzo-Soprano Repertory

To clarify the significance of the range, the key is given first. The right-hand column gives the PCG (pitch center of gravity) to the nearest quarter-tone. A plus sign (+) confirms that the center lies a quarter-tone above the note (e.g., b′ + lies between b′ and c″); a minus sign (−) indicates a PCG slightly (but not a full quarter-tone) lower than the given pitch.

A. Principal numbers in dramatic works

Date	Section	Key (range)	PCG (pitch)
1838	*Benvenuto Cellini* (Ascanio)		
	Act I "Cette somme . . ."	E (c♯′–b″)	19 (c♯″)
	Act II Air: refrain only	D (c♯′–g″)	17.5 (b′ +)
	1st episode	(c♯′–f♯″)	19 (c♯″)
	2nd episode A	(g–f♯″)	14.5 (g♯′ +)ᵃ
	2nd episode B	(c♯′–f♯″)	17 (b′ −)
ca. 1842	*La Nonne sanglante* (Agnès)		
	(Duet: Agnès's solo)	a (g′–b♭″)	20.5 (d″ +)
	Agnès's ballad	a (e′–g″)	16 (a♯′ −)
1846	*La Damnation de Faust* (Marguerite)		
	Recitative "Que l'air . . ."	− (d′–e″)	15 (a′)
	Section in 9/8	B (f♯′–f″)	20 (d″)
	"Le Roi de Thulé"	F (c′–f″)	15 (a′)
	Duet with Faust	E (d♯′–a″)	19 (c♯″)
	Finale to Part III (6/8 only)	F (f′–b♭″)	19.5 (c♯″ +)
	Romance (sections in 3/4)	F (c′–a″)	17 (b′)
	Romance (section in 9/8)	F (f♯′–f♯″)	19 (d♭″)
1854	*L'Enfance du Christ* (Marie)		
	Duet in Part I	A♭ (d♭′–f″)	16 (b♭′−)
	Response to the Angels	− (e′–g♯″)	16.5 (a♯′+)
	Duet in Part III	g (d′–g″)	18 (c″ −)
1856–1858	*Les Troyens* (Cassandre)		
	1. Act I recitative	− (e♭′–f″)	16 (b♭′)
	2. Air "Malheureux roi"	E♭ (d♭′–a♭″)	16 (b♭′)
	3. Duet recitative	− (e′–g″)	18 (c″)
	4. Duet	B (f♯′–b″)	19 (c♯″)ᵇ
	5. Air "Non, je ne verrais pas"	e♭ (c′–f″)	16.5 (b♭′ +)
	Les Troyens (Didon)		
	1. First recitative	− (d′–g″)	16.5 (b♭′ +)
	2. "Chers Tyriens"	G♭ (c♯′–b♭″)	17 (b′ −)
	3. Duet with Anna (4/4)ᶜ	E (d′–f″)	16 (a♯′)
	4. Duet with Anna (6/8)	E (d♯′–f♯″)	16.5 (a♯′ +)
	5. "Errante sur les mers"	F (c′–f″)	16 (b♭′ +)
	6. Recitative before III finale	− (e♯′–g″)	17.5 (b′ +)
	7. Quintette	D♭ (c′–g♭″)	15.5 (a′ +)
	8. Septuor	F (c′–f″)	16 (b♭′)
	9. Duet ("Nuit d'ivresse")	G♭ (c–g♭″)	16.5 (b♭′ +)
	10. Duet ("Errante sur tes pas")	b♭ (c♯′–a♭″)	16 (b♭′)
	11. "Va, ma sœur, l'implorer"	a (e′–g″)	18 (c″)
	12. Recitative "Qu'entends-je?"	− (c′–g″)	16.5 (b♭′ +)

Table 4.2. (*continued*)

Date	Section	Key (range)	PCG (pitch)
	13. "Je vais mourir"	– (d′–f″)	16.5 (b♭′ +)
	14. "Adieu, fière cité"	A♭ (e♭′–f″)	17.5 (b′ +)
	15. Final speech (No. 50)[d]	– (c′–g♭″)	17 (b′)
1862	*Béatrice et Bénédict* (Béatrice)		
	Duet—opening section	E (c♯′–g♯″)	16.5 (a♯′ +)
	Duet—Andantino	g♯ (e′–f♯″)	18 (c″–)
	Duet—Allegro sections	E (c♯′–a″)	18 (c″)
	Recitative	– (e′–f″)	16.5 (b♭′ +)
	Aria "Il m'en souvient"		
	Andante section[e]	E♭ (c′–f″)	15 (a′ –)
	Vision of war[f]	– (c′–f″)	15 (a′)
	"Oui, Bénédict . . ."	E♭ (e♭′–b♭″)	19.5 (d♭″ +)
	Trio	A♭ (e♭′–g″)	17 (b′ –)
	Scherzo–Duettino	G (f♯′–a″)	18.5 (c″ +)

B. Songs intended for mezzo-soprano (unless otherwise indicated)

Date	Title	Key (range)	PCG
1830	*L'Origine de la harpe*	G (e′–g″)	17 (b′)
	La Belle Voyageuse	A (c♯′–f♯″)	17 (b′)
1832	*La Captive*	E (b–f♯″)	15 (a′)
1848?	*La Captive* (orchestral)	D (a–f♯″)	13.5 (g′ +)
1833	*Le Jeune Pâtre breton*	E♭ (e♭′–g♭″)	17 (b′)
1834	*Je crois en vous*	D♭ (c′–f″)	14.5 (a♭′)
1839	"Premiers Transports" (contralto)	G (c′–e″)	15.5 (a′ +)
1840	*Les Nuits d'été*		
	Villanelle	A (e′–f♯″)	20 (d″ –)
	Le Spectre de la rose	D (c′–a♭″)	16.5 (a♯′ +)
	Sur les lagunes	g (c♯′–g″)	16 (b♭′)
	Absence	F (c♯′–f♯″)	17 (b′ –)
	L'Île inconnue	F (d♭′–g♭″)	17.5 (b′ +)
1842	*La Mort d'Ophélie*	A♭ (d′–g″)	17 (b′)
1843	*La Belle Isabeau*	e (b–f♯″)	15.5 (a′ +)
1845?	*Zaïde* (soprano)	F (e′–g″ or b♭″)	18 (c″)[g]
1850?	*Le Matin*	d (d′–g″)	16.5 (b♭′ +)
1850?	*Petit Oiseau*	f (e♭′–f″)	15 (a″)

[a] In Weimar, without the low g and a, this comes nearly a semitone higher.

[b] The PCG includes the sustained top b″ at the end of the duet, which is optional and can be replaced by f♯″; this lowers the PCG to below c♯″.

[c] Includes preceding recitative.

[d] Up to the point where she stabs herself, at the end of No. 50; dying words not included.

[e] Comprising "Je m'en souviens" to bar 73 and the reprise at bar 126 with coda.

[f] Lowered by the final bars (119–123) but in any case only a fraction higher than the rest of the Andante.

[g] *Zaïde* PCG measured without the optional top b♭″.

Example 4.2. *Benvenuto Cellini*, Act II, episode in Ascanio's second Air, in the Paris and Weimar versions.

instance the A and G below middle C in Ascanio's second aria (Paris version; see ex. 4.2)—we may be left with a false impression.[22]

"Mais qu'ai-je donc" vividly illustrates a facet of Berlioz's handling of tessitura (see table 4.2A). The refrain, in which Ascanio humorously expresses his anxious ennui, is noticeably lower than the episodes in which he reminisces about recent events. The tessitura in the Weimar version is raised relative to the Paris versions because of a plot change; the second episode recalls not the scene with the Pope/Cardinal, but rather the fracas at the Roman Carnival. Hence in the first part of the second episode, Ascanio no longer mimics the deep voice and descending fifths of the Pope; instead he mimics the perplexed Teresa, confronted with two "Capuchin monks" (ex. 4.2). As table 4.2A shows, this episode lies considerably lower than the rest of the aria, which is otherwise nearly identical in both versions. The Paris and Weimar versions, therefore, do not require different voice-types for Ascanio; both are for the "second soprano" type to which Stoltz belonged, or which was typical of her preferences and capabilities in 1838. In relation to Berlioz's comments on her début the previous year, the lower range and tessitura of the Act II aria may be significant, as is his praise for the fullness of voice in the medium range. His compositional practice, therefore, contributes to reclassifying Stoltz as a mezzo. Subsequently he advised her to accept that this was her destiny. Reviewing a revival of *La Juive* in June 1840, he praised her acting and the beauty of her voice, but added that while she can reach the high notes, they didn't sound well, and she "would be better appreciated in a mezzo-soprano or even a full contralto role ['contralto franc']."[23]

In the meantime, the next piece to connect Berlioz with Stoltz was Gluck's *Alceste*, as she performed extracts from the title role, including the aria "Ombre, larve," at his concert of 16 December 1838.[24] The aria reaches a sustained b♭" at the climax, presumably manageable to a singer able to negotiate the b" in *Benvenuto Cellini*. A month later, Berlioz found an excuse to write a glowing review of Stoltz's performance.[25] At a date that cannot be ascertained, Berlioz may have had her voice in mind for the song we now know as *Absence*. The text of part of the abandoned dramatic intermezzo *Erigone* may have been composed to music later adapted for this, the only song in *Les Nuits d'été* for which Berlioz altered the form of Gautier's poem.[26] We cannot know the key in which it might have appeared in *Erigone*, but the key of the original version of *Absence* (1840) and of the version orchestrated in 1843 and sung by Marie Récio is F-sharp Major. In 1839, Berlioz may have had Stoltz in mind when composing the *Strophes* ("Premiers transports") in *Roméo et Juliette*, even causing her name to be mentioned in advance publicity.[27] It was sung at the first performances by Emily Widemann, and is for "contralto," although the range (c'–e") and tessitura (15.5) were well within Stoltz's capabilities (or those of any mezzo). Stoltz was not offended, and sent Berlioz a charming note of congratulation.[28]

In 1840, when he was composing *Les Nuits d'été*, the mezzo-soprano voice inhabiting Berlioz's inner ear was surely not that of Récio, but of Stoltz. In December 1840, Stoltz created her most important new role, Léonor de Guzman in Donizetti's *La Favorite*—a title that aptly reflects her role in Pillet's life. This, and her possible connection to Berlioz's *Strophes*, raises the question of sound and in particular of "weight" of tone—an attribute, as we have seen, of the "mezzo-contralto" voice. Vocal weight—that sense that the sound is broader than the same pitch played on, for instance, the violin—is certainly an attribute of the full contralto, but also of the modern mezzo-soprano, including those who transpose down Berlioz's mezzo-soprano songs. It is not certain that Berlioz expected extra weight from a mezzo-soprano, but his description of Stoltz— "bien sonore dans le medium"—sounds like the definition of a modern mezzo. Donizetti's opera, composed explicitly for Stoltz, exemplifies the character of her preferred solo register, different from what she could achieve when supported by other singers in an ensemble or finale.[29] Her double aria lies relatively low, the introspective *cantabile* particularly so. The prayer in the final act lies rather higher, as if pushed by the character's desperation; and in the ensembles, where she takes the highest part, her tessitura is that of a soprano.[30]

The phenomenon of a role lower in its arias than in its ensembles recurs in Stoltz's next collaboration with Berlioz. In 1841, she sang Agathe in *Le Freyschütz*, with Berlioz's recitatives.[31] Berlioz confirms her ability to maintain a higher tessitura when buoyed up by other singers; he informs us of the downward transposition of the arias, which he deplores, adding, "She was, however, able to retain the original key, B Major, of the final sextet, and sang the top line with a fire and energy that invariably brought the house down."[32] The version she sang of Agathe is thus consistent, even to the approximate level of tessitura, to the role tailored for her by Donizetti.[33]

Despite Berlioz's astonishingly tactless remark about Stoltz in a feuilleton (see below), Pillet, in the autumn of 1841, invited Berlioz to work again for the Opéra, on *La Nonne sanglante*. In view of Stoltz's success as the tormented Léonor, it would seem natural for Berlioz to plan the role of Agnès for her, but the only part that survives, a short recitative and the incomplete duet, may suggest otherwise.[34] The opening Allegro of the duet seems high for Stoltz; in the second section, the ballad, a lower tessitura is to be expected in the narration of a ghost story (see table 4.2A). The final section is missing, but could be expected to return to a higher tessitura, especially as Rodolphe is a high tenor who rises to d♯″. On the basis of the poetic meter, Hugh Macdonald has plausibly suggested that the final section of the duet was removed from the manuscript of *La Nonne* to form the B-Major duet for Cassandre and Chorèbe in Act I of *Les Troyens*. If so, the tenor part was adapted for baritone; but there can be no certainty about the original key. Perhaps it was A Major, parallel major to the opening of the duet. Even in the key of B, much else could have been changed, but it is worth noting that Cassandre's tessitura is only slightly lower than that of Agnès in the first part of the duet in *La Nonne*. When the *Troyens* duet was performed in Baden in 1859, Cassandre was sung by Pauline Viardot.[35]

In 1855, Stoltz performed *La Captive*, apparently the published orchestral version in D, dedicated to Viardot, and not the earlier orchestral version in E Major that Viardot actually sang. The version in D, identical except for minor modifications, had been performed by the contralto Widemann. Even in E, the original song is low enough for a contralto, with a range b–f♯″ and a tessitura below that of the mezzo-soprano songs (see table 4.2B). The E-Major version should have suited Stoltz, and since Berlioz did not jettison the orchestral material, he may well have brought it out for her. On the other hand, perhaps Stoltz, by now a mezzo-contralto, preferred the lower key.[36]

Music for Récio

Working with Stoltz no doubt habituated Berlioz to considering the mezzo-soprano suitable for a dramatic heroine. However, well before reviving his *Faust* music of 1829, he became personally involved with a "second soprano" engaged at the Opéra in October 1841. It was on the occasion of her début (26 December) in a role that was once Stoltz's, Isolier in *Le Comte Ory*, that Berlioz, perhaps already *amoureux*, unwisely observed that "Mademoiselle Récio, without imitating Madame Stoltz [that is, without resembling 'un sac de noix posé sur un escabeau'—'a bag of walnuts sitting on a step-ladder'], lent to the character of Isolier a physiognomy at once spiritual and tender."[37] For Berlioz, Récio sang *Le Jeune Pâtre breton*, *Absence*, the "Cavatine du premier tableau de *Benvenuto*

Cellini," and *La Belle Voyageuse.* The "Cavatine" was presumably the Larghetto of Teresa's double aria ("Entre l'amour et le devoir"), which seems high for a mezzo-soprano, not only rising to a final b″ but generally elevated in tessitura.[38] Quite possibly it was transposed down.[39] Récio, in any case, never had sufficient vocal qualities to affect Berlioz's compositional plans, and we do not know that he wrote anything especially for her.

Virgins and Mothers

When Berlioz revised Marguerite's *Romance* for a concert in 1844, the intended soloist was Madame Nathan-Treilhet. Indisposed at the last minute, she was replaced by Récio, who sang *Absence.*[40] In 1846, for the première of *La Damnation de Faust,* Berlioz found himself unable to get the "most fashionable" singers.[41] He had probably hoped for performance with forces of the Opéra (perhaps including Stoltz), as suggested by his letter of 13 March 1846, in which he asks his friend d'Ortigue to tell the Opéra's chorus-master, Pierre Dietsch, that "I am preparing a job for him with my grand opera [*sic*] of *Faust.*"[42] In the end his Marguerite was Hortense Duflot-Maillard, for whom Berlioz transposed the ballad "Le Roi de Thulé" down from G to F. Yet even in its original key, "Le Roi de Thulé" is lower in tessitura than anything else in the role, including the *Romance.* Even in 1829, Berlioz had apparently exploited a lower tessitura for a dramatic reason: in the ballad, Marguerite's own passions are not involved; a note in the score of the *Huit Scènes* asks that it be sung without expression.[43]

We do not know whom Berlioz had in mind when composing the rest of Part III of *La Damnation de Faust*—the recitative for Marguerite's entrance, the duet with Faust, and the finale. The recitative quotes the 9/8 section of the *Romance,* which is distinctly higher than its surroundings on both occasions; in the *Romance* itself, this section places much emphasis on g″ (see table 4.2A). The *Romance,* duet, and finale all rise to a″. But the mere imposition of a few high notes in a state of emotional exaltation, especially when supported by another singer or singers, is perhaps less significant than the tessitura of the duet, higher than in the earlier scene, and the tessitura of the finale, higher still. In the duet, Marguerite begins a melodic reprise (at bar 62), but yields the melody to Faust, adding a descant in a distinctly lower register than she employs in their previous and subsequent dialogues. Nevertheless, the whole role, like those of Léonor and Agathe, lies lower in solos than in ensembles. And it is also clear that Marguerite's voice rises when she remembers her dream of Faust, recalling his person (in the 9/8 sections) and her erotic desire, just as it does when Faust is physically present.

The next dramatic role Berlioz conceived was that of Marie in *L'Enfance du Christ.* As with *Faust,* he performed this work with singers not particularly well known from major roles created or revived in opera. Opinions differ as to whether the role of Marie, taken by Marie-Stéphanie Meillet, is for soprano or mezzo-soprano, although Berlioz called her a soprano.[44] She has no arias, but opens the first duet (Part I) with a solo that rises only to f″. Even when Joseph is also singing, her range is only slightly lower, and overall the tessitura remains similar to those Berlioz designated for contralto (see table 4.2A). Marie is thus presented as a mezzo-soprano. The short agitated duet in which she and Joseph speak to the angels, and the longer duet in Part III when they are pleading for shelter, are not contrapuntal like the first duet, and the tessitura tends to rise. In the latter ("Dans cette ville immense") Marie when singing alone is confined to the range d′–e♭″. When singing above Joseph, increasing desperation causes her to rise to a double cadence on g″. Nevertheless these last bars—followed by a considerable rest before her next, quite short entries—scarcely change the voice-type, and most of the role lies lower than Marguerite's.

Heroic Virgins, Heroic Queen

Pauline Viardot (1821–1910) is generally labeled a mezzo-soprano; alluding to her early career in Paris, Joël-Marie Fauquet states that "Pauline's voice evolved towards contralto, making her a direct rival of Rosine Stoltz, whom Berlioz pre-ferred."[45] But Stoltz was not at this stage (if ever) a contralto. When Berlioz reworked the original tessitura of Gluck's *Orfeo* for Viardot, he described it as that of a contralto (although Stoltz had been considered for the role).[46] If Viardot sang it in the manner implied by surviving performance material, she retained a taste for ornamentation of a type Berlioz usually deplored.[47] What this actually sounded like cannot be recaptured; and while such flourishes could be permitted in the representation of the mythical singer, they could not, and as far as is known were not, included in the tragic role of the Thracian queen Alceste. Both Viardot and Stoltz sang *La Captive*, and we might imagine that both were competing for Berlioz's favors, something that would qualify our perception, based largely on his own testimony, of Berlioz as a perpetual outsider.

Nevertheless Berlioz wrote nothing entirely new for Viardot—unless we assume he intended her to sing in *Les Troyens*. He was at one point infatuated with Viardot and did seriously consider that she might sing both Cassandre and Didon, although he was otherwise careful to distinguish the two roles by various musical means.[48] Viardot sang extracts from both roles in 1859, including Cassandre's aria and the duet from Act I, and the love duet from Act IV. Meanwhile Berlioz sent Stoltz a copy of the libretto with a flattering dedication.[49]

During the period of composition, Berlioz no doubt wanted to keep his options open. When *Les Troyens* finally reached the stage—without the first two acts—there was of course no need to cast Cassandre. As for Viardot and Stoltz, who both pretended to Didon's Carthaginian throne, Berlioz wrote (making enemies of both): "they are unwilling to recognize the irreparable outrage committed by time"; "their voices have gone."[50] Instead, "Madame Charton will make a superb Didon. She delivers the whole of the last act admirably; in some places [. . .] she clutches at one's heart."[51] Anne Charton-Demeur (1824–1892) had already created the role of Béatrice in 1862. Early in her career, she had sung "Premiers transports," a piece hardly suited to a full soprano.[52] Thus comparison of two of his greatest roles is for the present purpose especially instructive.

Unlike Marguerite, Didon, when amorous, does not raise her voice—unless her words to Ascagne in Act III, which allude to his father's fame, indicate the working of some sort of sexual chemistry (Énée is present, but in disguise). In the Act IV septet and quintet, although supported by lower voices, Didon retains her medium tessitura, eschewing high notes. Even in the Act V duet "Errante sur tes pas," the last part of the role to be composed, her fury is stifled—this is a public scene, amid the bustle of the port—and only twice does she essay the top of the register. The duet is a dialogue, the voices scarcely ever singing together. It modulates extensively, B-flat Minor giving way to sharp keys, so that the notes of the chromatic scale are relatively evenly distributed, but there is a marked emphasis on the middle of the range; the pitch most used is c″ followed by b♭′ and a′. In her first two speeches Didon reaches f″, by far the most prominent high note, but she descends quickly each time, and again from the g♭″ in the third phrase, as she accuses Énée of tearing out her heart (ex. 4.3a).

In her fourth phrase, she ascends mainly by semitones to g″ (bar 57), the major mode of E-flat proclaiming her regal greatness; but again she sweeps down the arpeggio to conclude on f′ (ex. 4.3b). Another g♭″ appears as she insults Énée's ancestry, accusing him of being suckled by a wolf. Given the jagged nature of her opening phrases, the smooth line when she pleads with Énée to make her pregnant before leaving provides a radical contrast (bars 112–132), moving mainly by step within a narrow range. This depresses the tessitura as a whole, but leaves the voice rested before the magnificent final curse; a♭″ is the highest note since the happily floated b♭″ of "Chers Tyriens." Berlioz offered to suppress the duet "should the singer not be endowed with a voice filled with energy, in which case she might be exhausted before the final scene."[53] But it is partly because the role does not lie very high that so much energy needs to be expended.

Following the Trojans' departure, Didon's enraged recitative (no. 12 in table 4.2A) remains at a mezzo-soprano level, with high sections balanced by low; the former include the opening ("Qu'entends-je?"), the latter her determination to take control of herself and her situation publicly, by ritual ("Du prêtre de Pluton que l'on réclame l'office"). The variation in pitch shows Berlioz's concern for the singer, and his responsiveness to Didon's changing emotions. In the monologue and aria, the general tessitura is maintained with a strikingly reduced range; the aria is higher in tessitura despite a small reduction in range due to

Example 4.3. *Les Troyens*, Act V, Duet No. 44. (a) mm. 30–39; (b) mm. 54–61.

Didon's passionate surge to f″ at "Je ne vous verrai plus," and the lingering e♭″ which precedes her exit.

Is Didon in some sense Berlioz's final tribute to Madame Branchu? Although the role is radically different from that of Alceste, the handling of the voice, and its regal qualities in love and diplomacy, are comparable, and distinct from the other mezzo roles. The model for the "heroic virgin" Cassandre is surely that of the passionate Julie, in Spontini's *La Vestale*, which Branchu also sang, and which Berlioz hoped Stoltz would sing in a revival;[54] this, too, makes little use of high soprano tessitura. This passion reappears in Béatrice once she has decided to marry Bénédict. Béatrice sings only four numbers, but all but the last are complex. She leads the combative duet with Bénédict, the first section establishing a clear mezzo-soprano profile in range and tessitura. But in the short Andantino, and in the Allegro in which they comment aside on the strange delight they take in tormenting each other, her voice rises considerably, as does Cassandre's in her duet with Chorèbe (no. 4 in table 4.2A).

Both Héro and Béatrice are given double arias. In the slow sections, Héro's gentle sentiments use a soprano tessitura, the range d♯′–a″, and a center of gravity on c♯″, too high for a mezzo. Béatrice, in the slow section of "Il m'en souvient," maintains a tessitura a major third lower (see table 4.2A), even when she recalls her nightmarish vision of Bénédict killed in battle. In the subsequent Allegro, one can only admire her colossal burst of energy as she decides to accept the "slavery" of wifehood, which takes her into soprano territory. Her exalted Allegro and Héro's are differentiated less by tessitura and range (although Héro extends to b″ with a cadenza focused on a″) than by Héro's less dynamic, more ornamental coloratura. The contrast between Béatrice's direct, surging scales and distinct verbal underlay and Héro's teasing twists and turns, and excitably scrambled words, may be seen in examples 4.4a and b.

(a)

(b)

Example 4.4. *Béatrice et Bénédict*, (a) Héro's aria (Act I, no. 3), mm. 184–203; (b) Béatrice's aria (Act II, no. 10), mm. 246–265.

The Mezzo: A Lifelong Passion

Study of Berlioz's music for mezzos, or for individual singers of this type, suggests a few conclusions. One is that dramatic roles require a wider range than songs, by using higher notes, but are not necessarily higher in tessitura, as shown by tables 4.2A and 4.2B. The high notes—at most b″—are carefully positioned for maximum impact. This is nowhere more true than in Didon's contribution to "Errante sur tes pas"; cursing her departing lover, she rises no higher than a♭″. The tense beauty of her final aria partly derives from its relatively high tessitura, not its range. Such care with high notes is surely the essence of good composition for *mezzo*-soprano.

Certain songs from *Les Nuits d'été* that Berlioz assigned to mezzo-soprano are transposed down by modern mezzos. In *Villanelle* and *Absence*, the problem is not the range, but the extensive use of the top f♯″. In *Villanelle*, where there are no lower-lying episodes, the tessitura is within the norm of the full soprano, and higher than *Zaïde*. Unfortunately transposition down to F dulls the song's spring colors, despite singers' efforts to lighten their tone. *Absence* is transposed down a minor third, diminishing the sense of distance inherent in the ethereal diminuendo on f♯″. It was losing "three-quarters" of the marvelous *color* that worried Berlioz when he transposed Agathe's cavatina down for Stoltz.[55] Perhaps, given the modern understanding of "mezzo-soprano," these songs should be reallocated to soprano. *L'Île inconnue* when transposed down requires adjustments to the cello part that denature Berlioz's palette and distort the texture.

These wonderful songs are Berlioz's best known; they survive the impact of such changes and benefit from performance by superior artists. But they are also foundational works in the history of orchestral song and repositories of Berlioz's own most sensitive orchestral colors; so these reservations seem worth voicing. It is clear from other data that for Berlioz they were within the competence, at original pitch, of most mezzo-sopranos. In dramatic roles such transpositions are probably less common, although Berlioz did make provision for Stoltz, in *Le Freyschütz*, as we have seen.

Calculating levels of tessitura valuably demonstrates consistency or in some cases the consistent application of variability. With Didon, for instance, we find, first, a consistency of level despite changes of vocal range and of key (as in the duets in three different keys), and second, variation in tessitura consistent with dramatic effect. That higher notes appear in situations of excitement is hardly surprising, but information regarding the pitch center of gravity allows a more accurate perception of the type of singer Berlioz had in mind.

As for the classification of voice-types, it hardly matters whether a singer calls herself soprano, mezzo-soprano, or contralto, so long as she can negotiate a role. But it does matter that Berlioz seems to have composed five great dramatic roles for mezzo-soprano. The highest is Marguerite; she is followed by Cassandre and Béatrice; and they are followed by Marie and Didon—but on measurable grounds they all belong to the same general voice-type. Marguerite, Marie, and Cassandre maintain a higher tessitura when they are the highest voice in an ensemble. This seems natural, and thus raises an interesting question of characterization: Why does this *not* happen with Didon? Teresa and Héro are sopranos, their characters young and virginal. The relatively high mezzo Marguerite is perhaps Berlioz's response to similar characteristics (a version of Goethe's Gretchen). While the low tessitura of "Le Roi de Thulé" may be explained dramatically, singers could reconsider Berlioz's downward transposition, and perform it in the pristine G Major of its earliest versions, as this was Berlioz's first thought in composing *La Damnation de Faust* (the necessary transition exists).[56] Marie could be affected by the casting convention for mothers, lower and weightier than the soprano, typified by Fidès in Meyerbeer's *Le Prophète*, a role designed for Pauline Viardot.

Cassandre might have been a soprano had the composer followed the convention for mad scenes, of which the one in *Lucia di Lammermoor* is only the most famous. Berlioz chose differently, perhaps because he had Viardot in mind, perhaps because Cassandre is *not* mad, but overwrought and stressed by prophetic visions that are true but destined not to be believed. She should not seem mad to the audience. Her tessitura, which allows a thrilling (but optional) b″ at the end of the duet, is compatible with the weight of sound, and with the use of the chest register, that are useful for dramatic projection in the lower part of the range; but overall it is marginally higher than Didon's. Of all these characters, the Carthaginian queen seems least inclined to go for high notes, and most inclined to settle for a medium range. Although a higher alternative is provided, there is a delicious moment when she actually goes below Énée in the love duet (bars 95–98). Is it because Didon has already been married, and is a queen, that the tessitura is handled in this way?

Different weights of voice are valuable elements of contrast, particularly when two or more female voices representing different characters sing together. In the duets of Didon with Anna, and of Héro with Ursule, the subordinate characters are substantially lower-voiced. Anna is designated contralto, and Ursule, although nominally a mezzo-soprano, requires the same kind of voice.[57] The contrast is particularly pleasing in Berlioz's last important composition, the trio he added to Act II of *Béatrice et Bénédict* in time for the 1863 performances. Héro, soprano, and Béatrice, mezzo, are supported by Ursule, whose low notes are essential to the texture. Much of the trio is an exchange of solos, but when the voices join, Héro and Béatrice intertwine to exquisite effect around e♭″–f″ (bars 172–186); otherwise Béatrice's is a middle part to Héro's soprano. In the final section, Béatrice places a degree of emphasis on the tonic pitch, a♭′, that would be unusual in a principal line; but this pitch lies nearer to the center of the singer's range, whereas in her aria, the tonic in E-flat is relatively high or relatively low, and focus on the dominant (b♭′) is to be expected. Béatrice's magnificent *scena* is archetypal for a dramatic mezzo, and the entire role seems tailored for the singer who gave the première, as Didon, it seems, was not. Perhaps Berlioz's firm views on *Werktreue* meant that in the latter he would not make any adjustments to accommodate the slightly higher tessitura probably better suited to Charton-Demeur.

Finally, for the author at least, this study demonstrates the resourcefulness of Berlioz's deployment of the voice in general, and this category of vocal range and tessitura in particular. In his own time, he may not have been considered particularly grateful to singers, but that was also true of Mozart. Nowadays singers have developed a proper appreciation of Berlioz's greatest roles which, with several of his songs, are included in the repertories and aspirations of many excellent performers.

Notes

1. See Mozart's letter to his father, 28 February 1778, in *The Letters of Mozart and his Family*, ed. and trans. Emily Anderson, 3rd ed. (London: Macmillan, 1985), p. 497.

2. *NBE* 24, p. 380; the translation is from *Berlioz's Orchestration Treatise: A Translation and Commentary* [by] Hugh Macdonald (Cambridge: Cambridge University Press, 2002), p. 255.

3. See for instance *Mémoires*, chapters XV–XVI, on changes in orchestration and on Castil-Blaze's popular versions of Weber, and the comments of the protagonist in *Lélio ou Le Retour à la vie* on alterations by Fétis to the works of Beethoven.

4. Elizabeth Forbes, "Branchu, Alexandrine Caroline," in *The New Grove Dictionary of Opera* (henceforth *Opera Grove*), ed. Stanley Sadie (London: Macmillan, 1992), vol. 1, p. 582. See also *Mémoires*, chapters V, XV; and *NBE* 22a, p. xi.

5. Lamenting that he may never hear her in *Iphigénie en Tauride*, Berlioz mentions that if pitch were lowered, she might again sing Iphigénie and Armide (*CG* I, pp. 57–58). The Opéra had adopted the higher pitch normal in Parisian concerts, with a′ = 431.3. In Gluck's time standard pitch at the Opéra was low (a′ = 404), but it rose during Branchu's career to reach 423 in 1810. See Bruce Haynes, "Pitch I," in *The New Grove Dictionary of Music and Musicians*, ed. Stanley Sadie, 2nd ed. (London: Macmillan, 2001), vol. 19, pp. 793–802, here, pp. 799–800; and *CG* I, p. 58, note 1.

6. See *NBE* 22a, p. xi; and "Alceste" (Joël-Marie Fauquet) in *Dictionnaire Berlioz*, ed. Pierre Citron, Cécile Reynaud, Jean-Pierre Bartoli, and Peter Bloom (Paris: Fayard, 2003), pp. 18–19.

7. *NBE* 8b, p. 556.

8. Joel-Marie Fauquet, "Viardot," in *Dictionnaire Berlioz*, p. 576; April Fitzlyon, "Viardot, [née Garcia]," in *Opera Grove*, vol. 4, pp. 981–982.

9. Mezzo-soprano range is given as c′–a″, with extension to b–b″, by Wolfram Seidner, "Singen: Stimmengattungen und Stimmtypen," in *Die Musik in Geschichte und Gegenwart*, Sachteil 8, pp. 1424–1425. Berlioz gives the range of b–g″ for "Soprano II," but for choral voices. See *NBE* 24, pp. 358–359; and *Berlioz's Orchestration Treatise*, p. 248.

10. See "Mezzo-contralto" (anonymous), in *Opera Grove*, vol. 3, p. 372; and Owen Jander et al., "Mezzo-soprano," in ibid., vol. 3, pp. 372–374.

11. *NBE* 24, p. 381; and *Berlioz's Orchestration Treatise*, p. 257.

12. Ascagne/Ascanius is the same person as the title role in Mozart's *Ascanio in Alba*.

13. The early songs contain other obsolescent terms; *Amitié, reprends ton empire* is for soprano, "discante," and tenor; its second version, and *Le Montagnard exilé*, call for two "dessus."

14. In *Irlande*, *L'Origine de la harpe* is also suited to mezzo-soprano; it has a different range but the same tessitura as *La Belle Voyageuse* (see table 4.2B).

15. Paris: Schlesinger, 1830. A facsimile is found in Hector Berlioz, *Mélodies irlandaises: Les sources*, ed. Isabelle Poinloup (Courlay: Fuzeau, 2003).

16. On Récio's repertory, see Peter Bloom, "Récio" in *Dictionnaire Berlioz*, pp. 449–450.

17. On the history, see *NBE* 1a, pp. xiii–xiv; and *Mémoires*, chapter XLVIII.

18. See *inter alia* Karin Pendle, "A Night at the Opera: The Parisian Prima Donna, 1830–1850," *Opera Quarterly*, 4 (1986), pp. 77–89; Christian Merlin, "Stoltz," in the *Dictionnaire Berlioz*, pp. 530–531; *NBE* 1a; Mary Ann Smart, "The Lost Voice of Rosine Stoltz," *Cambridge Opera Journal*, 6 (1994), pp. 31–50; and idem, "Stoltz, Rosine," in *The New Grove Dictionary of Music and Musicians*, 2nd ed., vol. 24, pp. 428–429.

19. See *Benvenuto Cellini: Dossier de presse parisienne (1838)*, ed. Peter Bloom (Heilbronn: Musik-Edition Lucie Galland, 1995), passim; and *Mémoires*, chapter XLVIII.

20. *Journal des débats* (27 August 1837); *CM* 3, pp. 216–217.

21. D. Kern Holoman, "*Benvenuto Cellini*," in *Opera Grove*, vol. 1, pp. 411–412, here, p. 411; *NBE* 1a, p. 2. Holoman designates the role "M.-Sopr." in *NBE* 25, p. 176.

22. The inventor of the Pitch Center of Gravity (PCG) calls it "a purely numerical manipulation [that] permits objective calculation of a point-tessitura." See Richard Rastall, "Vocal Range and Tessitura in Music from York Play 45," *Music Analysis*, 3 (1984), pp. 181–199, here, p. 192. See also Julian Rushton, "Buffo Roles in Mozart's Vienna: Tessitura and Tonality as Signs of Characterization," in *Opera Buffa in Mozart's Vienna*, ed. Mary Hunter and James Webster (Cambridge: Cambridge University Press, 1997), pp. 406–425. (Duration may be measured in units of one's choice: measured in eighth notes, a quarter note appears as the number 2; measured in sixteenth notes, as the number 4.)

23. *CM* 4, p. 344.

24. *NBE* 22a, p. xii.

25. *Journal des débats* (22 January 1839); *CM* 4, pp. 15–16.

26. Gautier's poem is not in the refrain form of *Absence*. It has been suggested that Berlioz planned to incorporate *Absence* into *Erigone* (*NBE* 13, pp. xi, 137), but this chronology accommodates neither the probable date of *Erigone*, nor the alterations to the poem, perhaps made to accommodate preexisting music. Macdonald clarifies the chronology without suggesting that the music of *Absence* derived from *Erigone* (*NBE* 21, pp. x–xi).

27. *NBE* 17, p. xi.

28. *CG* II, p. 595.

29. On Donizetti and Stoltz, see William Ashbrook, *Donizetti and His Operas* (Cambridge: Cambridge University Press, 1982), pp. 442, 652–653; and Smart, "The Lost Voice," pp. 48–50.

30. The PCG for Léonor's *cantabile* is as low as 14 (equivalent to g♯′), with the *cabaletta* at 15.5 (a′ +). The prayer lies at 17.5 (b′ +), at the higher end of Berlioz's mezzo-soprano solos, and just above *Absence* when sung in F-sharp Major.

31. Vocal score, Paris: Schlesinger 1842; full score, *NBE* 22b.

32. *Mémoires*, chapter LII.

33. In the keys used by Stoltz, "Ma prière" ("Leise, leise") has PCG 14.6, below g♯′, with the recitatives, which are by Weber, slightly higher. The Allegro reaches nearly to 18, just below c″. The Cavatine, when sung in F rather than A-flat, has PCG 14.8.

34. See *NBE* 4, p. 264.

35. *Dictionnaire Berlioz*, p. 576; *NBE* 2c, p. 757.

36. The version in E (H. 60E) has not been published, being nearly identical to the version in D (H. 60F). See *NBE* 25, pp. 124–127; and *NBE* 13, p. ix–x. Stoltz sang *La Captive* with piano (and cello), no doubt in E, in 1839 (*CM* 4, p. 58).

37. *Journal des débats* (30 January 1842); *CM* 5, p. 32.

38. The range is f♯'–b'', the PCG 21 (d♯''), a semitone above Ascanio's first aria.

39. Teresa's aria was published with piano accompaniment in *Neuf Morceaux détachés* (Paris: Schlesinger, 1839). A competent pianist could transpose such a slow piece at sight.

40. Nathan-Treilhet, like Stoltz, had sung Rachel in *La Juive*. She had already let Berlioz down in Brussels in 1842. See *Mémoires: Premier Voyage en Allemagne*, first letter (chapter [LI-1]).

41. *Mémoires*, chapter LIV.

42. *CG* III, p. 325. Berlioz may have called *Faust* "grand opera" in default of any conventional term for a large-scale dramatic cantata. He surely did not expect the work to be staged.

43. *NBE* 5, p. 78. See also Julian Rushton, *The Music of Berlioz* (Oxford: Oxford University Press, 2001), pp. 175–176.

44. *NBE* 11, p. 2, has "Sainte Marie (Soprano)," as does the printed program (*CG* IV, p. 623). Berlioz called her a soprano (*CG* IV, p. 669), but Roger Fiske has mezzo-soprano, in Berlioz, *L'Enfance du Christ* (London: Ernst Eulenburg, 1971), p. ii.

45. *Dictionnaire Berlioz*, p. 576.

46. *NBE* 22a, pp. viii–xi.

47. The cadenzas (*NBE* 22a, p. 195) reach c'''. Berlioz earlier thought that Viardot was "too Italian," and a "diva *manquée*" (*NBE* 22a, p. viii; *CG* II, p. 531; and *CM* 4, pp. 39–40).

48. Julian Rushton, "Dido's *Monologue* and *Air*," in *Hector Berlioz: Les Troyens*, ed. Ian Kemp (Cambridge: Cambridge University Press, 1988), pp. 161–180, here, p. 176.

49. *CG* VI, p. 485.

50. *CG* VI, p. 485; *CG* VII, p. 40.

51. *CG* VI, p. 484.

52. Christian Merlin, "Charton-Demeur," in *Dictionnaire Berlioz*, p. 102.

53. See *NBE* 2c, p. 757.

54. *CM* 4, p. 260.

55. *Mémoires*, chapter LII.

56. *NBE* 8b, p. 504.

57. Designated "mezzo-soprano" (*NBE* 3, p. 2), Ursule surely ought to be a contralto or mezzo-contralto.

Part Three

Criticizing and Criticized

Chapter Five

Berlioz as Composer-Critic

GÉRARD CONDÉ

Il serait prodigieux qu'un critique devînt poète,
et il est impossible qu'un poète ne contienne pas un critique.
—Charles Baudelaire

In Part II of his essay on Wagner and *Tannhäuser* in Paris, Baudelaire suggests that "it would extraordinary indeed if a critic should become a poet; but it is impossible for a poet *not* to be a critic."[1] Earlier, Étienne Méhul, in the preface to his 1799 opera *Ariodant,* had urged composers, as "repositories of the secrets of their art," not to remain silent "in the midst of so many discussions in which they are seen now as idols, now as victims." Already in eighteenth-century Germany, Telemann and Mattheson had taken to writing prose, and they were followed by Abbé Vogler and by his disciple Carl Maria von Weber. But it is surely E. T. A. Hoffmann, in his own mind more a composer than a writer, who best exercised the critic's craft in the sense intended here: all of his essays, and especially those on Beethoven, reveal an understanding far beyond that of most of his contemporaries.

Berlioz was an extraordinarily prolific journalist. Reading through his nine-hundred-odd *feuilletons,* a modern edition of which began to appear in 1996,[2] requires far more time than listening to his complete musical works, so it is not surprising that most of his contemporaries saw him more as a journalist who composed music than as a composer who wrote about his art.

Robert Schumann was seen in the same light, although neither he nor Berlioz was the first artist to have taken up his pen to convey what was the central passion of his life, namely, musical composition. Despite the connotations of "music *critic,*" Berlioz, Schumann, and others were not primarily interested in pointing to others' imperfections; they rather wished to demonstrate the creative act as a perpetual questioning nourished by admiring masterpieces, past and present, and by reflecting upon the reasons for one's own failures and the failures of others.

The examples of Weber and Hoffmann were decisive for Schumann, who, for several years, devoted almost as much time to their works as to his own; and one might want to say the same thing about Berlioz, because he greatly valued the same two models. In fact the quantity and the literary quality of Schumann's and Berlioz's writings long hindered their acceptance as totally independent composers. (Wagner and Liszt also wrote a great deal of prose, but they concentrated less on particular composers and works and more on general questions of art and society.)

By the end of the nineteenth century and the beginning of the twentieth, the composer-critic had become a fixture. In France alone, Ernest Reyer succeeded Berlioz at the *Journal des débats*, and Paul Dukas, Claude Debussy, Alfred Bruneau, Gabriel Fauré, Florent Schmitt, André Messager, Reynaldo Hahn, Darius Milhaud, and a number of other lesser-known figures, had bylines in all the leading magazines and newspapers. This phenomenon was reversed in the second half of the twentieth century, when composers—other than occasionally reviewing new recordings in popular magazines—turned away from an activity now seen more as specialized journalism than as artistic criticism, or "critique artiste," as it was called at the time to lend it a certain distinction. And today's composers do not seem to suffer from having lost their place in the press. Convinced that "he who knows speaks not" and that "he who speaks knows not," they are perfectly happy to deplore the ignorance of critics who misunderstand their works. This is hardly a new problem. In his *Traité de la critique musicale* of 1946, for example, Armand Machabey urged critics to study composition, but not to the point of becoming themselves composers, for that would compromise their objectivity.[3] This was to forget that beyond the acquisition of basic skills, one learns to compose only in direct proportion to the intensity of one's personal engagement; it was also to forget that nothing is worse than a judgment founded on a little bit of half-baked knowledge. The demanding music lover, gifted with intuition and sensitivity and, more important, capable of communicating his thoughts and impressions, can accomplish the task of criticism far better than the amateur composer.

Ought we to worry that the judgments of the composer-critic will be prejudiced by his own aesthetic principles? Such a concern, it seems to me, is futile, for no one can entirely separate himself from current trends and attractions, or from the prevalence of certain traditional views. The crucial difference between the journalist-critic and the composer-critic, then, is one of vocation: for the former, music is a kind of spiritual food as well as an object of contemplation; for the latter, it is the very source of his existence. The journalist-critic speaks of what arrives from outside; the composer-critic, of what lives inside. Less diversified in his interests than the journalist, the composer-critic does not usually tend to succumb to the desire to achieve recognition solely by the brilliance of his critical judgments.

Critic because he was a composer, as Baudelaire would have it, Berlioz, with regard to writing about music, also burned with one of those debts of gratitude whose flame, it is said, is never really extinguished. Educated as a youth in the rudiments of music, he did not wait to start composing until he entered the Conservatoire in Paris, as we know from his youthful *romances* and from the instrumental pieces (now lost) that he played with his friends at La Côte-Saint-André. But it was his reading of articles in Michaud's *Biographie universelle* that fired up his imagination and gave rise to an artistic ambition that went well beyond the acquisition of elementary competence. "The description of the tempest in *Iphigénie*," Berlioz wrote, "and of the *Danses des Scythes*, and the dissertation on the sleep of Orestes [which Berlioz found in Michaud], simply made my heart pound with an ardent desire to hear all these miracles."[4]

Once arrived in Paris, Berlioz could simply not keep away from the Opéra, where he was obviously overwhelmed—but not entirely satisfied. He felt the need to experience those supreme emotions of which the encyclopedia-writer had given him an inkling. So he threw himself, more or less as an autodidact, into the composition of large-scale works, among them a *Messe solennelle*, two operas, and an oratorio. Aware as he was of the eloquence of certain writings on music, he likewise attempted simultaneously to express his opinions in the newspapers. The effect of reading the *Biographie universelle* was so strong that, speaking of Gluck some years later, Berlioz inadvertently yet almost literally cited the article from Michaud's dictionary.

The title of chapter XXI of the *Mémoires*, "Fatalité! je deviens critique," is thus to be taken with a grain of salt, because our repentant *feuilletoniste* had early on taken of his own accord the first steps on the road to a journalistic career.[5] Indeed, in the months following his move to Paris, Berlioz wrote to Michaud, at that time editor-in-chief of the newspaper *La Quotidienne*, to propose an article he later saw as "in itself highly disorganized and quite badly conceived," as he puts it in the *Mémoires*, "one which furthermore went well beyond the boundaries of even the most heated polemics." Michaud apparently suggested that he revise the article, but Berlioz preferred to take up his arguments in several letters addressed to *Le Corsaire*, a newspaper treating opera and theater, fashions and fads, which as a rule endorsed convictions quite opposite to Berlioz's own.

Open to polemical writing, *Le Corsaire* was more addressed to the youthful dandy and to the amateur of *bel canto* singing than it was to the admirers of Gluck, Méhul, Cherubini, and Spontini, whose music was at that time going out of fashion. It is important to note, given the complex nature of Berlioz's particular genius, which was innovative in its love of the past, that by assailing fashionable *dilettanti* in order to preach the eternal values of the "ancients" (his third letter, appearing in *Le Corsaire* on 29 December 1825, takes violent issue with the opinions expressed by Castil-Blaze, the then critic for the *Journal des débats*, regarding the revival of Gluck's *Armide*, which Castil-Blaze simply found old-fashioned), by thus confirming his earlier attacks upon the *rossinistes*, Berlioz was adopting a conservative attitude that curiously made him the spokesman for the professorial establishment at the Conservatoire—well before he even dreamed of becoming a student at that institution.

Three years would go by before Berlioz submitted to the newspaper *Le Correspondant* some critical "Considérations sur la musique religieuse" and a

"Biographie de Beethoven," in 1829, and, in 1830, an "Aperçu sur la musique classique et la musique romantique." These are more professions of aesthetic faith than critiques, and here, having meanwhile discovered *Der Freischütz* and the Beethoven symphonies, Berlioz distanced himself from the values of his teachers Jean-François Lesueur and Anton Reicha. At the same time, to the *Berliner allgemeine musikalische Zeitung*, he sent reviews of the première of Boieldieu's *Les Deux Nuits* and of various performances given by a German company visiting Paris, as well as a description of the École royale de musique. Such journalism "is poorly paid," he wrote at the time to his mother, "but it may turn out to be highly useful by giving me a little bit of celebrity in Prussia."[6]

It was only after his return from Rome, and for essentially pecuniary reasons, that Berlioz began, after 1833, regularly to deliver articles to *L'Europe littéraire*, which offered generous honoraria, and to *Le Rénovateur*, which paid less well. The *Gazette musicale de Paris*, founded in 1834 by the music publisher Maurice Schlesinger for the purpose of promoting the works of his stable of French composers as well as the German repertory issued by the main branch of the firm, in Berlin, immediately hired Berlioz because, among other things, he was known as an enemy of the Italian school. But it was finally the prestigious *Journal des débats*, the unofficial mouthpiece of the administration of Louis-Philippe, that gave Berlioz his legitimate place at the summit of the hierarchy of Parisian music criticism. In chapter XLVII of the *Mémoires* he tells us how he was offered this position (long the pulpit of Castil-Blaze) without really having sought it out:

> One day, not quite knowing where to turn in order to earn a few francs, I wrote a sort of short story called *Rubini à Calais*, which appeared in the *Gazette musicale*. I was in very low spirits when I wrote it, but even so the story was entirely light-hearted—a very common contradiction, as everyone knows. A few days after its appearance it was reproduced in the *Journal des débats*, preceded by a very flattering comment from the editor-in-chief. I immediately went to thank Monsieur Bertin, who then suggested that I take over the music column of the *Journal des débats*.

Berlioz's tenure at the *Débats*, from 1835 to 1863, was largely peaceful. He was appreciated, respected, and apparently not overly hampered in his work except by the endless obligation to fill by precise deadlines the *rez-de-chaussée* or "ground floor" of the journal. Berlioz almost always projected himself into his discussions, defending his own gods while speaking of others, and Armand Bertin, the owner's son and the newspaper's principal editor during Berlioz's tenure, clearly was not troubled that he did so. In his biography of Benedetto Marcello, for example, which appeared in the *Débats* on 4 August 1837, it becomes clear as one reads along that Berlioz is establishing a parallel between his own life and that of the Italian composer: the boy does not immediately display extraordinary musical talent; his father gives him his first music lessons; he overcomes familial opposition to a musical career only after the brilliant success of a mass. Indeed, in a letter of 31 August 1824, one year before the first performance at Saint-Roch of his own *Messe solennelle*, Berlioz invokes that very the example, and at length, in order to convince his father to allow him to pursue his chosen career.[7] The short story *Le Premier Opéra*, too, is very closely linked to the trials and tribulations Berlioz experienced with the authorities at the Ministry of the Interior, after the commissioning of the *Requiem*, in 1837.

The *feuilletons* could weigh heavily upon him because they were (like the present article) of a not insignificant length, and he had often to plumb the depths of his fertile imagination in order gracefully to fill his column. And yet, despite what other scholars have said of his dislike of the job, Berlioz clearly felt a powerful need to express himself in writing, as his forty-year career suggests. At the time of his first polemical publication, in 1823, he had just been accepted into Lesueur's private studio; when he signed his last article (on Bizet's *Les Pêcheurs de perles*) for the *Journal des débats*, on 8 October 1863, he had also just retired as a composer—two months shy of his sixtieth birthday. Overextenuated by illness and disappointment, he then enveloped himself in silence during the five remaining years of his life.

In fact silence, for Berlioz, was already a kind of death. One need only read his correspondence to realize how intensely he desired to share his enthusiasms, to analyze his feelings, to substantiate them in writing. The precision and lucidity of his style and expression bear elegant witness to this need. When he was composing—let us not forget—we find exactly the same thing. The same clarity and conviction that characterize his music are quite naturally found in his prose, so much so that some of his more evocative critical writings can touch us even more profoundly than can the very pages of Gluck or Spontini, for example, that inspired them.

Is this the result of a discourse that is in some sense magical, or of an especially brilliant rhetoric? Rather than ask such a futile question it is more useful simply to note that Berlioz devotes himself energetically to the task of re-creation, and by his example he incites us to do likewise. If it is true, in art as in love, that lack of imagination gives rise to indolence, then Berlioz effects the opposite. To measure the remarkable power of suggestion of which he was capable, and which he worked on his readers, it suffices to locate, in the score of *Iphigénie en Tauride*, any one of the notes and chords that Berlioz found surprising and irresistible, but that we, now, may well find of little consequence.[8] Clearly we have become accustomed to much stronger progressions—are there any music lovers out there who can still be flabbergasted by the "false" entries of the horn in the *Eroica* and *Pastoral* Symphonies?—but we may still lack minds open to novelty, and readiness, because of our fear of being duped, to throw caution to the winds.

It is precisely this fear of compromising emotions, of strong reactions, of allowing our own sensibilities to speak instead of the judgments of others—a fear common to both listeners and artists—that Berlioz wanted to combat: his writings persistently and obstinately demonstrate awareness that such timidity put at risk the survival of the masterpieces which nourished him; that timidity also compromised the understanding of his own music, which of course derived from those very *chefs-d'œuvre*. He explains himself on this point in chapter XXI of the *Mémoires*, where he speaks of the attractiveness of the idea of becoming a critic and thus of having in his hands a powerful arm with which "to defend the beautiful and to attack whatever seemed to [him] opposed to it"; and he adds, justifying his letters to *Le Corsaire:*

> [T]he blasphemous diatribes that appeared in the Rossinian journals against Gluck, Spontini, and the whole school of good sense [. . .], and all the arrogant stupidities put forth by those who don't even know the notes of the scale, threw me into paroxysms of rage. In reading the hallucinations of one of those madmen, I was one day overcome by the temptation to reply.

Seen at first, then, as a means of expression and retaliation, criticism would gradually become for Berlioz an important source of income, his sole such regular source, as a matter of fact, because the performances of his music—once the musicians' honoraria, the rental fees, and the poor-relief taxes were paid—were by no means always profitable. Furthermore, he rarely got commissions, he was unable to obtain a professorial post at the Conservatoire, he was not a virtuoso performer, and, apart from some guitar lessons, he almost never taught.[9]

The *Gazette musicale de Paris*, transmogrified into the *Revue et Gazette musicale* in 1835, reached only a small and musically inclined public. Upon joining the *Journal des débats*, however, Berlioz, found himself in a situation in which he would be read and understood, he hoped, by readers without musical sophistication. It is really quite remarkable to see an artist—who in his music scrupulously avoided petty commonplaces and thus the likelihood of immediate understanding—perfectly capable of presenting certain artistic principles to the general public in a grand and straightforward way. He did so willingly, in a lively manner, and sometimes with great humor. Although he rejected the traditional Italian comedic adage of "Castigat ridendo mores" because he was convinced that laughter was in fact useless in reforming moral customs, Berlioz nonetheless never stopped making fun of the banal librettos of *opéras comiques* and of the noisy triviality of their settings.

He succeeded in doing so without employing the technical musical jargon behind which certain writers tend to hide when they have nothing to offer other than inconsequential details. Music criticism cannot be reduced to sneak attacks; of that Berlioz was convinced. His *feuilletons* are not critiques in the traditional sense of the term; nor are they circumspectly elaborated aesthetic theories. They are rather *responses to*, they are literary *fantasies on* serious subjects (such as *Euphonia* of 1844), they are polemical texts through which we sense the desire to convince by infectiousness (as in *Le Suicide par enthousiasme* of 1834), precisely as would music itself. This surely results from the fact that Berlioz harbors no illusions; speech about music, legitimate though it may be, is always chimerical. At best one hopes to attract the attention of readers by thought-provoking phraseology or by shocking ideas and words; one hopes to surprise them and make them laugh, to touch a momentary chord in their heart, and, by means of a mysterious sort of complicity, to render them sympathetic to the work in question. Berlioz knows all the resources of the French language and deploys them well as composer, poet, and artist.

Could it have been otherwise, given that he possessed neither the special inquisitiveness of the true critic nor the scholarly erudition of the musicologist? He was a fertile writer essentially because of his sensitivity and imagination, and because of the sonorities that resonated within him when he heard the works of Gluck, Beethoven, and Weber, those summits to which he himself aspired. Certain visceral and sometimes unjustified hatreds—of fugues in sacred music (he disapproved of the *In Gloria Dei Patris* fugue in the *Missa Solèmnis*), of *vocalises* in dramatic music (Donna Anna's second act aria "Non mi dir" was his *bête noire*), of the formulaic cadences of the Italian style (of which he found traces in Beethoven's Eighth Symphony)[10]—in a sense legitimized his enthusiasms and gave them the appearance of impartiality; and it is not difficult to find in his writings a number of hasty and biased judgments based in some cases upon nothing more than anecdote.

The composer of his own generation for whom Berlioz displayed continued interest and admiration, odd though it may seem, was Mendelssohn. Meyerbeer impressed him, as we learn from so many musical citations in the *Traité d'instrumentation et d'orchestration modernes*, but Berlioz soon saw in the German operatic composer the limitations of an incomplete genius. He said almost nothing about Schumann, and while he genuinely admired Liszt's pianism, he never took very seriously Liszt's vocation as a composer. Chopin, like Bellini, gained his sympathetic understanding, as we see in the obituaries he wrote for both, but he felt that he had little to learn from either one. Such was not the case for Verdi and Wagner. To the former he consecrated only a few but nonetheless highly complimentary lines on *Les Vêpres siciliennes* in the *Journal des débats* of 2 October 1855. To the latter he devoted considerably more space, in the *Mémoires* and in the articles (later included in *À travers chants*) about Wagner's Parisian concerts of 1860. In fact the path that Wagner was following so closely resembled his own that Wagner's departures from it seemed to Berlioz all the more contradictory. This, in point of fact, is generally the greatest obstacle faced by the composer-critic.

Whatever Berlioz's biases, they in no way discourage our continuing curiosity about his writings. Berlioz's *feuilletons* interest us first and foremost because they flow from the same pen that created the *Symphonie fantastique*, the *Requiem*, *Roméo et Juliette*, and *Les Troyens*. They also interest us because of that inner unity which was so powerful in Berlioz, and which, propelling his entire existence towards a single goal, established so many compelling and complex links among his personality, his writing, his music, and his life.

One must of course not conclude from this that all his *feuilletons* are of equal interest, for a music critic can hardly limit his activity to doing battle in behalf only of composers he admires. With his eyes fixed upon the horizon, Berlioz had to walk for some thirty years through the muddy highways and byways of Parisian musical life with an all too heightened awareness of the necessity of having often to write sweet nothings about nullities. "The *feuilletoniste*," he writes in chapter LIII of the *Mémoires*, "very often has no opinion at all regarding the subject of the *stuff* ['des *choses*'] about which is forced to write; that *stuff* arouses neither his ire nor his admiration; it doesn't really *exist*. [. . .] On one occasion I remained imprisoned in my room for three full days, unable even to begin to write a *feuilleton* on the Opéra-Comique." And he concludes by begging someone to bring him some music stands to carry, some double basses, and some harps, because "to *feuilletonize* in order to live [. . .] is the height of humiliation."

Be that as it may, because of the very oneness of Berlioz's personality, because of that inner unity we have mentioned, the fact that he *had* to write criticism to survive never spoiled his style or sapped his thinking. When it came to defending his noble causes—the opportunities to do so were admittedly drenched by the tidal wave of insipid comic operas he was obliged to review (he always called them "des opéras comiques très plats")—Berlioz remained as able at fifty as he was at thirty to find great freshness of expression. At certain times, in inspired moments, he casts aside the subject to hand with a few politely or sardonically formulaic remarks, then entertains the reader with considerations of a far more serious or intriguing sort.

At other times, trapped by respect or friendship or even indifference into publishing disingenuous praise, like all critics unable to exercise the requisite willpower, Berlioz had no recourse other than to confide the truth elsewhere, to family or to friends. Feeling pressed to say something positive about Louis Niedermeyer's opera *Alessandro Stradella*, for example, premiered on 3 March 1837, Berlioz wrote to his sister: "[. . .] I warn you in advance not to believe a word of what I shall write about the score, because in the fifteen years I've been listening to music, *never* have I encountered anything as unflappably boring as this."[11] He was surely exaggerating, but this kind of remark, of which there are more than a few examples in his collected correspondence, makes it possible to accuse Berlioz of being overly indulgent if not utterly duplicitous. He was surely more prepared to scoff at the little inventors of *opéras comiques* than he was at the stars of his day; and he was always ready to ridicule the plot of a ballet or the libretto of an opera, while he was sometimes forced to praise its musical setting, which in truth was probably neither better nor worse than the text.

We might note two exceptions to this self-imposed circuitousness, however, which won for Berlioz a good deal of long-lasting animosity. First, in an article on *Zampa*, which appeared in *Le Rénovateur* on 6 September 1835, Berlioz rather severely criticizes Ferdinand Hérold's score even though the recent death of the composer had in fact revived the work's popularity. Second, in an article on

Donizetti's *La Fille du régiment* for the *Journal des débats* of 16 February 1840, Berlioz accuses the composer of having "colonized" all the theaters of the French capital. We also find Berlioz squabbling with Cherubini, whom he much admired in certain ways and whom he hoped possibly to succeed at the Conservatoire (and at the Institut de France); and we find him systematically minimizing the undeniable gifts of Auber, who would in fact accede to Cherubini's job. Berlioz's taunting of Rossini (and of Palestrina for that matter) is more an expression of annoyance, because he sincerely admired *Le Barbier*, *Le Comte Ory*, and *Guillaume Tell*, and offered, in the prologue to *Roméo et Juliette*, one of the first examples of the neo-Palestrinian style, at least as Berlioz and his contemporaries might have imagined it, with its straightforward recitation for four-voiced choir.

Far more frequently can we be surprised by Berlioz's indulgence, even to the point of questioning the integrity of his judgment. But Berlioz knew perfectly well that a critic is impotent in the face of triumphant mediocrity, and that ill-understood severity leads only to incomprehension from the reader and resentment from the composer, the performer, and the conductor. He also knew that such severity would cause the work neither to get better nor to fail. Nonetheless Berlioz, like all critics, can seem untrustworthy for having perhaps caved in under the pressure of fashion and friendship, and untrustworthy, even more, for *not* having sacrificed his compositional career upon the altar of absolute candor and truth.

On the last point he has the right to plead extenuating circumstances. Had he been merely an obscure composer, he would never have been able to amass the exceptional forces required for his musical inspirations. His notoriety and widely acknowledged competence as a critic, however, combined with his recognition as a laureate of the Institut de France, rendered him a redoubtable public figure to whom one could lend a concert hall or a chorus, for whom one could exempt a portion of the poor-relief tax (which, for concerts, was exorbitant), and with whom players from the Conservatoire and singers from the Opéra could indeed be ready and willing to work. Did not all of this justify a little bit of creative praise and diplomatic silence, given the likelihood that the contrary would have produced strong and, knowing Berlioz, even excessive opposition? "My position at the *Journal des débats* is growing in importance," he wrote to his father in March 1837:

I am besieged by a horde of other newspapers that seek my collaboration. I think I will accept to work with the *Chronique de Paris* and the *Encyclopédie du XIXe siècle;* the prestige of those two papers can only increase the already considerable influence of my column at the *Débats*. All of that takes an enormous amount of time, however, and if I were to compose a good symphony, it would produce ten times more, optimistically speaking, than what I might earn from a full year's worth of all my articles added together. But mainly I must get to the Opéra! My battle plan is to break down the doors of that immense theater.[12]

Ten years later (having gotten to the Opéra in 1838, but still fighting to survive), Berlioz had to admit that the very persons whom he had so often "indulged and supported in his *feuilletons*" had almost "never demonstrated any real gratitude." "Do you really believe," he wrote to his friend Auguste Morel in 1848, "that I am the dupe of all those people with sycophantic smiles who hide their teeth and nails because they know that I have claws and backers?"[13]

In 1856 Berlioz confided to Adolphe Samuel that he was worried about the difficulties that Samuel was getting into because of the seriousness of his criticism:

> Look at what has happened to me as the result of my rare expressions of candor. My fists were full of verities. I lifted one little finger that allowed a few of them to get out— and you want to open your whole hand. . . . I don't know if the false prophets of art are worth the effort we make to do battle against them. Furthermore, whenever art becomes tied up with business (as is always the case with works destined for the theater), it always gives us fifty thousand reasons to justify its crimes, and its commercial success proves its critics wrong. And yet, in the long run, our protests do have some effect, because old-fashioned common sense does eventually win out. But how very long that takes! . . .[14]

Finally, in 1861, Berlioz, ill, admitted to his son that "my pen keeps falling from my hand, but I have to keep trying in order to earn my miserable hundred francs"—the amount he was usually paid for an article for the *Journal des débats*— "and to keep up my guard against so many buffoons who would attack if they weren't so afraid of me. And my head is full of new ideas, of projects I cannot carry out because of this enslavement."[15] On may justifiably wonder, in the face of this sort of confession, what Berlioz's life and work would have been like had he in fact been able to devote to his own music the time he devoted to the music of others, or had he been able to write, like Schumann and Wagner, about only those who sincerely interested him. And yet, looking collectively at his four symphonies, his overtures, his operas and oratorios, his *mélodies*, cantatas, and sacred music, one has the impression that they form a whole to which nothing need be added. Each score is at once original and complementary to the others. In fact Berlioz only once abandoned a serious project—a symphony in A Minor to which he alludes in chapter LIX of the *Mémoires*—not because he lacked the time, but rather because he lacked the money to cover the inevitably enormous expenses that such a work would entail. When we hear the fragments that remain to us of *La Nonne sanglante*, we may regret out of curiosity that he did not finish the opera, but Scribe's libretto, later offered to Gounod, is so implausible that whatever Berlioz may have written might not have redounded to his advantage.

In contrast, and perhaps the point needs emphasizing, however humiliating it may have been, Berlioz's work as music critic *released* him from having to compose in order to live. In fact, having neither the facility of an Auber or an Adam nor the fortune of a Meyerbeer, he would have been *unable* to do so: despite his romantic illusions about finding himself eventually crowned with popularity, Berlioz realized early on that the originality of his music rendered it of interest to only a limited number of connoisseurs and elevated minds. He may well have regretted this situation, but he was clearly aware of precisely how it came about.

Exercising the profession of *feuilletoniste* over the years clearly drained Berlioz, but he must nonetheless have felt the necessity of setting down his thoughts in words as strongly as he felt the necessity of setting down his feelings, otherwise inexpressible, in notes. Berlioz was extremely sensitive in the realms of both word and tone. It follows that, contrary to what has so often been alleged, Berlioz's music has no need of support from words. Indeed, who *really* knows the program he wrote for the first listeners to the *Symphonie fantastique*? And is it not true that if this work *really* depended on the program for its survival, it would have long ago vanished from the repertory?

On the other hand, Berlioz's prose is itself essentially musical, not only by the equilibrium of its phrases, the sonority and rhythm of its words, the momentum of its paragraphs, but also by its astonishing capacity to find equivalents in speech to the subjective effects produced by the music under consideration, be it the symphonies of Beethoven, the overtures of Weber, or the operas of Gluck. By evoking scores impressionistically, Berlioz accentuates the emotional evidence, the powerful convictions that emerge from so many masterpieces. Contrary to received opinion, it is not the obvious literary artifice, but rather the finely elaborated verbal construction, that makes an impact upon the general reader, and that makes the "how it's done," almost always incomprehensible, disappear behind the "why it's done"—which is, in modern terms, the definition of communication. Great art must of necessity be complex. But complex does not mean complicated. Indeed, complex is the opposite of complicated, because an artist produces not a book of spells but rather a work of art. And when Berlioz speaks, for example, of the former repertory of the Opéra-Comique (the works of Grétry, Monsigny, Dalayrac) and abandons his own day for the richer works of the past, he knows how to make us feel the difference between the essential if somewhat primitive elements of the genre and so many of its superfluous elements, which must not pull the wool over our eyes as to its real worth.

Berlioz's writings on music, whether we consider the *feuilletons*, the anthologies he made of them (*Les Soirées de l'orchestre, Les Grotesques de la musique, À travers chants*), the *Mémoires*, or even the correspondence, do not offer the rigor of a treatise on musical aesthetics. In their most fantastical digressions and desperate avoidances of prosaic reality, we always hear the voice of the composer, or, to speak more broadly, the voice of the artist, because we never sense a lessening of expressive intensity. Even when Berlioz feels it necessary to stretch out a line or broaden a paragraph, he does so in the manner of the virtuoso violinist who improvises a cadenza—with grace and imagination.

(Translated by Peter Bloom)

Notes

1. The full text, of which I use the last sentence as epigraph, reads as follows: "Ce serait un événement tout nouveau dans l'histoire des arts qu'un critique se faisant poète, un renversement de toutes les lois psychiques, une monstruosité; au contraire, tous les grands poètes deviennent naturellement, fatalement, critiques. Je plains les poètes que guide le seul instinct; je les crois incomplets. Dans la vie spirituelle des premiers, une crise se fait infailliblement, où ils veulent raisonner leur art, découvrir les lois obscures en vertu desquelles ils ont produit, et tirer de cette étude une série de préceptes dont le but divin est l'infaillibilité dans la production poétique. Il serait prodigieux qu'un critique devînt poète, et il est impossible qu'un poète ne contienne pas un critique." See Charles Baudelaire, "Richard Wagner et *Tannhäuser* à Paris [1861]," in *Curiosités esthétiques: L'art romantique et autres œuvres critiques*, ed. Henri Lemaître (Paris: Garnier Frères, 1962), pp. 689–728, here p. 706.

2. See the volumes abbreviated *CM* in the List of Abbreviations.

3. Armand Machabey, *Traité de la critique musicale* (Paris: Richard-Masse, 1946), p. 131.

4. *Revue et Gazette musicale* (9 November 1834).

5. [No English word quite captures the sense of Berlioz's "fatalité." "Calamity," David Cairns's choice, may not sufficiently convey the element of inevitability—as suggested by Baudelaire's "fatalement" (see note 1)—as well as of doom. —*Ed.*]

6. *CG* I, p. 253. Berlioz was already thinking ahead to the visit to "Germany" that was required of winners of the Prix de Rome, for he believed he was going to win the prize in the summer of 1829. See *CG* I, p. 256.

7. *CG* I, p. 64.

8. Berlioz delivered four articles on *Iphigénie en Tauride* to the *Gazette musicale de Paris* in November and December 1834. On this subject, see Joël-Marie Fauquet, "Berlioz and Gluck," in *The Cambridge Companion to Berlioz*, ed. Peter Bloom (Cambridge: Cambridge University Press, 2000), pp. 199–210.

9. ["Berlioz might feel benevolently disposed towards some of the younger composers like Reyer, Massenet, Bourgault-Ducoudray, Adolphe Samuel, the Dane Asger Hamerik and Saint-Saëns" (*Cairns 2*, p. 741), but none of these was a pupil, with the possible exception of Hamerik. See the article on Berlioz and Hamerik by Christopher Follet at www.hberlioz.com/others/hamerik.htm#3hberlioz.com. —*Ed.*]

10. For Berlioz, the end of the second movement of the Eighth is nothing more than a copy of the Italianate, "felicità" cadence. See *À travers chants*, p. 68: "I have never been able to fathom this prank."

11. *CG* II, p. 333. In the review of the opera that Berlioz published in the *Journal des débats* of 5 March 1837, the comments on the music are polite but hardly overflowing with praise.

12. *CG* II, p. 336.

13. *CG* III, p. 504.

14. *CG* III, p. 388.

15. *CG* VI, p. 200.

Chapter Six

"A Certain Hector Berlioz": News in Germany about Berlioz in France

GUNTHER BRAAM

An average sentence, in a German newspaper, is a sublime and impressive curiosity.

—Mark Twain

Berlioz made his first appearance in a German music newspaper on 6 June 1829;[1] the first German concert review of one of his works came out six months later, on 30 December.[2] By the mid-eighteen-thirties, information on Berlioz in the press *d'outre-Rhin* is no longer rare. How in fact did news about Berlioz find its way from Paris to Germany? This is the subject of the current article, whose purpose is to call attention to important and hitherto little-known or neglected sources of early Berlioz reception in Germany—little-known or neglected in part because they exist in German, and many modern Berlioz scholars, particularly the English speakers and the French, have yet to take the full measure of their import.

In collaboration with Arnold Jacobshagen, I have, in the volume mentioned in note 1, assembled a substantial amount of new material from the German press. Some significant documents, however, did not find their way into that book. I shall thus include quotations from those documents in this article, which the reader may wish to regard as a complement to *Hector Berlioz in Deutschland*.

Precisely how would a German journalist working in the earlier decades of the nineteenth century have done research about Berlioz's life, work, and impact? In what follows, I should like to suggest, in the form of a "journalist's handbook," with historical examples as needed, seven ways he might have gone about that task.

1. Consult the Paris "Yellow Pages"

The first step would be to consult a "Who's Who" of the contemporary world of Parisian culture—for in fact such directories did then exist. The following entry is taken from a dictionary of artists edited in 1831 by the painter Charles Gabet:

> BERLIOZ (Hector), compositeur de musique; Paris, r. de Richelieu, 96; né à la Côte St.-André (Isère) en 1803; él[ève]. de MM. Lesueur et Reicha. Il a composé Une messe en musique qui fut exécutée d'abord à l'église St.-Roch, à Paris, et ensuite à celle de St.-Eustache par l'orchestre et les chœurs de l'Opéra. Il a donné, en 1828 et 1829, à l'École royale de musique, plusieurs concerts composés de morceaux de sa composition. Il a fait la musique des *Francs-Juges*, opéra écrit pour l'Odéon, et que la nouvelle destination de ce théâtre n'a pas permis de représenter. Cet artiste a publié, chez Schlesinger, la grande partition de 8 scènes de Faust de Goëthe; 9 Mélodies de Th. Moore, avec accompagnement de piano; Plusieurs romances, etc., etc. M. Berlioz a remporté, en 1828, un second grand prix de composition musicale. Il donne des leçons particulières de composition, d'harmonie et de chant.[3]

It is highly likely that Berlioz himself is the author of this text because, apart from its odd capitalization and mixture of words and figures, it is, *mirabile dictu,* correct. Important to notice is the comment at the end, which informs us that Berlioz was prepared to teach not only composition and harmony but also singing. We know that he often sang in formal and informal settings, but we may not have known that, in his student years, he also actually taught voice.

This reference book, of more than seven hundred pages, contains a *Supplément* on a single leaf bound in at the end, in which only eight persons are mentioned, one of whom is Berlioz:

> BERLIOZ (Hector), compositeur (*ajoutez à son article*). Il a remporté au concours de l'Institut, en 1830, le grand prix de composition musicale. Il est auteur d'une *Symphonie* en cinq parties, exécutée le 5 décembre 1830 devant un nombreux auditoire.[4]

For a short while after the première of the *Symphonie fantastique,* on 5 December 1830, Berlioz seems to have been the talk of the town. He then left Paris for almost two years, in 1831–1832, and this absence was reflected in the German musical press. One article appeared in 1831 concerning the première of the *Fantastique,* one other in 1832. In 1833 Berlioz was mentioned in three articles.[5] For information concerning his private life, the author of the third of these seems to have drawn directly or indirectly from Joseph d'Ortigue's *Le Balcon de l'opéra,* published in April 1833: the passages there dealing with Berlioz's *curriculum vitae* were taken from the article d'Ortigue earlier published in the *Revue de Paris,* on 23 December 1832, for which Berlioz himself had supplied an autobiographical sketch in order to enhance his reentry, after the *voyage en Italie,* into the musical world of the French capital.[6] German journalists would have had access to the *Revue de Paris*, but if not, they would have had to wait until 1833 for the publication in book form of this (auto)biography of Berlioz—a short biography, to be sure, but one already highly seasoned with anecdotes.

The first long biographical entry on Berlioz was not published in a German dictionary until 1842: this appeared in the supplementary volume added in that year to Gustav Schilling's *Encyclopädie der gesammten musikalischen Wissenschaften oder Universal-Lexicon der Tonkunst.*[7]

2. Ask Travelers for News from Paris

Another step for our German journalist *à la recherche de Berlioz* would be to try to find eyewitness reports, such as the one we have from Carl Schwencke (born in 1797), the son (one of fifteen siblings) of the Hamburg music director Christian Friedrich Gottlieb Schwencke. According to Schwencke's nephew, Friedrich Gottlieb Schwencke, who edited Carl's *Erinnerungen* in 1884, Carl had been,

> since he was nineteen years old, [. . .] constantly on tour in Germany, Austria, Denmark, Sweden in particular, Norway, Russia, and France. [. . .] In 1840 he even visited Constantinople [. . .] In the early days, before the era of railways, he several times made the journey from Hamburg to Paris on foot—as his Paris doctors had advised him to do for reasons of health. [. . .] His last home was in Nussdorf near Vienna [. . .]. Carl S. vanished in January 1870 and all inquiries as to his whereabouts have been futile. [. . .][8]
>
> In Paris, where he often would spend the winter, he found a patron in Cherubini and an intimate friend in the director of the concerts at the Conservatoire, the famous Habeneck, who had some of his works performed, e.g., a mass and his symphony. It was also there that he found publishers for several of his piano works and quartets.[9]

In the *Journal des débats* of 25 April 1838 Berlioz mentions a *Benedictus* by Schwencke, and he wrote a favorable review of it in the *Revue et Gazette musicale* of 20 May 1838.[10] In his *Erinnerungen*, Schwencke drops the name of Berlioz:

> Since 1827 I have spent five winters in Paris [. . .]. In 1838 I had the pleasure of hearing my *Benedictus* for four voices with accompaniment of four solo cellos and wind instruments played in one of the [Conservatoire] concerts and of finding a friendly reaction even from maestro Cherubini. Furthermore, Berlioz wrote a long and interesting article about it in the *Gazette musicale.*[11]

The performance of a *Sinfonie in D* by Schwencke at the Conservatoire, on 12 February 1843, repeated on 11 February 1844, led Berlioz to mention him in the same breath as Mozart, Haydn, Mendelssohn, and Beethoven.[12] And in his *Erinnerungen*, speaking of the spring of 1833, Schwencke noted the following:

Some days later [after visiting Paganini] I made the acquaintance of the young Berlioz, who won the first prize in composition at the Conservatoire a few years ago and who was receiving three thousand francs per year, as he would for a total of five years, for cultural traveling. He had recently returned from Italy, and could hardly find the words to report to me on the miserable and wretched state of music there, especially in Rome, where the quality of instrumental music must be beneath contempt. According to the official regulations, he was supposed to spend three of those five years in Italy, yet he asked for—and indeed has been granted—permission, from the directors of the Conservatoire, to return after one year and to spend the remaining twelve thousand francs in Paris. A Symphony by him, performed here just recently [on 9 December 1832], is reported by some to be a most ingenious piece of work, and by many others to be a silly hodgepodge. I shall not comment on it until I have heard it myself. He seems to be an eccentric and fantastical fellow and to have a high regard for his own musical capacities. Moreover he is a man with a scientific education, having first studied medicine and only later dedicated himself exclusively to music, thus exposing himself to the tremendous ire of his father, a medical doctor. His favorite composers are Gluck, Beethoven, and Weber; his judgments of many others are one-sided and biased due to his lack of a broad ["vielseitige"] musical education.[13]

A later entry among Schwencke's recollections gives us a small indication of Berlioz's outward appearance:

Berlioz, seen as the greatest of geniuses by some, as a madman by others, had his long, broad, and shapeless overture to *Les Francs-Juges* performed. The audience's reaction was disparaging; one even heard hissing, which made me feel rather sorry for him, as he sat in the orchestral loge, dressed in an unusually elegant manner, perhaps expecting torrential cheers of enthusiasm. I sat in Habeneck's loge, where I met the composer Paër, who is almost forgotten over here; he was sitting to my immediate right and caused me a good deal of amusement because, throughout the overture, he criticized more than he listened, highly irritated as he was by this young fellow who wanted to compose but who succeeded only in putting together an *olla potrida* [a potpourri, or hodgepodge].[14]

Schwencke seems certain about the identity of the overture he heard, and about the fact that Berlioz himself was not conducting. This, together with the fact that he was sitting in Habeneck's loge—which means the Conservatoire—suggests that the concert he attended was that of 30 December 1832 or that of 14 December 1834.

Schwencke's last mention of Berlioz is undated:

If we compare the scores of German and French composers [. . .], we are constrained to say that there is no question of the superiority of the latter in terms of multifarious and individualized instrumentation. [. . .] It is by this means, and by this means alone, that even very mediocre talents among [the French] win names for themselves as composers. One would be astonished by the sterility and aridity of the ideas of a Halévy or a Berlioz, etc., if ever one were to separate them from their instrumental dress.[15]

Schwencke's *Erinnerungen* were published posthumously. Yet his impressions may well have found their way into the German musical newspapers because he traveled widely, because he had met Berlioz in person, and because oral transmission was a prime source for journalists of the day.

3. *Discover What German Celebrities Think of the Composer*

Felix Mendelssohn-Bartholdy and Ignaz Moscheles—equally famous in England and on the continent—became friends in 1824 and exchanged numerous letters after that time. In the Berlioz literature, the remark that is most frequently quoted from their published correspondence, edited in 1888 by Moscheles' son Felix, is that one has to wash one's hands after touching one of Berlioz's scores. Other remarks from Mendelssohn's side of the exchange have rarely been noticed.

On 6 February 1834, the orchestra of the Royal Philharmonic Society in London rehearsed, under the direction of Moscheles, Mendelssohn's *Melusine* Overture and Berlioz's *Grande Ouverture des Francs-Juges*. Of the latter, Moscheles wrote to Mendelssohn on 12 February 1834:

> After yours [the *Melusine* Overture], I had Berlioz's Overture, *Les Francs Juges*, to conduct. We were all curious to know what the result of French genius would be. I say French, for so far no other country but France has recognized Berlioz as a genius. But, oh! What a rattling of brass, fit for the Porte-Saint-Martin! What cruel, wicked scoring! as if to prove that our ancestors were no better than pedants! And, oh! again, for the contrast of the middle subject, that would console us with a vaudeville melody, such as you could not hear to more advantage in *L'Ours et le Pacha*,[16] or in *Die Wiener in Berlin*.[17] Then the mystic element—a progression of screeching harmonies, unintelligible to all but the cats of March! To show that something terrible is agitating the fevered brain of the composer, an apoplectic stroke of the big drum shakes to shivers the efforts of the whole orchestra, as well as the auditory nerves and diaphragm of the assembled audience.[18]

Mendelssohn replied to Moscheles at the end of April 1834:

> What you say of Berlioz's Overture I thoroughly agree with. It is a chaotic, prosaic piece, and yet more humanly conceived than some of his others. I always felt inclined to say with Faust, "He ran around, he ran about, / His thirst in puddles laving; / He gnawed and scratched the house throughout, / But nothing cured his raving; / And driven at last, in open day, / He ran into the kitchen."[19] For his orchestration is such a frightful muddle, such an incongruous mess, that one ought to wash one's hands after handling one of his scores. Besides, it really is a shame to set nothing but murder, misery, and wailing to music; even if it were well done, it would simply give us a record of *atrocités*. At first he made me quite melancholy, because his judgments on others are so clever, so cool, and correct, he seems so thoroughly sensible, and yet he does not perceive that his own works are such rubbishy nonsense.[20]

Two months later Mendelssohn mentioned Berlioz again, in a letter to Moscheles of 26 June 1834:

> If in his latter days he [Henri Herz] should take to the Romantic and write melancholy music, or to the Classical and give us fugues—and I should not be surprised if he did—Berlioz can compose a new symphony on him, "de la vie d'un artiste," which I am sure will be better than the first.[21]

Even when Moscheles lets drop a few positive words about one of Berlioz's symphonies (presumably the *Fantastique*), Mendelssohn objects, as he wrote to Moscheles on 25 March 1835:

> What you say about Berlioz's symphony is literally true, I am sure; only I must add that the whole thing seems to me so dreadfully boring—and what could be worse? A piece of music may be a piece of uncouth, crazy, barefaced impudence, and still have some "go" about it and be amusing; but this is simply insipid and altogether without life.[22]

Five months later, on 13 August 1835, Mendelssohn complains to Moscheles about all the attention that is being lavished upon Liszt's *Harmonies poétiques et religieuses*, published in 1835, because the work appears to him to be "very stupid." He goes on:

> What annoys me is that there is so little to throw into the other side of the balance; for what our Reissiger & Co. compose, though different, is just as shallow, and what Berlioz writes is not music either, and even old Cherubini's *Ali Baba* is dreadfully poor and borders on Auber. That is very sad.[23]

Mendelssohn may have been too polite a person to publish his private opinions in the newspapers. It was his custom to suggest that it was better to make real contributions to music than endlessly to talk and write about it.[24] If his personal views were mirrored in the contemporary press, it would have been in an indirect manner. We do not know whether Moscheles quoted Mendelssohn's statements beyond the circle of his own family and friends.

4. Join the Staff of a German Avant-Garde Music Journal

Information on Berlioz begins to flow with some continuity only in 1834. In that year, the *Neue Zeitschrift für Musik*, recently founded by Robert Schumann, mentioned Berlioz for the first time in the issue of 28 April 1834.[25] On 2 June we find an announcement of the arrangement of the *Symphonie fantastique* for piano "four hands"—in fact it is for two—by Franz Liszt,[26] and on 20 and 24 November 1834, the first autobiographical text signed by Berlioz in a German journal, which Schumann offered as a part of his commentary on the *Gazette musicale*.[27]

Subsequently, Schumann found information on Berlioz in the French newspapers, in the communications from his Paris correspondents (among them Stephen Heller, who went to Paris in 1838 and soon became Berlioz's close friend), and in communications with Berlioz himself.

In 1835, Schumann published the longest review of a single work that he would ever bring into print: a comprehensive treatment, in six installments that appeared between 3 July and 14 August, of Liszt's piano arrangement of the *Symphonie fantastique*.[28] He had already printed two articles on the same subject, on 27 February and 3 March, by Heinrich Panofka, and, on 19 and 23 June, by F.-J. Fétis.[29] Schumann's grand analysis of Berlioz's first symphony marked the first highpoint, and a lasting highpoint, of German Berlioz reception.[30]

Schumann asked his future father-in-law, Friedrich Wieck, to show Liszt's piano arrangement to the music publisher Raimund Härtel; he then asked Härtel on 22 December 1835 to return it.[31] Clara Wieck—later no fan of the Frenchman's—was apparently touched by her fiancé's early enthusiasm for Berlioz and in mid-1835 composed an *Impromptu*, *Le Sabbat*, and a *Scène fantastique: Le Ballet des revenants*; these were subsequently incorporated into her *Quatre Pièces caractéristiques pour le pianoforte*, Op. 5 (1836).

If we are to take seriously a comment by Joseph Mainzer (another future enemy of our composer), Berlioz's position in the world of European music, in the eyes of the German press, was rising quickly. In the *Neue Zeitschrift* of 5 July 1836, in which he announces the death of Anton Reicha, Mainzer wrote: "Among [Reicha's] many pupils I name but two, Onslow and Berlioz. They alone will surely outstrip all others."[32] A few months later, on 14 September 1836, while explaining to Heinrich Dorn, Kapellmeister in Riga, the nature of his fictitious *Davidsbund* (his critical "band of David"), Schumann himself wrote that "Mozart was as great a member of the *Bund* as is now Berlioz."[33]

This positive point of view was challenged by Wilhelm Florentin von Zuccalmaglio, who provided a conservative voice in the *Neue Zeitschrift* under the *nom de plume* of Dorfküster Gottschalk Wedel. On 4 November 1836, Zuccalmaglio, in the course of a review—in the form of a dream monologue—of Franz Lachner's Fifth Symphony, Op. 52, subtitled "Passionata," inserted some gratuitously ironic comments about Berlioz's "program music," in which he implies that the *Fantastique* had fulfilled the legacy of such major artworks as Papa Haydn's "Toy Symphony" and Beethoven's (notorious) *Battle of Vittoria*.[34]

Before printing Zuccalmaglio's "dream," Schumann wrote to the critic, on 18 October 1836, to tell him that his text was inappropriate for the *Neue Zeitschrift*:

In one of your earlier letters you suggest that some of your articles remain unpublished. That is true of only one of them—the dream about [Lachner's] "Prize Symphony."[35] I often look at this article with genuine sadness: it has many good things in it, but I would rather read it in a magazine other than the *Neue Zeitschrift*, which is dedicated primarily to the young and to progressive movements. Furthermore, we have written so positively about that very symphony of Berlioz that the publication of a point of view so opposite to our own would be of little value.[36]

Schumann eventually resolved the dilemma by printing the following editor's note at the head of the second part of the review:

How our gentle Gottschalkian Wedel became enraged about the "Frank" [i.e. French; Schumann mocks Zuccalmaglio's old-fashioned usage] Berlioz! Yet in the sphere of the arts we are not all so pious a village sexton as you are ["So fromme Dorfküster, als du"] and people pray to the deity in many ways. Indeed, every man does so differently. When Berlioz slays men at the altar, when he behaves like an Indian fakir, he has the same righteous intentions as does Haydn, for example, when he makes the offering of a cherry blossom with a devout look upon his face. Yet we do not wish forcefully to impose our beliefs upon anyone.[37]

It should be noted that when Zuccalmaglio conceived his article, no work of Berlioz's had as yet been performed in Germany. Despite the fact that Zuccalmaglio alludes to the *Fantastique* as the latest excrescence of romantic ecstasy (he knew the symphony only from Liszt's arrangement), he could also have been acquainted with one of the two piano arrangements of the *Grande Ouverture des Francs-Juges*—either the version Berlioz made himself, with Chopin's help, which was published by Richault in Paris in February 1836;[38] or the version unauthorized by Berlioz that was published by Hofmeister in Leipzig shortly thereafter. On 22 March 1836 Schumann commented on the pirated arrangement, pointing out perspicaciously that one cannot judge Berlioz from a piano arrangement—especially one of such poor quality.[39] This review had immediate consequences: first, Berlioz published an open letter in the *Revue et Gazette musicale* on 8 May 1836, "À Mons. Hofmeister, éditeur de musique à Leipsick," in which he excoriates the unauthorized arrangement. One month later, on 7 June 1836, Schumann kindly printed a translation of Berlioz's letter.[40] And he soon noted in his diary, on 10 August 1836, that that act of kindness had produced a result: "Berlioz sends me his overture."[41] It was Schumann, then, who was in effect responsible for the first performance of a work by Berlioz in Germany. For at the same time that he brought out the (authorized) piano arrangement, Richault in Paris issued the full score: that is what Berlioz sent to Schumann, and that is what Schumann offered to the Euterpe Concert Society in Leipzig. The conductor of the Society, Christian Gottlieb Müller, prepared a set of orchestral parts (which have been preserved[42]) and they were used when, on 7 November 1836, under Müller's direction, this orchestra of amateurs performed the overture to *Les Francs-Juges*. Aside from the 1834 rehearsal of the same piece, in London, which we have mentioned above, this was the first extra-Parisian performance of any work by Hector Berlioz. The performance was repeated on 21 November 1836. The sum total of what we know about this historically if not artistically important German première is contained in two notices, the first of which appeared in the *Allgemeine musikalische Zeitung* of 4 January 1837:

> Among other compositions, the society performed the first orchestral work that we have heard here by Mr. Hector Berlioz: this was the overture *Les Francs-Juges*. The execution of the work, heavily scored with brass, was well done, yet the overture appealed to only a few in the audience and passed almost unnoticed. Nevertheless we have to thank the direction for programming music by the man who, with his novel-like symphonies, has stirred up a good deal of interest in Paris. By request the overture was repeated at one of the same society's subsequent concerts, where it made an only slightly better impression. What is particularly original about this overture is its strange inclusion of a number of curious harmonic progressions, and not its melodies, which are rather less distinguished than we might have hoped.[43]

Six months later, on 30 June 1837, in the context of a review of the musical season, a critic in the *Neue Zeitschrift* wrote:

> We have had a fine selection of older concert overtures [. . . and] among the newest have been one each by Attern, Conrad, and Berlioz: the latter's "Judges of the Secret Court" [*Les Francs-Juges*] is considered a notorious monster, but I find it nothing if not well shaped and clearly structured, still immature in some parts but no doubt the work of a French musical genius who enjoys casting bolts of lightning here and there as though announcing in his symphonies the coming of thunder.[44]

In an open letter to the *Revue et Gazette musicale* that appeared on 19 February 1837, Berlioz thanked Schumann for the performance of his overture.[45] Schumann translated and reprinted the letter in the *Neue Zeitschrift* of 3 March. There, Schumann explains:

> [The performance] may have occurred at my request, but I was very happy to make it. As far as Mr. Berlioz's gratitude is concerned [. . .], it should be lavished not upon me but rather upon the director of the Euterpe Concert Society, Mr. C. G. Müller, who copied out the parts from the score that I gave him, and upon the orchestra of that honorable society, which, after only a few rehearsals, gave a clear and thoughtful performance of the work.[46]

The *Grande Ouverture des Francs-Juges* was performed again in Leipzig by the Euterpe in 1837 and in 1839; in 1838, both Berlioz and Schumann were made honorary members of the that concert society, as Schumann announced in the *Neue Zeitschrift* of 9 January 1838.[47]

The next German performance of this work took place in Weimar, on 19 March 1837, and caused something of a stir. In the *Neue Zeitschrift* of 9 May 1837, Schumann published an "Open letter to Mr. Hector Berlioz" from Johann Christian Lobe, who reported enthusiastically on the Weimar performance.[48] In due course Zuccalmaglio prepared a reply to Lobe, which he submitted to

Schumann. In a private letter of 20 August 1837, Schumann explained to Zuccalmaglio the genesis of Lobe's "Open Letter":

> Your letter concerning Berlioz [i.e., Zuccalmaglio's reply to Lobe] has caused me some embarrassment, as did Lobe's, which does indeed exaggerate. I should like to tell you the reason for its inclusion in the journal; this may not be the best reason, but it is always better to be honest and frank. Lobe sent me the letter and along with it he asked for a sum of money—which I was happy to give him—but I did not wish to lose money on the transaction; I have been working for the journal for years; I did not wish to pay him from my own funds. That is how it happened [that the letter was printed in the journal]. And then, please forgive me for saying so, but you judge the overture without even having heard it! You have no idea how capable Berlioz is at handling the orchestra. If, after hearing the overture properly performed, you still wish to have your article printed, I will be glad to see to it. By the way the whole subject does not deserve all of this attention; it was adequately treated in the short announcement of the overture in an earlier volume [of the *Neue Zeitschrift*]. What I said then still seems valid to me now. Still, it troubles me that you should have written your excellent article in vain.[49]

Two months later, on 20 October 1837, Schumann made this public:

> It is for the same reason [i.e., lack of space], dearest Wedel, that we regretfully cannot publish your rebuttal to Mr. Lobe, in Weimar, concerning the Berlioz's Overture to "The Judges of the Secret Court"; we also feel that the overture does not merit more discussion, as it has been properly considered in volume 6, p. 101, of our journal. Finally, even though we are not in total agreement with the eccentric eulogy from Weimar, we find your reproach to be too harsh.[50]

Zuccalmaglio soon revised his article, which Schumann then published in the issues of 12, 19, and 22 December 1837.[51] In the meantime, however, the impatient Zuccalmaglio had sent the original text to the *Allgemeine musikalische Zeitung*, Schumann's immediate competitor. There, too, it was put on hold. But when the director of the *AmZ*, Gottfried Wilhelm Fink, read the *revised* version in Schumann's journal, he took advantage of the occasion and, on 3 January 1838, brought out Zuccalmaglio's *original* article.[52] It is for this reason that Schumann wrote to Zuccalmaglio on 13 January 1838:

> I am sure you were just as surprised as I was to see your article, which eventually appeared in my journal, appearing again in Fink's. This made me a feel a little jealous, too, since in fact I have little or no esteem for Fink's public demeanor. Thus play the Gods of Chance—and the article, about whose original appearance you had doubts, now appears in two forms. Lobe has already sent some "thoughts" ["Bedenken"] about it. But at this moment I have no space for them. If this continues, I will send his piece back to Weimar. Frankly, I regret even paying for the paper of this dispute, because I am as clear in my mind about Berlioz as I am about the clear blue sky. Still, the issue is an important one. I really do believe that we are at the dawn of a new musical era, a dawn that is needed and long overdue.[53]

In the end Lobe's "Bedenken" were not published. But he long remained an admirer of Berlioz, as we know from further letters and documents, including his composition treatise of 1844, in which he mentions Berlioz in a very positive light:

> As a rule one deploys individualized and dissimilar themes for the separate movements of a large compositional form such as a symphony or a sonata. Recently, however, the ingenious Frenchman Berlioz has made use of a single leading theme throughout all the movements of his symphony entitled *Épisode de la vie d'un artiste*. This opens the way to a new and expanded procedure of thematic development, which could soon lead to a number of grand tone poems.[54]

Schumann, meanwhile, continued to proselytize for Berlioz's music. On 28 May 1839 he wrote to the Leipzig composer Herrmann Hirschbach to ask if he knew anything of Berlioz: "He is highly extravagant; he has little sense of beauty; but he is well aware of what is true, and of what is profound."[55] On 22 November 1839 he wrote again to Lobe: "We have heard an overture to *Waverley* by Berlioz. Try to get hold of it and to have it performed. It will deeply move you."[56] And on 19 February 1840, when asked to submit samples of his journalistic writings in order to receive an honorary doctorate, Schumann quoted not only his article about the Beethoven monument but also his article about Berlioz's *Symphonie fantastique*.[57]

These glimpses of Robert Schumann's editorial procedures reveal him in a very sympathetic light. While he himself stood firmly in support of Berlioz's "cause"—in part because he was intimately acquainted with the *Fantastique*, whose treasures are greater than those of *Waverley* and *Les Francs-Juges*—he nevertheless opened the pages of his journal to those of differing opinions, even those who appeared to the editor to be somewhat old-fashioned. Later on, however, Schumann's enthusiasm for Berlioz would begin to cool.

5. Become a Pen Pal of One of the Composer's Enemies

From 1836 to 1850 the French composer Adolphe Adam maintained a regular correspondence with Samuel Heinrich Spiker, librarian for the King of Prussia, in Berlin, and included in his letters a lot of green-room talk from various Parisian musical venues. We quote one passage here in order to illustrate how a comment made by a composer-colleague of Berlioz's, but by no means his kindred spirit, might find its way into the German musical press. For it is likely, in this case, that Spiker gave Adam's letter to Ludwig Rellstab for use in *Iris im Gebiete der Tonkunst*, the journal he edited from 1830 to 1841. In what follows, we present Adam's original French text and indicate all the words and phrases that were cut either by Rellstab or, earlier, by Spiker, by placing them in square brackets. Thus, on 11 December 1837, Adam wrote to Spiker as follows about the first performance of the *Requiem*:

[Nous avons eu une chose curieuse, c'est] une messe des morts de Berlioz, qu'on a exécutée [aux Invalides] pour le général Damrémont [, tué devant Constantine]. Il y avait quatre cents musiciens et on lui avait alloué pour cela vingt-huit mille francs. Vous ne pouvez vous figurer rien de pareil à cette musique, qui, outre un orchestre considérable dans les proportions ordinaires, comprenait l'adjonction de vingt trombones, dix trompettes et quatorze timbales. [Eh bien! tout cela n'a pas fait le moindre effet, et pourtant vous allez voir tous les journaux, à bien peu d'exceptions près, proclamer cette messe comme un chef-d'œuvre. Cela vient de ce que Berlioz est lui-même journaliste: il écrit dans le *Journal des débats*, le plus influent de tous, et tous les journalistes se soutiennent. Il faut dire que s'il est un détestable musicien, en revanche il écrit fort élégamment; mais vous pensez que les idées d'un pareil homme doivent être fort singulières en musique.] Il nie tous les musiciens, excepté Beethoven et Meyerbeer [; et ce qu'il admire chez le premier, ce sont les défauts que nous sommes obligés de reconnaître; il n'admet pas la mélodie, et ce qu'il admire le plus dans Meyerbeer, c'est un roulement de timbales d'un finale des *Huguenots*. Il admire et ne cherche que les combinaisons bizarres d'instruments; ainsi, dans sa messe, un des passages qu'il affectionnait était ainsi conçu: c'était deux flûtes tenant une tierce à l'aigu, pendant que les trombones faisaient entendre les notes graves de pédale inusitées sur cet instrument; et puis rien du tout dans l'intervalle . . . On ne peut imaginer rien de plus niais, si ce n'est ceux qui admirent de telles platitudes.] Il paraît que Schlesinger va graver la messe [, et, par curiosité, je vous engage à vous la procurer].[58]

And here, as point of comparison, we present the note (in translation) as it is found in Rellstab's *Iris* on 29 December 1837:

II. Review of recent events. / Paris. [. . .] Berlioz's *Requiem*, performed at the funeral service for general Damrémont, was played by four hundred musicians; to cover his expenses, he received an indemnification of twenty-eight thousand francs. There can hardly be a music more bizarre than this. Beyond employing an already colossal orchestra, he employed an additional twenty trombones, ten trumpets, and fourteen timpani! The composer Berlioz recognizes no masters other than Beethoven and Meyerbeer (!)—a splendid combination that tells us a great deal about the composer. Schlesinger will probably have the full score engraved.[59]

This sort of editorial reduction was and is common enough. We find Robert Schumann doing precisely the same thing, for example, in an article for the *Neue Zeitschrift* that he received from Richard Wagner—a well-known document in which Wagner speaks admiringly of the *Symphonie funèbre et triomphale* and sympathetically (as enhanced by Schumann) of Berlioz's isolation in Paris.[60]

6. Give the Above-Mentioned German Celebrity a Second Chance

But more positive news of Berlioz's *Requiem* crossed the border as well, as Moscheles knew, for example, when he wrote to Mendelssohn (the above-mentioned celebrity) on 23 December 1837: "The *Gazette Musicale* exalts Berlioz's *Requiem* above all music of all times. A new vista, it says, is opened! You know I am not a believer in this genius; tell me whether anything of his has been to your taste."[61] Two years later, however, Mendelssohn, apparently ready to give Berlioz another try, had not changed his mind. On 30 November 1839 he wrote to Moscheles: "Berlioz's program, which you send me, is a very silly production. I wish I could see any pluck or originality in it, but to me it seems simply vapid and insipid. Has not Onslow written anything new? And old Cherubini?"[62]

7. Go to Paris, Meet the Composer, Make a Written Report

Berlioz research has tended almost completely to ignore the comments on the French composer left by Anton Felix Schindler, otherwise well known as Beethoven's somewhat shady amanuensis in the later years of the master's career. Schindler traveled to Paris in 1841 in order to do research on French views of Beethoven, and to Berlin in 1842 in order to sell to the King of Prussia some of Beethoven's papers that he, Schindler, may have obtained by devious means. (The Royal Library in Berlin did purchase these things in 1845.) In his diary Schindler mentions Berlioz on several occasions:

> On Saturday 30 [January 1841] I visited Mr. Habeneck, for whom I had brought with me the score of Handel's *Judas Maccabaeus*. But he had gone hunting. [. . .] Together with Friedland, I went in the evening to see Berlioz, rue de Londres 31, but he had already gone out because we had kept him waiting too long.[63]

(Ferdinand Friedland was a businessman, a friend of Heine's, and a generous admirer of Berlioz's. It has been thought that Berlioz first met Friedland in Frankfurt in 1842 or 1843, but Schindler's note suggests that he probably met Friedland in Paris in 1841.)[64]

> Tuesday, 2 February [1841] . . . At 7 p.m. I went to see Berlioz (rue de Londres 31). We then went together to a café, in the rue Lepelletier, where we spent a good hour chatting and becoming acquainted. As a kindness to me, Berlioz promised to organize within a few weeks a large-scale performance of his works, with an excellent orchestra, in order that I might come to know them as well as possible. He has already given three concerts and is therefore still exhausted from the effort and time he spent doing so.[65]

The "three concerts" mentioned by Schindler are presumably those of 7 August 1840 in the Salle Vivienne (repeated on 14 August), of 1 November 1840 at the Opéra (the grand festival concert that Berlioz gave in the presence of Louis-Philippe), and of 13 December 1840 at the Conservatoire. It seems unlikely that Berlioz would actually try to organize an orchestral concert specifically to please Schindler, whose greatest claim to fame, as he put it on his visiting card, was to have been "l'ami de Beethoven." It is conceivable that the concert Berlioz mentioned to Schindler is the one that eventually took place on

25 April 1841, which Berlioz and Liszt organized in support of the Beethoven monument to be constructed in Bonn; but it is more likely that he referred to a forthcoming concert of the Société des Concerts du Conservatoire. Still, when, at the beginning of February 1841, Schindler offered Berlioz a copy of his biography of Beethoven, Berlioz returned the favor by making him the extraordinary gift of the score of the *Requiem*—as we learn from Berlioz's letter of 4 February,[66] and from Schindler's diary entry of the next day:

> Friday, 5 [February 1841] [. . .] In the evening I went to the concert given in the rue St. Honoré, which had a larger audience than the last two times. [. . .] When I returned home, at about 11 p.m., I found a parcel, opened it, and saw the full score of Berlioz's *Requiem* with the inscription "à monsieur Schindler, Hommage de l'auteur. H. Berlioz." I immediately started reading it and continued until about 1 a.m. I was very pleasantly surprised by many things in it.[67]

> On Monday, 8 [February 1841], after 12 noon, Mr. Berlioz came to see me, and I promised to give him [the score of] the First Overture to *Fidelio* for the concert he intends to organize in my honor.[68]

The "first" *Fidelio* overture was in fact rehearsed privately by musicians from the Société des Concerts, but at their sixth annual concert, on 21 March 1841, they preferred to play the work we know as *Leonore* No. 2, which Berlioz preferred as well. In his review of that concert, Berlioz mentions that the manuscript of No. 1 had been provided by Schindler, "artiste distingué lui-même et ami de Beethoven."[69]

> Sunday, 21 [March 1841] [. . .] After 1 p.m. I went to the concert at the Conservatoire. The Overture to *Leonore* (the second version) was given extraordinarily well. The *Ave verum* [of Mozart] had to be repeated. The Concertino by Ernst suffered the fate I had feared and did not please. [. . .] The Ninth Symphony was played with the highest conceivable integrity. It represents this orchestra's greatest triumph, and Habeneck's, too. [. . .] But it is too bad that the audience is not given a program book with the sung text, for without it they cannot comprehend the character of the music, especially of the fourth movement, because they do not know what it's about. Mr. Berlioz sat next to me during the symphony. The enthusiasm of the musicians was just as high as the quality of their playing. By 8 p.m. I was already back at the hotel.[70]

The following note was set down when Schindler was in Berlin, where he saw the German soprano Henriette Sontag, whom he had earlier met in Vienna when she sang in the première of the Ninth Symphony, on 7 May 1824. Berlioz heard Sontag when she was in Paris in the eighteen-twenties but we do not know if they met. By 1842 she certainly knew who he was, as Schindler's testimony makes clear:

> On Wednesday, July 26 [1842], at noon, I visited [in Berlin] the countess Rossi (Henriette Sonntag). [. . .] She believes that Berlioz and Liszt will find greater recognition in the future; that the current period of transition has yet to reach its apogee.[71]

The result of Schindler's trip to Paris was the book, *Beethoven in Paris*, first published in Münster in 1842 and still of considerable interest. Here Schindler introduces Berlioz in his role as a critic:

> At the third [Conservatoire] concert I had already heard Haydn's B-Major Symphony (in 4/4 time), performed impeccably. The A-Major Symphony by Beethoven had been repeated in the concert on 18 April [1841]; in his review for the *Gazette musicale* [of 25 April], Berlioz simply says this: "Pour la symphonie en *la* qui terminait la séance. . . . !!!! C'est tout ce que je puis en dire de nouveau! Et vive l'empereur de la symphonie!" ["As for the A-Major Symphony that closed the program. . . . !!! That is the only new thing I can say about it! And long live the emperor of the symphony!"][72]

Apparently Schindler placed great value upon Berlioz's judgments of Beethoven's symphonies. In the following passage he develops more fully a notion briefly mentioned in his diary. It is unlikely, as Schindler suggests, that Berlioz should have forgotten the meaning of Schiller's *An die Freude*, since he had included Chrétien Urhan's complete translation of it in his review of the Ninth Symphony that appeared in the *Revue et Gazette musicale* on 4 March 1838. Indeed, here Berlioz himself regrets the lack of a printed text, and says quite specifically that an exact translation of the German poetry is necessary to understand the logic of Beethoven's score.[73] So Schindler's comment, not without interest, is exaggerated:

> Now let us imagine a French audience of at least a thousand persons, which is the number the auditorium of the Conservatoire can accommodate, of whom not a single one knows Schiller's ode *An die Freude*, and not a single one has been provided a translation. What is such an audience to make of the fourth movement of the Ninth Symphony, especially when not a word of the singers is understood? Even Berlioz, my neighbor during the performance of the symphony, a fervent admirer and profoundly knowledgeable about Beethoven, admitted to me that he was not particularly enthusiastic about the fourth movement because he did not really know the text; he had once studied it but had now forgotten its meaning. Why all these strange phrases? What feelings lie behind them? The reason that there is singing at all in the fourth movement of the symphony remains unknown to those one thousand listeners, so it is in no way surprising that every man and every woman in attendance can hardly wait for the end of this totally enigmatic music![74]

A short note on Berlioz as conductor gives Schindler the opportunity to deal with Berlioz for the first time in an extended way, albeit in a footnote:

> As conductor of Beethoven's music, Habeneck stands in the forefront, an accomplishment that can in no way be minimized; and even when Mr. K[astner], in the *Gazette musicale* of 2 May of this year, compliments Mr. Berlioz on his conducting of Beethoven, writing that "personne ne sait donner aux œuvres du grand maître une expression

plus colorée et plus vraie" ["no one renders the works of the great master with more genuine and colorful expression"]—I have no doubt at all, considering Mr. Berlioz's(*) exemplary modesty, and would even be willing to bet, that he would himself award first place in this category to the veteran Habeneck.

(*) The name of this artist and critic is surely already known in Germany; but will those works that he has written up to now ever become known to the Germans? Of his major works I know only the *Requiem*, which in Paris has caused more censure than approval. Unfortunately I have not had the opportunity to hear any of his symphonies. Berlioz, this splendid, amiable man and artist, should have received his musical education in Germany, where he would have had better and stricter guidance, especially since his whole character is already more German than French. Had he done so, he would not have taken the perilous path upon which he has embarked, towards a goal that seems impossible to reach; German music is already so deeply rooted in the French mindset[75] that music of a non-Germanic sort is for the French all but unfathomable. This is the reason that the ingenious Berlioz has so many adversaries among Parisian artists, in particular among those who are enlightened and held in high esteem. If he were to dedicate his talent and energy to works that are simple, natural, and therefore readily understood, he would surely gain enduring renown and render essential service to music! —For my judgment on Berlioz as critic of art see below.[76]

An entire chapter of *Beethoven in Paris* is dedicated to the subject of Parisian music criticism. Here Schindler draws a striking picture of Berlioz as journalist and author using as a point of comparison Berlioz's colleague Henri Blanchard. Like Schindler's suggestion that Berlioz should have written music that is easy to understand—precisely the opposite, of course, of what Berlioz intended to do— his comments on Berlioz's writings are critical of the very literary elements that cause his texts to live on today.

The *Gazette musicale* is a remarkably longstanding institution, much read in France, and in terms of the quality of its contributors it is among the finest such journals of its kind in Europe. Its main collaborators are Henri Blanchard, Berlioz, Kastner, Maurice Bourges, Paul Smith, and A. Specht, who are essentially in charge of the "revue critique." Others, including Richard Wagner (*), Jules Martin, Lafage, Anders (**), Spazier, A. Morel, and d'Ortigue, contribute articles that should not go unnoticed in the German world of music, since they are in most cases of broad general interest and have the same noble purpose: to provide information in an agreeable way and to bring about progress in the recognition of the Good, the True, and the Beautiful. [. . .]—Not unintentionally do I put Mr. Blanchard at the head of this list of wise men, and at his side Mr. Berlioz as vice-president. [. . .]—Hector Berlioz is no less a learned and highly educated musician than Blanchard, no less a fighter in the forefront of the battle for truth and justice, yet he lacks the consistency and strict logic of his superior officer. In his reports he frequently goes too far, amuses himself by making historical deductions that do not always seem to me to be entirely valid, and digresses instead of going right to the point and playing it safe. As brilliant and entertaining as his style may be, one often regrets that his articles are not more concise in the expression of their principal ideas, since in that way they would be more valuable and more immediately useful. Far more regrettable is the fact that Berlioz, as I have remarked above, was not educated in Germany. As a creative and highly knowledgeable artist, as a man with ideals, with unequalled energy, with great determination, Berlioz would without a doubt have followed a path different from the one he has chosen; he would have earned the esteem of all of those in the educated classes, and he would have seen the products of his creativity passed along to posterity. That his lot has not been happier is due to Fate. Fate—which caused him, with all his genius, to fall into a series of unpleasant, rough and tumble, and romantic entanglements, under the burden of which he completed his studies and reaped their fruits in the form of odd and disagreeable compositions that manifest a very strange taste indeed. (***)[77]

> (*) [A footnote commenting on the serious and outspoken nature of Wagner's reports from Paris.]
>
> (**) [A footnote on Anders not relevant to the present discussion.]
>
> (***) An extensive biography of this artist is contained in Dr. Schilling's *Tonkünstler-Lexicon.* [See section 1 above, p. 103.]

Even from the brief selections considered here, it becomes obvious that very early on Berlioz reception in the German press was marked by piquant opposition and contrast. Determined enemies such as Adolphe Adam, and loyal friends such as Joseph d'Ortigue, Stephen Heller, and Georges Kastner, used their influence as correspondents to try to mold opinions on the other side of the Rhine. Professional approval and condemnation of Berlioz's music, by such figures as Schumann and Zuccalmaglio, resulted from silent score reading and not live performance. (That is how Berlioz learned Schumann's piano music and a great deal of other music as well, including, for example, the full score of Wagner's *Tristan.*) The friendly or reserved comments and eyewitness accounts of such figures as Schwencke and Schindler are revealing, but found their way only indirectly into the mainstream daily and weekly press. Almost all "reporters" focus on the unusual and sensational aspects of Berlioz's writings, and time and again they note his affinity to things German. To Berlioz, no one remained indifferent. If his music criticism was rather broadly accepted, his music triggered rejection—from Mendelssohn, from Zuccalmaglio—or enthusiasm—from Schumann, from Lobe.

When he began his first great trip to Germany at the end of 1842, German enemies and admirers were waiting in suspense to find out if this fellow was the "greatest of geniuses" or a "madman," as Schwencke put it. Schwencke's words prefigured a hundred fifty years of criticism concerning "a certain Hector Berlioz."

Notes

1. This is a text written by Berlioz, published in the *Berliner Allgemeine musikalische Zeitung,* pp. 183–184; cited in *Hector Berlioz in Deutschland: Texte und Dokumente zur deutschen Berlioz-Rezeption (1829–1843),* ed. Gunther Braam and Arnold Jacobshagen

(Göttingen: Hainholz, 2002), p. 330 (and in *CM* 1, pp. 17–18). In the present article, references to citations found in *Hector Berlioz in Deutschland* are indicated by the reference "B/J" ("Braam/Jacobshagen").

2. *Allgemeine musikalische Zeitung (AmZ)*, col. 863 (B/J, p. 331). It is here that we find the phrase "ein gewisser Hector Berlioz" ("a certain Hector Berlioz").

3. Charles Gabet, *Dictionnaire des artistes de l'école française, au XIXe siècle: Peinture, sculpture, architecture, gravure, dessin, lithographie et composition musicale* (Paris: Mme Vergne, 1831), p. 49.

4. Ibid., p. 709.

5. See B/J, pp. 335–339.

6. See Sylvia L'Écuyer, *Joseph d'Ortigue: Écrits sur la musique, 1827–1846* (Paris: Société française de musicologie, 2003), pp. 277–290. The notes Berlioz prepared for d'Ortigue are also available on Monir Tayeb and Michel Austin's remarkable website, www.hberlioz.com.

7. Gustav Schilling, *Encyclopädie der gesammten musikalischen Wissenschaften, oder Universal-Lexicon der Tonkunst*, 6 vols. (Stuttgart: Franz Heinrich Köhler, 1835–1838). See B/J, pp. 83–87.

8. Carl Schwencke, *Erinnerungen*, ed. H. Benrath, Hamburgische Liebhaberbibliothek, Herausgegeben im Auftrage der Gesellschaft Hamburgischer Kunstfreunde von Alfred Lichtwark, Vertrieb durch die Commetersche Kunsthandlung (Hamburg: Lütcke & Wulff, 1901), pp. xiii–xv. In November 1824 Beethoven dedicated to Schwencke the canon *Schwenke dich ohne Schwänke* (WoO 187). In this article, all translations from the German have been made by the author and further Englished by the editor. The translations aim for fidelity, not literalness.

9. Schwencke, *Erinnerungen*, p. xiii.

10. See *CM* 3, pp. 454, 467–468.

11. Schwencke, *Erinnerungen*, pp. 155–156.

12. *CM* 5, p. 420.

13. Schwencke, *Erinnerungen*, pp. 140–141. The concert of 9 December 1832 featured the revised *Symphonie fantastique* with the first performance of its sequel, *Le Retour à la vie*.

14. Ibid., pp. 144–145.

15. Ibid., pp. 225–226.

16. *Der Bär und der Bassa* (1823), comedy with music by Karl Ludwig Blum (1786–1844), after Eugène Scribe's play *L'Ours et le Pacha* (1820).

17. *Die Wiener in Berlin* (1824), comedy by Karl Eduard von Holtei (1798–1880), music by Karl Ludwig Blum. Moscheles refers to the melody that first appears at bar 119 of Berlioz's overture.

18. *Briefe von Felix Mendelssohn-Bartholdy an Ignaz und Charlotte Moscheles*, ed. Felix Moscheles (Leipzig: Duncker & Humblot, 1888), pp. 81–82; *Letters of Felix Mendelssohn to Ignaz and Charlotte Moscheles*, ed. and trans. Felix Moscheles (Boston: Ticknor, 1888), pp. 93–94. (The translation has been slightly adjusted by this author and the editor of the current volume.) Two days earlier Moscheles wrote a similar letter to Sigismond Neukomm, in which he spoke of Berlioz's overture as "a ridiculous explosion of music and dance and pathos, accompanied by the bass drum and more noise than you can imagine, so deafening and excessive that, on more than one occasion, listeners and players alike broke out laughing" (*CG* II, p. 328).

19. Here Mendelssohn paraphrases Brander's Song from Goethe's *Faust I* (*Auerbachs Keller in Leipzig*).

20. *Briefe von Felix Mendelssohn-Bartholdy*, p. 85; *Letters of Felix Mendelssohn*, p. 97. By this time Mendelssohn had read through Liszt's transcription of the *Symphonie fantastique*, which he found—as he later told Ferdinand Hiller on 26 February 1835—"insipid, boring, and philistine." See Ferdinand Hiller, *Felix Mendelssohn-Bartholdy, Briefe und Erinnerungen* (Köln: DuMont-Schauberg, 1874), pp. 38–39.

21. *Briefe*, p. 97; *Letters*, pp. 112–113.

22. *Briefe*, p. 116; *Letters*, p. 133.

23. *Briefe*, p. 120; *Letters*, p. 136 (modified). In chapter XLVII of the *Mémoires* Berlioz himself lampoons Cherubini's *Ali-Baba, ou les quarante voleurs* (1833).

24. Evidence of this, moreover with specific reference to Berlioz, is found in a letter that Mendelssohn wrote from Leipzig to his sister Fanny on 4 April 1843: "Now let me answer your questions [as posed in a letter of 28 March 1843]. I cannot say anything about the article on Berlioz, because I haven't seen a single music journal since I have arrived here, nor do I want to see one." See Fanny und Felix Mendelssohn, *"Die Musik will gar nicht rutschen ohne Dich": Briefwechsel 1821 bis 1846*, ed. Eva Weissweiler (Berlin: Propyläen, 1997), p. 363. In her letter to Felix of 28 March 1843, Fanny had asked who might have written the article on Berlioz that appeared in the *AmZ* on 15 March 1843 (B/J, pp. 535–539); she found this article "too musical for a philosopher and too philosophical for a musician." See *The Letters of Fanny Hensel to Felix Mendelssohn*, ed. and trans. Marcia Citron (Stuyvesant, NY: Pendragon Press, 1987), p. 316.

25. *Neue Zeitschrift für Musik*, 1 (1834), No. 8, p. 32 (B/J, p. 341).

26. *NZfM*, 1 (1834), No. 18, pp. 71–72 (B/J, p. 342).

27. *NZfM*, 1 (1834), No. 67, pp. 266–268; No. 68, pp. 270–271 (B/J, pp. 342–345). The autobiographical text concerned Berlioz's travels in Italy, first published in the *Revue européenne* (15 March 1832), and later reprinted in 1834 in the *Gazette musicale de Paris* and in *Le Rénovateur*.

28. *NZfM*, 3 (1835), No. 1, pp. 1–2; No. 9, pp. 33–35; No. 10, pp. 37–38; No. 11, pp. 41–44; No. 12, pp. 45–48; No. 13, pp. 49–51 (B/J, pp. 17–41).

29. *NZfM*, 2 (1835), No. 17, pp. 67–69; No. 18, pp. 71–72 (B/J, pp. 7–11); and No. 49, pp. 197–198; No. 50, pp. 201–202 (B/J, pp. 12–15).

30. Among the many treatments of Schumann's review are those by Leon Plantinga, *Schumann as Critic* (New Haven, CT: Yale University Press, 1967), pp. 235–250; Rainer Kleinertz, "Schumanns Rezension von Berlioz' *Symphonie fantastique*," in *Schumann Forschungen 6*, ed. Ute Bär (Mainz: Schott, 1997), pp. 139–151; and Edward Cone, "Schumann Amplified," in *Berlioz: Fantastic Symphony*, ed. Cone (New York: Norton, 1971), pp. 249–277.

31. *Robert Schumanns Briefe, Neue Folge*, ed. F. Gustav Jansen (Leipzig, 1904), p. 417.

32. *NZfM*, 5 (1836), No. 2, p. 5 (B/J, p. 364).

33. *Schumanns Briefe*, p. 78.

34. *NZfM*, 5 (1836), No. 37, pp. 147–148 (B/J, pp. 371–373). The "Toy Symphony" has been variously attributed to Joseph Haydn, Michael Haydn, Leopold Mozart, and others.

35. With his fifth symphony Lachner had won first prize in a competition sponsored by the *Kunstverein* of Vienna; the symphony then became known as the "Prize Symphony."

36. *Schumanns Briefe*, p. 80.

37. *NZfM*, 5 (1836), No. 38, p. 151 (B/J, p. 373).

38. *Hofmeisters Monatsberichte* had already announced publication of that piano arrangement in the issue of November/December 1834. On Chopin's assistance, see *CG* II, p. 281.

39. *NZfM*, 4 (1836), No. 24, pp. 101–102 (B/J, pp. 361–362).

40. *NZfM*, 4 (1836), No. 46, p. 192 (mentioned in B/J, p. 363).

41. "Berlioz schikt mir seine Ouverture" (Robert Schumann, *Tagebücher*, vol. 2, *1836–1854*, ed. Gerd Nauhaus [Basel and Frankfurt am Main: Stroemfeld/Roter Stern, 1987], p. 24).

42. In *F-Pn*, Collection Macnutt.

43. *AmZ*, 39 (1837), No. 1, col. 13 (B/J, pp. 377–378).

44. *NZfM*, 6 (1837), No. 52, p. 209 (B/J, pp. 382–383). Little is known of Wilhelm Attern (1812–1843) and Carl Eduard Conrad (1811–?).

45. *Revue et Gazette musicale*, 4 (1837), No. 8, pp. 61–63; *CM* 3, pp. 37–40 (*CG* II, pp. 327–332).

46. *NZfM*, 6 (1837), No. 18, pp. 71–72 (B/J, pp. 378–380).

47. *NZfM*, 8 (1838), No. 3, p. 12 (B/J, p. 397).

48. *NZfM*, 6 (1837), No. 37, pp. 147–149 (B/J, pp. 42–45).

49. *Schumanns Briefe*, p. 91.

50. *NZfM*, 7 (1837), No. 32, p. 128 (B/J, p. 385).

51. *NZfM*, 7 (1837), No. 47, pp. 185–187; No. 49, pp. 193–194; No. 50, pp. 197–199 (B/J, pp. 386–394).

52. *AmZ*, 40 (1838), No. 1, cols. 7–17 (B/J, pp. 48–59).

53. *Schumanns Briefe*, p. 106.

54. Johann Christian Lobe, *Compositions-Lehre oder umfassende Theorie von der thematischen Arbeit und den modernen Instrumentalformen* (Weimar: Voigt, 1844), p. 174.

55. *Schumanns Briefe*, p. 156.

56. Ibid., p. 174.

57. Ibid., p. 183.

58. Adolphe Adam, "Lettres sur la musique française (1836–1850)," *La Revue de Paris* (1 August 1903), pp. 468–469. (A modern reprint of the *Lettres sur la musique française*, with an introduction by Joël-Marie Fauquet, appeared from Minkoff, in Geneva, in 1996.)

59. *Iris im Gebiete der Tonkunst*, 8 (29 December 1837), No. 53, p. 212 (B/J, p. 395).

60. *NZfM*, 16 (22 February 1842), pp. 63–64 (B/J, pp. 500–501).

61. *Briefe von Felix Mendelssohn-Bartholdy an Ignaz und Charlotte Moscheles*, p. 150; *Letters of Felix Mendelssohn*, p. 165.

62. *Briefe*, p. 185; *Letters*, p. 198. The "program" in question, which Mendelssohn calls a "Zettel," or "scrap of paper," is that of *Roméo et Juliette*, premiered in Paris one week earlier, on 24 November 1839.

63. Anton Schindler, *Sein Tagebuch aus den Jahren 1841–1843*, ed. Marta Becker, Veröffentlichungen des Manskopfschen Museums für Musik- und Theatergeschichte; Im Auftrage des Kulturamtes der Stadt Frankfurt a. M, ed. Joachim Kirchner, 1 (Frankfurt am Main: Waldemar Kramer, [1939]), pp. 35–36.

64. See *CG* III, p. 41n; *CG* VIII, p. 384n.

65. Schindler, *Tagebuch*, p. 40.

66. *CG* VIII, p. 192. Schindler's *Biographie von Ludwig von Beethoven* appeared in Münster in 1841; an English translation by Ignaz Moscheles appeared in London in the same year.

67. Schindler, *Tagebuch*, p. 43–44.

68. Ibid., p. 46.

69. *Revue et Gazette musicale* (28 March 1841); *CM* 4, p. 477.

70. Schindler, *Tagebuch*, pp. 75–76.

71. Ibid., p. 98.

72. Anton Schindler, *Beethoven in Paris* (Münster: Aschendorff'sche Buchhandlung, 1842), p. 25n. In the 1860 edition of his biography of Beethoven, Schindler added *Beethoven in Paris* as an appendix, but that appendix represents a much abbreviated version of the very informative 1842 monograph, which is rare (copies may be found in the Bayerische Staatsbibliothek, in the Bibliothèque nationale de France, and in the library at Duke University). [In the original version of the article quoted by Schindler, Berlioz's comment on Beethoven's Seventh Symphony is, more precisely: "......... !!!!!!" —*Ed.*]

73. *CM* 3, pp. 408–409.

74. Schindler, *Beethoven in Paris*, pp. 48–49.

75. Schindler presumably refers to the fact that the Beethoven symphonies were then much appreciated in France.

76. Schindler, *Beethoven in Paris*, pp. 53–54.

77. Ibid., pp. 87–91.

Part Four

The "Dramatic Symphony"

Chapter Seven

Berlioz's Lost Roméo et Juliette

HUGH MACDONALD

If a man will begin with certainties, he shall end in doubts;
but if he will be content to begin with doubts, he shall end in certainties.
—Francis Bacon

Berlioz's third symphony *Roméo et Juliette* was composed in 1839 in response to a gift of twenty thousand francs from Paganini, to whom the work was dedicated. It has always been classed among the handful of his finest works, along with *La Damnation de Faust* and *Les Troyens,* and Berlioz himself retained a special affection for it to the end of his life. As part of the accepted history of the work it is well known that when he sat down to compose in the early months of 1839 this was not the first time he had contemplated music for Shakespeare's play; in any case it was his usual practice to allow projects to mature slowly in his mind before taking their eventual form. This is certainly true of the *Requiem,* which grew out of several large-scale plans that he had been talking about for some years, and of *La Damnation de Faust,* which is a masterly expansion of the *Huit Scènes de Faust* composed seventeen years earlier. Most of his larger works have a prehistory threading back through his life.

In the case of *Roméo et Juliette* the prehistory can be traced in the reports of two of Berlioz's collaborators with whom he shared confidences about earlier plans and in one memory from his own pen. The first is by Émile Deschamps, who wrote the verses for the 1839 *Roméo et Juliette.* Writing of his early friendship with the composer Deschamps recalled:

> It was at that moment that Monsieur Hector Berlioz told me about his plan for a dramatic symphony on *Roméo et Juliette.* Shakespeare fever was all the rage and I went along with it. I was delighted by this new homage to my divine poet and to collaborate with a great artist. We worked out the plan of this musical and poetic work; melodies and verses came to us in profusion, and the symphony appeared . . . ten years later.[1]

This reminiscence appeared in 1844, accompanying a publication of Deschamps's translations of *Macbeth* and *Romeo and Juliet.* The time-lapse, ten years, sounds a little approximate, so it would be rash to give any date to their earlier conversations. There is no evidence of any contact between Berlioz and Deschamps before 1833, although they could easily have met before Berlioz's departure for Rome in 1831.

The second reminiscence is found in Auguste Barbier's posthumous memoirs, published in 1883.[2] Berlioz met Barbier, one of the librettists of *Benvenuto Cellini*, in Italy in 1832. Berlioz apparently asked Barbier to write the libretto for a *Roméo et Juliette*, probably an opera, which he was contemplating at that time. Barbier refused, pleading lack of time.

The third report is found in Berlioz's own *Mémoires*. In a footnote to his description of wanderings in the country near Rome he wrote:

> It was on one of those excursions on horseback [. . .] with Felix Mendelssohn that I expressed my astonishment that no one had ever thought of writing a *scherzo* on Shakespeare's dazzling little poem on Queen Mab. He was as surprised as I was, and I immediately regretted having put the idea into his head. For several years I was afraid of hearing that he had tackled this subject. Then it would have been impossible or unwise for me to make the double attempt as I did in my symphony *Roméo et Juliette*.[3]

This footnote did not appear in earlier accounts of his Italian travels, but was added sometime after 1844.

A symphony, an opera, a scherzo. These three mentions hardly add up to a coherent picture of an *Ur-Roméo*. They tell us only that Berlioz allowed the subject to pass through his mind in the years 1829–1832, which should not surprise us in view of the profound impression the play made on him when he first saw it in 1827. Those commentators who have studied *Roméo et Juliette* in depth have accepted these bare traces as an archaeologist might, on unearthing pottery and shards, accept the fact of an ancient civilization, but without digging for the habitations buried beneath.[4] If we look for evidence of an actual early composition based on *Romeo and Juliet*, there is no manuscript and no mention of such a piece in his *Mémoires* or correspondence, it is true. There is nonetheless a good deal of evidence that Berlioz embarked on a work which, like many of his early projects, came to nothing.

It is a fundamental assumption that sensitive composers write music in response to things that move them. Berlioz, known above all for his intense response to literary stimuli, described the impact on him of seeing Shakespeare's play in vivid detail, a paradigmatic example of extrovert romantic sensibility. Having seen *Hamlet* at the Odéon on 11 September 1827 played in English by Charles Kemble's company, Berlioz returned, already thunderstruck by Shakespeare's genius and Harriet Smithson's playing of Ophelia, to see *Romeo and Juliet* four days later. Whether this play made a deeper impression on him than *Hamlet* is hard to say, but Smithson undoubtedly moved him even more as Juliet than she had as Ophelia. Berlioz was thrown into a turmoil of passion by the combination of poetic genius and ideal feminine beauty. What happened next? In his own record of the months that followed he says he lost the ability to sleep and all ability to work.

> I wandered aimlessly along Paris streets and in the country nearby. Out of sheer exhaustion, I recall, there were only four occasions during that long period of suffering when I truly slept a deep death-like sleep: one night in a cornfield near Villejuif, one night in a field near Sceaux, another in the snow beside the frozen Seine at Neuilly, and lastly on a table in the Café Cardinal.[5]

He roused himself from this state of "desperate degradation" ("abrutissement désespéré"), dreaming ceaselessly of Shakespeare and of the actress, by resolving to give a concert which would bring his name to Harriet's notice. Since the Seine was probably not frozen before January and the concert did not take place until 26 May 1828, this period lasted at least four months, perhaps seven, in Berlioz's recollection.

Our knowledge of these months in Berlioz's life from sources other than the *Mémoires* is unusually slender; indeed it is hard to know what exactly he was doing. There are very few surviving letters, even to his family, and perhaps he wrote fewer than usual. We have only four letters from the seven months that follow the *coup de foudre* in September:

13 October 1827	to Laforest
22 October 1827	to Quatremère de Quincy
29 November 1827	to Ferrand
11 January 1828	to his mother[6]

He was presumably attending his classes at the Conservatoire, but he was no longer working at the Théâtre des Nouveautés. In November while lunching with the Lesueur family he described the cemetery scene in *Hamlet* to the eldest daughter, aged twenty, of whom he was certainly fond. Only a week later, to everyone's horror, she died. Berlioz attended the funeral. On the 22nd of that month, at Saint-Eustache, he gave the second performance of his *Messe solennelle*, conducting the performance himself; the labor involved in assembling and rehearsing an orchestra, a chorus, and three soloists, and in dealing with tickets and officials on a day when street riots were in progress nearby hardly fits with his own image of listlessness and sleeplessness. A great many of his friends attended the performance and a group of thirty went out to dinner afterwards. Despite the strong impression it made, this performance convinced him that the *Messe* was unworthy of him and he soon "burnt" it (or at least, as we now know, destroyed all the performance material). A factor in his rejection of the *Messe* may well have been the new worlds of feeling and expression revealed to him by Shakespeare and his own determination to strike out on a new musical path. Of his emotional condition at this time he gives a brief picture in the letter to Laforest and a pointed hint in his letter to Ferrand.

Between 22 November 1827 and 9 March of the following year, when the newly formed Société des Concerts du Conservatoire gave its inaugural concert, we have really no idea of what Berlioz was doing. We have a continuous record of what he was composing from 1823 until the summer of 1827, assuming that the *Waverley* Overture was written in the early part of 1827. The same applies from the summer of 1828 until his departure for Rome at the end of 1830. But between the Prix de Rome cantata of July 1827, *La Mort d'Orphée*, and the preliminary rounds of the next competition in June 1828, there is no surviving record of any compositional activity at all. Not until the early eighteen-fifties, and for very different reasons, is there any sign of his muse running dry. He told his mother on 11 January 1828 that he had "never been so busy both at home and elsewhere." Is this just an invented excuse for not writing earlier? He mentions a family friend who lived in a street he went down "nearly every day," going where?

According to the *Mémoires* (chapter XVIII) he did compose one piece at this time under the impact of intense emotional feeling for Harriet Smithson, and that was the *Élégie*, the last of nine settings of Thomas Moore later published under the title of *Neuf Mélodies*. But he was wrong, since he had not yet read Moore and the piece in question was composed around January 1830.[7] What then did he write in the circumstances he describes? The only possible answer is some kind of Shakespeare piece.

Quatre Scènes Composed

A probable sequence of events, it seems to me, would have been the following: if he had not bought French translations of *Hamlet* and *Romeo and Juliet* at the theater, he would buy them very soon afterwards; eventually he had Letourneur's complete translation of Shakespeare, but perhaps not yet.[8] In 1828 he was taking evening classes in English, but within days of the performances he would have read both plays in French with a consuming passion, committing many lines to memory. It is impossible to imagine that he would not have singled out certain scenes as being in some sense suitable for music. That is what happened when he saw Saurin's *Beverley*, also at the Odéon, in 1823: he picked out a scene of particular appeal and set it for bass voice and orchestra. More pertinently, that is what happened a year later when Berlioz discovered Goethe's *Faust*, a play which he read but did not see in the theater. He selected a number of scenes in the drama and set them to music, without any attempt at a unified composition or any suggestion of dramatic continuity.

That, surely, is how he approached *Hamlet* and *Romeo and Juliet*. To compose an opera on either play was unthinkable since opera librettos of the day belonged to a quite different genre. From *Hamlet* he presumably responded to the scenes with the ghost, the account of Ophelia's death, the suggestion of funeral music at the end, and perhaps the play within the play. Whether or not he composed any *Hamlet* music at this time, he later provided music that relates in some way to all of these. In the case of *Romeo and Juliet* he would most likely have selected the following: Mercutio's Queen Mab speech, the scene of the Capulets' ball, the balcony scene, and the scene in the Capulets' vault with the lovers' deaths. A dirge for the supposedly dead Juliet was part of Garrick's 1748 version of the play and became an exquisite movement in the 1839 *Roméo et Juliette*, but since it was not included in the 1827 production Berlioz would not have included this in any selection of scenes at that time. By 1839 he and Deschamps, having studied the "authentic" Garrick version, found an appropriate place for it in their symphony.

In all his deranged wanderings he must have been thinking *musically* about these scenes, and when he says on 11 January 1828 that he had "never been so busy at home," he surely refers to composition. What else would keep him busy at home? To picture Berlioz wrestling in his mind, and on paper, with musical settings of Shakespearean scenes at this time in no way contradicts his own later memory of listless wandering in cornfields or on the banks of the Seine. So let us suppose that Berlioz composed *Quatre Scènes de Roméo et Juliette* in this period. What happened to the music and why did he never mention it? I believe there are plausible answers to both questions if we look closely at Berlioz's career in the following two years. To take the first question first, it is a fact that most of the music he wrote in the eighteen-twenties displeased him to the point where he destroyed, or at least rejected, it. *Estelle et Némorin, Le Passage de la Mer rouge, Beverley,* the *Messe solennelle, Les Francs-Juges,* and *Huit Scènes de Faust* were all victims of his own contempt or rejection. Most of this music has disappeared. Some was absorbed in later works. It is not hard to see how either eventuality applied to our imagined *Roméo et Juliette,* when we consider each possible movement in turn.

1) *Queen Mab.* Perhaps there was a setting of Mercutio's Queen Mab speech. The existence of two separate Queen Mab pieces in the definitive *Roméo et Juliette* confirms Berlioz's delight in it, as does his reported conversation with Mendelssohn in 1832. On the face of it, when he said that "no one had ever thought of writing a *scherzo* on Shakespeare's dazzling little poem," he should have been including himself. He could, on the other hand, have been disingenuously concealing the fact that he had himself attempted one, especially if he had rejected his effort. We have a musical shard in the form of the *Ballet des ombres,* composed between April and December 1829, set to spooky words by Albert du Boys, "imitées de Herder." If Berlioz had already rejected his original Queen Mab piece, part of it would have been suitable and available as a phrase at the end of each verse of the *Ballet des ombres* (see ex. 7.1). When this piece was in its turn withdrawn, the figure found its way first into the Carnival scene in *Benvenuto Cellini* and then, after this was also rejected, into the scherzo *La Reine Mab* in the 1839 *Roméo et Juliette.*

Example 7.1. *Ballet des ombres*, mm. 71–79.

2) *The Capulets' ball.* If there was ballroom music composed in 1827–1828 we have to look no further than the *Symphonie fantastique*, composed in 1830, for its later incarnation as *Un Bal*, the second movement. According to the symphony's program, the artist, who would not normally be likely to attend balls, finds himself in a variety of different surroundings, in this case in the middle "du tumulte d'une fête brillante," as Romeo himself does. In the symphony the *idée fixe*, representing the beloved, interrupts the music from time to time, although it is easy to reconstruct the movement without these interruptions if they were merely inserted in 1830 to recall the *idée fixe*. There are two alternatives: the *idée fixe* was added in 1832 in Italy, when the movement was revised (this part of the symphony's autograph dates from the Italian period); or, conversely, the *idée fixe* was always part of the movement, since, after all, Romeo first sets eyes on Juliet at the Capulets' ball.

3) *The balcony scene.* Berlioz admired the play above all for its poetic representation of amorous passion. In the 1839 symphony the *Scène d'amour* is at the emotional heart of the work. Surely, in the heat of his reaction to the play, he would write a movement to represent such powerful feelings, incorporating a melody as an idealized expression of Juliet herself. Berlioz's own state of high emotional tension was exacerbated by the temptation to identify with Romeo as Juliet's/Harriet's adorer. Any love music that represented the balcony scene would also be his own ardent declaration to the object of his passion, Harriet Smithson, and it would be natural to represent this passion musically with a theme of an impetuous, striving character, perhaps sounding like the theme shown in example 7.2.

Example 7.2. *Herminie, Introduction*, mm. 2–6.

A few months later, when he entered the Palais de l'Institut to compose a cantata for the Prix de Rome, he had the melody at hand with its restless accompaniment, adequate certainly for the depiction of Herminie's troubled soul. The first fifty-three bars of *Herminie* could easily be borrowed from a *Roméo et Juliette* love scene without damaging its integrity, even if the work itself had still not been rejected, since Prix de Rome cantatas did not qualify in his mind as the composer's authentic work. Later on, of course, this music was adapted as the main Allegro of the *Symphonie fantastique*'s first movement.

In that context the music is preceded by a slow introduction which depicts, according to the program, the *vague des passions*, a concept which Berlioz derived from Chateaubriand. Before he sees the beloved for the first time the artist suffers from a sickness of the soul, both misery and joy, without any object. In Chateaubriand's *René* this condition is described as:

> that which precedes the development of great passions, when all the faculties, young, lively, and whole, but closed, have acted only on themselves without aim and without object. [. . .] The imagination is rich, abundant, and marvelous, the reality is poor, dry, and disenchanted. With full heart one lives in an empty world; and having experienced nothing, one is disillusioned with everything. [. . .] Oh, if only I could have shared my feelings with someone else! O God! If only you had given me the woman of my desires! If only you could have brought me an Eve, formed out of myself, as you did for our first father! [. . .] O celestial beauty, I would have thrown myself at your feet; then taking you in my arms I would have begged the Almighty to give you the rest of my life.[9]

Berlioz found another expression of the *vague des passions* in Walter Scott's *Waverley*, whose hero Edward Waverley is susceptible to the same gnawing feelings: "In the corner of the large and sombre library [. . .] he would exercise for hours that internal sorcery by which past or imaginary events are presented in action, as it were, to the eye of the muser."[10] The susceptible Waverley then encounters Flora McIvor at a Highland chieftain's merry-making (the *tumulte d'une fête*) and is soon obsessed with her image.

It seems hardly coincidental that Romeo sees Juliet for the first time at the Capulets' ball having earlier suffered from intense feelings without any clear object, the character of Rosaline (Romeo's earlier love) having been removed in Garrick's version of the play as seen in 1827. Romeo's father speaks of his son thus in Act I, scene ii (in Garrick's version), a perfect picture of the *vague des passions*:

> Many a morning hath he there been seen
> With tears augmenting the fresh morning dew.
> But all so soon as the all-cheering sun
> Should in the farthest east begin to draw
> The shady curtains from Aurora's bed,
> Away from light steals home my heavy son,
> And private in his chamber pens himself,
> Shuts up his windows, locks fair daylight out
> And makes himself an artificial night.
> Black and portentous must this humour prove
> Unless good counsel may the cause remove.

Any music Berlioz composed to express Romeo's aimless longing, followed by the distracted passion once he had spied his Juliet, would have taken the form of a slow movement followed by an Allegro, easily described as *Rêveries, Passions.* The first movement of the *Symphonie fantastique* was so labeled, and its form is not unlike that adopted by both the *Waverley* Overture and the *Roméo seul* section of the 1839 *Roméo et Juliette* leading into the noisy *Fête.* If such a movement were also part of the 1827–1828 *Scènes*, it would have depicted Romeo's passion as Berlioz saw it (and felt it). September 1827 thus represented the moment when his own pent-up passions found the object they had been unconsciously seeking; they needed to be expressed as "the rage, the fury, the madness that takes control of all our faculties and makes us capable of achieving everything," as described in the letter to Laforest of a few weeks later.

Since this scenario does not reflect the mood of the balcony scene, we might postulate a second love scene of a more tranquil character since one of the melodies in the 1839 *Roméo et Juliette* has an earlier origin. The oboe melody in *Roméo seul* is shown in example 7.3. This was earlier a setting of the words "Étoile du matin prends ta lyre" in the 1830 Prix de Rome cantata *Sardanapale.*[11] Again it would not surprise us if Berlioz had composed it for some other purpose before entering the Institut for the composition of that cantata. Its treatment in the 1839 symphony suggests that Berlioz regarded it as a love theme, which points significantly to a lost work such as the scenes we are attempting to reconstruct. Close to it in *Sardanapale* is another theme probably depicting the languorous charms of oriental Bayadères, who sing:

> Venez, bayadères charmantes,
> Et, par vos danses séduisantes,
> Troublez ma raison et mes yeux.[12]

There seems no place for such a thing in the set of scenes we are describing; in 1839 the theme was radically transformed from a seductive 3/4 into the vigorous 4/4 Allegro of the Capulets' ball.

Example 7.3. *Roméo et Juliette, Roméo seul,* mm. 81–86.

4) *The scene at the tomb of the Capulets' vault.* In Garrick's version this was the last scene of the play, closing with the death of the lovers. Its emotional charge was very great, intensified by the alteration that brought Juliet to life before, not after, Romeo dies from taking poison. In 1839 Berlioz adopted a realistically

narrative approach to this scene, whereas in 1827–1828 the evidence points to a setting of a slightly different episode in the play. When Berlioz sat for the 1829 Prix de Rome and composed the cantata *Cléopâtre*, he set Cleopatra's invocation to the Pharaohs as a somber piece with a heavy throbbing rhythm. "O my dear Ferrand," he wrote soon after, "I wish I could let you hear the scene where Cleopatra reflects on how her shade will be received by the shades of the Pharaohs entombed within the pyramids. It's terrifying, horrifying! It is the scene where Juliet meditates on her entombment, still alive, in the Capulets' vault, surrounded by the bones of her ancestors and Tybalt's body."[13] The words "It is the scene" ("C'est la scène") are significant, surely. Juliet does not of course meditate thus in the churchyard scene itself but in an earlier scene (IV, iii) when she is alone and about to take Friar Laurence's potion:

> How if, when I am laid into the tomb,
> I wake before the time that Romeo
> Come to redeem me? there's a fearful point!
> Shall I not, then, be stifled in the vault,
> To whose foul mouth no healthsome air breathes in,
> And there die strangled ere my Romeo comes?
> Or, if I live, is it not very like,
> The horrible conceit of death and night
> Together with the terror of the place,—
> As in a vault, an ancient receptacle,
> Where, for these many hundred years, the bones
> Of all my buried ancestors are pack'd:
> Where bloody Tybalt, yet but green in earth,
> Lies festering in his shroud.

In the autograph manuscript of *Cléopâtre*, as if to make the same point ("c'est la scène . . .") to the jury, Berlioz inscribed the first line of this speech at the top of the first page of the Invocation (with the word "How" replaced by "What"). The harmonic rhythm of the piece is broad and the tempo is slow, so it is impossible to know if the cantata's words "Grands Pharaons, nobles Lagides" were overlaid on a melody invented for different words. Berlioz at least had no difficulty when he decided to recycle the movement as the *Chœur d'ombres* in *Le Retour à la vie* in 1831, substituting a chorus in place of Cleopatra and giving them syllables from an imaginary language to sing: "Ô sondre foul, sondre foul leimi," etc. Finally, when this work was revised as *Lélio* in 1855, the words were changed once again, to "Froid de la mort, nuit de la tombe." As a further connection with *Roméo et Juliette*, Ian Kemp has observed a resemblance between Cleopatra's line and the brass declamation at the beginning of the 1839 symphony where the Prince of Verona intervenes to put a stop to the feuding in the streets.[14]

Quatre Scènes Absorbed

If such a set of scenes was planned, sketched, or composed in the winter of 1827–1828, what happened to them subsequently? Two events may have shaken the state of "desperate degradation" which he admits he had fallen into. On 3 March 1828 Harriet Smithson reached the apogee of her Parisian stardom when at her benefit performance at the Théâtre-Italien in the presence of royalty the stage lay deep in flowers, an event enthusiastically reported in the press. Even if Berlioz was not there, he would have heard about it. He resolved to give a concert of his own works: "Contrasting her dazzling reputation and my own miserable obscurity, I resolved I would by a supreme effort make my name shine to such a degree that even she would catch a glint of it."[15]

Less than a week later the Société des Concerts du Conservatoire gave the first of its momentous series of concerts introducing Beethoven's symphonies to Parisian audiences for the first time. Berlioz almost certainly heard the *Eroica* on 9 March and again on 23 March, when the concert also included the first movement of the *Emperor* Concerto, the Violin Concerto, parts of the *Missa solemnis*, and the oratorio *Christus am Ölberge*. On 5 April the Fifth Symphony and the *Egmont* Overture were played.

Berlioz went into high gear to plan and mount a concert consisting entirely of his own works. This took place on 26 May, an event described in detail in chapter XIX of the *Mémoires*. The program did not include any *Roméo et Juliette* music, only pieces that were at least a year old. There is no evidence that Harriet Smithson knew anything about it. In the wake of the Beethoven concerts the idea of composing a symphony must have been revolving in his mind that summer, but for the next year and a half he could find no way to write such a thing since the Beethovenian model required a formidably positive conclusion to its four movements. The *Roméo et Juliette* material could not possibly be fashioned into a symphony (whatever Deschamps said many years later) because of its unavoidably tragic ending.

Berlioz entered once more for the Prix de Rome that summer but won only the second prize. Perhaps his enthusiasm for *Roméo et Juliette* was cooling, displaced by a new enthusiasm. This was for Goethe's *Faust*, which came to his notice in the summer and absorbed him throughout the autumn. Like *Roméo et Juliette* (if our hypothesis is correct), *Faust* offered a number of scenes for music, and the settings were varied and original. Unlike *Roméo et Juliette* these scenes were completed to Berlioz's satisfaction. He had them engraved and the score was ready for circulation in April 1829. At the head of each piece is a quotation in English from *Hamlet* or *Romeo and Juliet*.

Almost immediately Berlioz regretted publishing this work and attempted to retrieve as many copies as he could. The curse of damning self-criticism was still upon him, as it had been for almost everything he had ever written. The *Ballet des ombres* was similarly condemned soon after. No wonder that the summer months of 1829 seem filled, in his correspondence, with agonizing over his future, over the intense inner passion that was driving him, and the vehemence of his feelings. *Cléopâtre*, that year's cantata, channeled some of this pent-up feeling. In Thomas Moore, whose poems captured his attention that year, he found an outlet for some of his rising musical sap, but the creative problem was not resolved until early in 1830 when in a rapid flurry of events the incredible *Symphonie fantastique* came into being.

Barely two months separate the day when he started to set down the symphony and its provisional completion, and we may well wonder at the speed of its composition. But it had been gestating for at least two and a half years, in fact since the evening when he saw *Romeo and Juliet* at the Odéon. The *Symphonie fantastique* is, in many respects, a *Roméo et Juliette* symphony. Up to this point he had found no satisfactory solution to the problem of genre. Opera? No. Symphony? No. Scenes? Perhaps. The trigger that fired the *Symphonie fantastique*'s starting gun seems to have been the person of Camille Moke, the attractive and talented pianist he met in the winter of 1829–1830 through his friendship with Ferdinand Hiller. She could only have won Berlioz's affection if all thought of Harriet Smithson were removed from his mind. When he began to speak of Harriet as though she were a worthless individual with a doubtful "theatrical" reputation, it is more than likely that Camille had fed him the necessary gossip. So his symphony did not have to end in a tragic love affair and the death of two lovers; it could be transformed into a celebration by having the lover murder his beloved and both descend into a riotous hell where infernal creatures dance in glee over their new victims.

Obviously this was no longer about Romeo and Juliet. It was now, as it always was, about Berlioz and Harriet, or, in the coy language of the symphony's program, about the artist and his beloved. But Berlioz knew that the first two movements of the symphony, at least, described Romeo's aimless search for love, his discovery of Juliet as the ideal beloved, and the ball where he saw her for the first time. To this sequence he added a slow movement, the *Scène aux champs*, which appears to have no connection with *Roméo et Juliette*, the *Marche au supplice*, which pictures the artist's execution, and the final *Ronde du sabbat*, taking both artist and his beloved into the nether circles of hell.

No doubt a work that had been over two years in gestation used borrowed music. The introduction to the first movement draws on a childhood melody "Je vais donc quitter pour jamais"; the first movement may be largely built out of *Roméo et Juliette* music; the second movement may be the music for the Capulets' ball; the third movement draws on a theme from the *Messe solennelle;* the fourth movement was retrieved from the opera *Les Francs-Juges;* the finale may have its origins in music for *Faust.* It is impossible to know how much (or how little) music was newly composed for the symphony in 1830. The important thing is that he found at last the form in which to express two or three years' accumulation of intense feeling.

Having made no public reference whatever to *Roméo et Juliette* in the program of the *Symphonie fantastique*, Berlioz was free to continue with thoughts about his favorite Shakespeare play. Seeing Bellini's *I Capuleti e i Montecchi* in Florence in 1831 he was outraged at its lack of Shakespearean passion, unaware that Bellini's sources were pre-Shakespearean Italian sources he knew nothing about. Before entering the theater Berlioz pictured to himself the scenes he expected to see and enjoy:

> First, the glittering ball in the Capulets' house where young Montague sees *sweetest Juliet* for the first time amid the swirling torrent of beautiful women. Then the furious fighting in the streets of Verona over which the raging Tybalt presides like the spirit of hatred and vengeance. The inexpressibly beautiful night scene on Juliet's balcony where the lovers murmur a concert of tender love as sweet and pure as the starlight smiling down upon them. The amusing silliness of Mercutio, the naive cackling of the nurse, the grave character of the hermit. [. . .] Then the terrible catastrophe with joy and despair interlocked, sighs of pleasure mingling with the rattle of death. Finally the solemn oath of the two families . . .[16]

Disgust at Bellini's failure to live up to his expectations led him to talk with Auguste Barbier about a *Romeo and Juliet* opera and with Mendelssohn about a possible Queen Mab scherzo. Perhaps after his return to Paris he mentioned the idea of a symphony on the subject to Émile Deschamps. By 1839 his determination finally to do full justice to the play became a reality thanks to Paganini's generous gift. He had been married to Harriet for over five years and had, we may suppose, read through the play many times with her, finding new meanings and allusions. The symphony that emerged was no longer the product of a spontaneous ardent response as the 1827–1828 pieces must have been, but the fruit of long reflection, no less intense in its depiction of the fire of love, but broader in scale and unified in its large-scale control of seven movements. Beethoven's Choral Symphony now contributed, if only marginally, to the main strand. But some of the music Berlioz might have wanted to use was no longer available. The scene of Romeo's discovery of Juliet and the ballroom music was embedded in the *Symphonie fantastique* and the vault scene was in *Le Retour à la vie*. All these had to be composed anew. Berlioz drew on rich sources of inspiration for the long movement *Roméo seul—Fête chez Capulet* and of course for the new *Scène d'amour*. Of the vault music there is a reminiscence in the sixth movement, *Roméo au tombeau des Capulet*, when over a throbbing rhythm in 12/8 a somber theme arises in the English horn, four bassoons, and horn. But this time it is Romeo, not Juliet, who is contemplating the gloomy awe of the vault.

Much of the argument presented here is obviously speculative. Fresh documents might one day emerge to support my findings, while it is impossible to prove that Berlioz did *not* write any *Roméo et Juliette* music at the time I propose. At the very least I hope we may accept that his creative mind was in a state of great turbulence and agitation in the years following the revelation of

Shakespeare and of Miss Smithson, and that his finished compositions belong to one another in a web of connecting threads, many of which are no longer visible to us today.

Notes

1. Émile Deschamps, *Macbeth, et Roméo et Juliette, tragédies de Shakespeare, traduites en vers français, avec une préface, des notes et des commentaires* (Paris: Comptoir des imprimeurs réunis, 1844), p. 230.

2. Auguste Barbier, *Souvenirs personnels et silhouettes contemporaines de 1830 à 1880* (Paris: Dentu, 1883), p. 230.

3. *Mémoires*, chapter XXXVI (p. 198n).

4. See Ian Kemp, "*Romeo and Juliet* and *Roméo et Juliette*," in *Berlioz Studies*, ed. Peter Bloom (Cambridge: Cambridge University Press, 1992), pp. 37–79, here, p. 47; and Julian Rushton, *Berlioz: Roméo et Juliette* (Cambridge: Cambridge University Press, 1994), pp. 10–12.

5. *Mémoires*, chapter XVIII.

6. *CG* I, pp. 159–174; and *CG* VIII, pp. 18–25. The letter to Nancy with the date 10 January 1828 in *CG* I, pp. 167–172, should be dated 1829.

7. See *CG* I, p. 306.

8. The available editions of Shakespeare in French and English are described by Kemp in "*Romeo and Juliet*," p. 39n.

9. This text is given in full in French in *NBE* 16, p. 192.

10. Quoted on the title page of the autograph of *Waverley*, but later crossed out. See *NBE* 20, p. viii, and facsimile, p. 308.

11. See *NBE* 6, p. xv.

12. The melody is given in *NBE* 6, p. xv.

13. *CG* I, p. 270.

14. Kemp, "*Romeo and Juliet*," p. 55.

15. *Mémoires*, chapter XVIII.

16. *Revue européenne* (15 March 1832); *CM* 1, p. 70.

Chapter Eight

Beethoven, Shakespeare, and Berlioz's Scène d'amour

JEAN-PIERRE BARTOLI

Shakespeare et Beethoven
sont les deux plus grands paysagistes peut-être qui aient jamais existé . . .
—Hector Berlioz (27 August 1854)

For most commentators, the *Scène d'amour* that constitutes the instrumental Adagio at the heart of Berlioz's *Roméo et Juliette* is a faithful illustration and a scrupulous rendering of the dramatic narrative of the balcony scene in Act II, scene ii of Shakespeare's play. Jacques Chailley, in the nineteen-seventies, was one of the first to present a strictly programmatic exegesis of this movement.

Berlioz according to Shakespeare

Chailley began on the basis of the information presented by the chorus in the Prologue, whose text forms an authentic literary "program" that is not presented apart from, but is rather integrated into, the musical fabric itself. As he has it:

> The Prologue of *Roméo et Juliette* is not, as it might seem to the superficial listener, a use- less redundancy. As an element of the dramatic structure it creates a link that justifies the selection of the various episodes by situating them within the larger action of the play. More important, it offers a veritable musical analysis of the score inserted into the score itself. Thanks to this analysis, we are able to fathom the precise meaning of a theme when it appears without words, because that theme will already have occurred, with an "explanation," in the Prologue.[1]

On the basis of information provided by Berlioz, Chailley proposes a seman- tic interpretation of the movement that has the music describe in chronological order the actions of Shakespeare's scene. The result is far from unpersuasive. More recently, Ian Kemp has undertaken to follow with even greater rigor and exactitude the path of Berlioz's literary and dramatic sources—namely, the Garrick version of the text and the version played at the Odéon in 1827. Kemp systematically applies to all the instrumental movements of the symphony the kind of analysis earlier undertaken by Chailley. For the *Scène d'amour*, he connects Berlioz's musical continuity, measure by measure, to the poetic dialogue. He synthesizes his findings in a highly-detailed comparative table.[2]

These two exegetical narratives lead in some quarters to enthusiastic acceptance and in others to categorical rejection. The latter results from a refusal to acknowledge that one of Berlioz's most admirable symphonic works should be exclusively based upon an underlying verbal scenario, from a refusal, that is, to believe that a successful symphonic movement could have an architectural framework resting on an entirely extramusical foundation. If that were the case, would we not have to say that Berlioz errs as to the essential purpose of the art of music? That he manifests arch naïveté in thinking that music can be so comprehensively illustrative? To these questions Jacques Chailley replied that it could not be otherwise. From his point of view, we simply must listen to such movements as the *Scène d'amour* with the assistance of the Prologue-Program:

> [O]nly in that way can we perceive, in addition to the lovely elements accessible to us without preparation, the discursive logic that I defy any analyst otherwise to discover if he gives in to the tendency, now in vogue, that consists of considering the least verbal support as an "impurity," when in fact what we have is a key generously supplied by the author himself.[3]

Ian Kemp wittily attempts to avoid this sort of reproach, suggesting that the conclusion to be drawn from the close correspondences he demonstrates between text and tone is not "that Berlioz's structure is naive, but rather that is dramatic, that Shakespeare is musical, and that both derive from the same archetypal source."[4]

Kemp moves beyond his comparative table by presenting the broad outlines of a formal structure articulated in four well-defined musical sections corresponding to the four sections of Shakespeare's scene. The first section, "introduction/exposition" (bars 125–180), subdivided into two "strophes," corresponds to the appearance of Romeo below Juliet's balcony, to his emotional asides, and to his confessions in response to those of Juliet, who, believing herself alone, has confided them "to the night" (Berlioz writes in the Prologue that Juliet "confie son amour à la nuit"): the opening measures establish the nocturnal landscape and the presence of the two protagonists (strings for Romeo, and winds, sighing, for Juliet) while Romeo's "declaration of love" appears twice (at bars 146 and 172). The second section (bars 181–249), likewise divided into two strophes, gives us a recitative that speaks of Juliet's anxieties and Romeo's reassurances. The third section is entirely devoted to the musical incarnation of Juliet's monologue (lines 85–92): this is the melodic development in a vocal style, played by the flute and English horn, that we hear in bars 250–274. There follows a final section, which corresponds to the love duet properly speaking (from bar 274 to the end). According to Kemp, this section is based on the principle of the rondo, whose refrain—in this case an amalgamation of "Romeo's theme" and "Juliet's theme" from section three (bar 250)—is presented seven times, at bars 274, 286, 322, 332, 341, 362, 367, with a final addition, at bar 375, of a few further melodic fragments.

Kemp's analysis of the passage is highly methodical: he succeeds in attaching the textual dialogue to the smallest musical inflections, though not without being compelled at times to superimpose certain lines of the drama, a practice that is, of course, perfectly common in opera. He furthermore divides the movement into segments that are readily audible on first hearing. His semantic divisions are thus in no way arbitrary with regard to the succession of musical events.

The comparison of the analyses of the narrative by Chailley and Kemp is significant because it reveals more similarities than disparities: Chailley, using as a guide only the Prologue and the dramatic flow of the scene, hears the unexpected interventions of the strings in bars 332–334, for example, as representing the nurse's "call from within" (after line 136), as does Kemp. But Chailley interprets the sweeping thirty-second-note line in the strings at bar 363 as a translation of the lovers' apprehensiveness, while Kemp understands it as the second call (lines 149, 152) of the nurse. Still, the large-scale divisions of both analyses are compatible. While Chailley limits himself to the larger dramatic situations, Kemp risks a literal transposition of the texts of Shakespeare and Garrick. Neither critic, it should be noted, takes into account the significant changes that Berlioz made in this movement after the first performance of the work.

Beyond establishing formal divisions founded essentially upon the dramatic action, some analysts have further wanted to underline the multiple motivic relationships that may be found among the various melodic materials of the movement, relationships that may be understood as having allowed the composer to avoid what might otherwise have been taken as a series of incoherent musical gestures. In his fine monograph on the symphony, Julian Rushton develops this notion.[5] Below I cite an example from Rushton's text (exx. 8.1a–c) and add two of my own that tend to confirm the point. It will be seen that examples 8.2a and b illustrate an idea suggested by Kemp and merely reinforce the narrative structure of the movement. Example 8.3 derives from the sort of thematic analysis that was commonly practiced by Rudolph Reti.[6]

These examples require no special commentary, and I would urge interested readers to consult the works of the three authors in question. Here I should like to return to the delicate question of the nature of the larger architecture of the Adagio. As a result of recent trends in musicological study, narrative readings of Berlioz's symphony have found renewed favor, while structuralist exegeses, tending towards formalism and thus departing from the pursuit of illustrative connotations and external semantic references, are lately looked upon with misgivings.

(a)

(b)

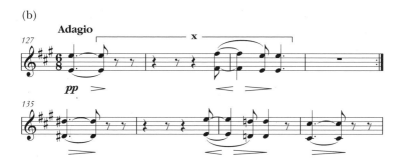

(c)

Example 8.1. *Scène d'amour*, Julian Rushton's analysis of Juliet's "voice." From Julian Rushton, *Berlioz: Roméo et Juliette* (Cambridge: Cambridge University Press, 1994), p. 38. Used by permission. (a) mm. 125–126; (b) 127–138; (c) 181–188.

(a)

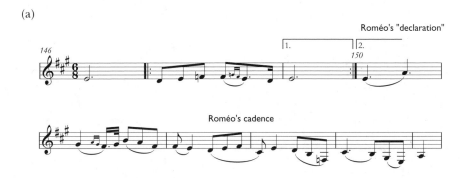

(b)

Example 8.2 (a–b). *Scène d'amour*, the two main forms of the principal theme. (a) First form, mm. 146–155; (b) Second form, mm. 274–280.

Example 8.3. Motivic relationships in the *Scène d'amour*.

Nevertheless, I am convinced that if Berlioz's *Roméo et Juliette*, so often performed and recorded by the finest orchestras and conductors, continues to appeal to the larger public, it is not because of the work's descriptive virtues, not because of its careful balance of literary and musical progression, and not because of its graceful themes and sonorous configurations, but rather because of its successful, intrinsically musical superstructure. If this were not the case, then we would have difficulty explaining why Félicien David's *Le Désert* and Benjamin Godard's *Symphonie légendaire*, for example, with all their undeniable illustrative merits, are not equally appreciated and celebrated. Furthermore, whether Berlioz's movement is or is not narrative is by no means the crucial question. The debate ought not to take place in these terms. The fact that at least two scholars so reasonably insist upon the narrative structure of the movement demonstrates at the very least that it does indeed possess narrative qualities. Nor is there any doubt that the composer himself partially if not totally conceived the movement in such a way as to render those narrative qualities audible. The question, rather, is whether the structure of this Adagio turns *uniquely* on narrative principles.

For my part, I am convinced that the movement closely follows the progression of the Shakespearean action, but I refuse to believe that its value rests on that progression alone and on the perfection of the musical formulas that it engenders. It seems to me that the movement does indeed contain a "discursive logic," to employ Chailley's expression, but that it exists independently of the verbal discourse, of the dramatic unfolding proposed by Shakespeare, even if this does serve as a "pretext." It is difficult to define such a discursive logic, but if its existence is real, then only musical analysis, using analytical metalanguage, can reveal its contours and uncover what motivates the form and the musical development of the movement. The value of the movement is thus intrinsically musical; its explication need not depend on literary elements. It is the *musical discourse*, referring to the music itself, that is responsible for much of the movement's success.

A more recent article by Vera Micznik brings a new perspective to Berlioz's Adagio by offering a narratological analysis based rather more on "topics" than on the musical imprint of the colloquy in Shakespeare-Garrick.[7] Micznik's comprehensive analysis tends more to separate Berlioz's symphonic development from the strictly illustrative development presented by Chailley and Kemp. One of her most interesting points is the resemblance she finds between the Adagio of Beethoven's String Quartet in F Major, Op. 18, No. 1, and two movements of the Berlioz: the *Scène d'amour* and *Roméo au tombeau des Capulets*. Insisting on the French composer's familiarity with Beethoven's quartets, Micznik does indeed uncover several undeniable analogies. Still, she herself admits that there remain numerous divergences between the two works, of which the most important is the fact that regardless of whether it may be heard as a dramatic *scena*, Beethoven's slow movement is clearly a sonata form that is perfectly audible as such, while Berlioz's *Scène d'amour* is not a sonata form and could never be mistaken for anything of the kind.

Micznik's comparative analysis is nonetheless reinforced by two historical facts. First, according to the recollection of Beethoven's friend Karl Amenda, as first reported by Wilhelm von Lenz, the slow movement of the string quartet was inspired by Shakespeare's tomb scene and Romeo's death.[8] Second, and to my way of thinking more decisive, one of Beethoven's sketches for this movement carries inscriptions in French that clearly pertain to this particular scene and thus confirm Amenda's remembrance. These sketches did not become known until their publication by Gustav Nottebohm, in 1872, three years after Berlioz's death, but Micznik suggests that they were probably known to Mendelssohn and might conceivably have been the subject of one of his conversations with Berlioz in Rome in the summer of 1831, especially since it is known (from chapter XXXVI of the *Mémoires*) that they did indeed discuss *Romeo and Juliet*.

It is not my intention here to challenge Micznik's hypothesis regarding an instance of musical intertextuality, but rather to propose another that seems to me more convincing from the point of view of the historical sources—relying as it does on an article written by Berlioz shortly before conceiving *Roméo et Juliette*—and from the point of view of musical structure. Engaging like Micznik in the game of finding a Beethovenian model for Berlioz's work, I find that the *Scène d'amour*, as the slow movement of a symphonic complex, reflects not the slow movement of the F-Major Quartet from Opus 18 but rather the Adagio of the Ninth Symphony. Let it be said at the outset that these two hypotheses are not mutually exclusive, nor does the one invalidate the other, for Berlioz might well have had both models in mind. But the intertextuality proposed here, because it is founded on purely musical relationships exclusive of Shakespearean literary references,[9] underlines more strongly our recognition of the tremendous influence exerted by the author of the Ninth Symphony upon the composer of *Roméo et Juliette*, and our contention regarding Berlioz's *Scène d'amour* as an independent or, if you will, "absolute" symphonic composition.

Beethoven according to Berlioz

Berlioz was profoundly affected by Beethoven's Ninth Symphony. Already in 1829 he wrote that the work seemed to him to represent "the culmination of [Beethoven's] genius," and he rejected the criticisms of a number of his contemporaries who, like Fétis, took the Adagio molto et cantabile as indicative of the decline of the creative powers of the master from Bonn.[10] Traces of the direct influence of the Ninth Symphony are everywhere in Berlioz's work. In the slow movement of the *Symphonie fantastique*, Berlioz—who at the time knew the Ninth Symphony only from having read the score in the library of the Conservatoire—remembered a way of writing employed by his German mentor that we would call the principle of variation via heterophony (see exx. 8.4a and 8.4b).[11]

Example 8.4a. Heterophony in the Adagio of Beethoven's Ninth Symphony, mm. 98–101.

The opening of the finale of *Harold en Italie*, with its recollections of themes from previous movements, bears renewed witness to Berlioz's admiration of the Ninth.[12] (In addition, we know that *Harold* was initially to be called "Les Derniers Instants de Marie Stuart," and was to feature a chorus.) In *Roméo et Juliette* the external marks of the Ninth are legion, including the deployment of voices, of instrumental recitative, and of thematic foreshadowing of later movements—which turns Beethoven's "parade of reminiscences" on its head. In the article mentioned above Ian Kemp calls attention to the use in both works of a first-movement coda based on an obstinately repeated motif, and to the use on the large-scale of a "crescendo" of instrumental means, as the both finales assemble the totality of the forces earlier employed.

With these things in mind let us consider the celebrated article on the Choral Symphony that Berlioz published in the *Journal des débats* on 4 March 1838, an

Example 8.4b. Heterophony in the *Scène aux champs* of the *Symphonie fantastique*, mm. 131–134.

article later incorporated into *À travers chants*. "In the Adagio cantabile," Berlioz writes,

> the principle of unity is so little observed that it might be regarded as two distinct movements rather than one. The first melody, in B-flat and in 4/4 time, is followed by one in D Major, absolutely different from the first, in 3/4 meter. The first theme, slightly changed and varied by the first violins, makes a second appearance in the original key, bringing back the melody in triple time without alteration or variation, but in the key of G Major, after which the first theme becomes solidly established and no longer allows the rival phrase to share the listener's attention.
>
> One must hear this splendid Adagio several times in order fully to appreciate such a singular disposition of materials. As to the splendor of all these melodies, the infinite grace of the ornaments that adorn them, the feelings of tender melancholy, of passionate dejection, and of religious meditation that they express: if my prose could give even an approximate idea of all of this, music would have found in the written word a rival that the greatest of all poets himself could not even begin to challenge. This is an immense creation, and when you are under its powerful spell, you are able to reply to the critic who would reprove the composer for having violated the law of unity: too bad for that law![13]

We must inquire into precisely what Berlioz means by "unity." Is he speaking of a general motivic unity across the entire movement? Or is he speaking only of what he calls the "second theme"? Is it impossible to imagine that Berlioz failed to perceive the motivic unity of Beethoven's Adagio, which is conceived on a thematic grid that is not difficult to discern.[14] In addition, a reading of contemporary composition treatises, such as those by Berlioz's teacher Anton Reicha, reveals that the notion of motivic unity was every bit as prominent in France as it was in the German-speaking lands. Motivic unity in Berlioz's own music attests to this fact, as may be observed above in examples 8.1, 8.2, and 8.3. The last sentence of the quotation from the article on the Ninth extends the sense of the opening of the paragraph, which would have Beethoven entering into a certain formal process and then, suddenly, moving on to something else. Berlioz is thus singing the praises of a piece that seems blithely to abandon in mid-stream the principle upon which its opening continuity is built. At a given moment, the music departs from the path that it seemed at first predestined to follow; it refuses to accept the role that conventional usage doled out.

In order better to understand the originality of the formal analysis implicit in Berlioz's comment, we may compare it with the more traditional approach offered by Heinrich Schenker. This is summarized in table 8.1, taken from the volume that Schenker devoted to Beethoven's work.[15] Schenker describes the movement as a theme followed by two variations—a description shared by most musicologists.[16] On the model provided by Haydn, these variations are preceded by an alternative theme (a *Zwischenthema*) which, in this case, is not varied but rather presented in two different tonalities; the second variation is also preceded by a free transition (a *freie Überleitung*) and followed by a coda in the form of a further motivic development.[17]

Berlioz, on the other hand, hears the movement in two parts: the first (bars 1–82) is articulated by the alternation of two "rival" themes of which one is varied while the other is content merely to appear in two different keys; the second (bar 83 to the end) has the first theme as "definitively established" and as "no

Table 8.1. Schenker's Analysis of the Adagio of the Ninth Symphony

1–2	*Introduction*	
3–24	*Main theme for variation*	Adagio, B-flat Major, ₵
25–42	*Alternative theme*	Andante moderato, D Major, 3/4
43–64	*First variation*	Adagio, B-flat Major, ₵
65–82	*Repeat of alternative theme*	Andante moderato, G Major, 3/4
83–98	*Free transition to second variation*	Adagio, E-flat Major, ₵
99–120	*Second variation*	Adagio, B-flat Major, 12/8
121–157	*Coda*	

longer permitting the rival phrase to share with it the listener's attention." For this second part, Berlioz does not speak of variation but alludes to a process whereby the first theme is deployed in the manner of a grand melodic development. In truth, he privileges the ear over the eye and insists more on describing the resulting sonorous effect than on the means by which Beethoven has constructed the movement. He is preoccupied and fascinated by the perceived effect of a ruptured unity. But how, in view of the thematic continuity, can we explain the perception of such a rupture? Simply by noting that the second variation (of the principal theme) is preceded by a motivic development of that same theme—the free transition evoked by Schenker—and followed by a coda subject to the same motivic working out. Taken as a whole, the passage does effectively sound like one long melodic development that turns on the initial theme, and not like a variation. Indeed, the beginning of Berlioz's second section (bar 83) is found at the midpoint of the movement in terms of numbers of bars (the literal midpoint would be bar 78) as well as in terms of duration, which, from the experiential point of view, is of course more relevant. For the ear, it is clearly a question of the second part of a movement and not of one more variation linked to earlier variations.

Berlioz according to Beethoven

Berlioz's article appeared in March 1838; his work on *Roméo et Juliette* began in January 1839. Such temporal proximity suggests that it is not unreasonable to compare and perhaps associate the procedure of thematic alternation that occurs at the beginning of both works' Adagios. I should like to pursue this path and examine Berlioz's movement in its entirety in light of his commentary on the Adagio of the Ninth. Table 8.2 presents a synthesis of the similarities and differences I find between the two movements, which seem to me to be significant.

The most immediately analogous point here, from an auditory point of view, is the effect of the pedal in fifths, with thematic fragments in the winds, in the two codas (see exx. 8.5a and b). But the impact of Beethoven's design upon Berlioz is to be read far less in detailed musical figurations such as these than in larger compositional procedures, for the two movements do not resemble each other in their themes or rhythms. Their affinities rather occur on the more profound level of the construction of the musical discourse. In both, it is possible to hear three episodes, with the middle episode serving as a bridge between a first period and a second period that is elaborated without returning to the first. Both undertake harmonic progressions by third but conclude by coming to rest in the tonic, which is then embroidered by moves to neighboring harmonies. Both exploit the processes of variation and motivic development, combining the two towards the end. Both, finally, seem to engender a spirit of continuous development. In addition, Berlioz, like Beethoven, breaks what he earlier called the

Table 8.2. The Adagio of the Ninth Symphony and the *Scène d'amour*. (Similarities are preceded by ▲; differences by ▼.)

Beethoven	Berlioz
▲ **Part I** alternating two themes of opposing characters. Change of tempo. Two presentations of each theme.	▲ **Part I** alternating two themes of opposing characters. Change of tempo. Two presentations of each theme.
▼ The first theme is the principal theme of the movement.	▼ The second theme is the principal theme of the movement.
▲ The first theme is always in I; the second in III or VI (relations by third).	▲ The first theme is always in I, the second in iii or flat-III (relations by third).
▲ The principle of ornamental variation is applied to the first theme; the other is merely transposed and reorchestrated, thus providing a contrast between repetition and change.	▲ The principle of variation (via transposition and reorchestration) is applied to the second theme; the other is practically unchanged, thus providing a contrast between repetition and change.
▲ The alternative theme disappears. (▼ Its motives will not later be exploited.)	▲ The first theme disappears. (▼ Its motives will later be exploited.)
Transition ▲ Motivic development of the first theme (retransition from E-flat to C-flat to B-flat): the effect is one of delaying the arrival of the first theme.	**Transition** 1. Dramatic interpolation (the dialogue of Juliet and Romeo) ▲ with motivic development of the first theme. ▲ 2. Development of the principal [second] theme in the form of "Juliet's monologue" (in F-sharp and A); the effect is one of delaying the arrival of the principal theme.
(This is the chronological center of the movement.)	(This is the chronological center of the movement.)
Part II ▲ Variation of the principal theme and final developments in the form of a coda.	**Part II** ▲ "Rondo"[a] with an important variant of the principal theme [the second form of the theme] adding motivic developments.
▲ The tonal activity remains centered upon I; modulations are "parenthetical" and merely ornament I and V.	▲ The tonal activity remains centered upon I; modulations are "parenthetical" and merely ornament I.

Table 8.2. (*continued*)

Beethoven	Berlioz
▲ Two remarkable and unexpected harmonic parentheses to IV and flat-III (bars 121–125; 131–136).	▲ Two remarkable and unexpected harmonic parentheses to flat-iii and flat-VI (after bar 308; after bar 354).
▲ These parentheses disrupt the expressive climate of the passage via the sharp contrast of the brass at bars 121–123 and 131–133.	▲ Two parentheses disrupt the expressive climate of the passage via the "nurse's call from within" in the strings in bars 332–336 and 362–363, to which one may add the two contrasting shifts, *animato*, at bars 358 and 372.
▲ After the variation of the theme, a motivic development of fragments of it (on the antecedent phrase, bar 127; on the consequent phrase, bar 141, etc.).	▲ Between statements of the principal theme (varied by transposition, new accompaniment, and reorchestration), motivic development of fragments of it (on the antecedent, bars 280, 341, 362; on the consequent, bar 350; on the first theme, bars 300, 360).
▲ Coda, with fragments of the theme (from bars 5–6), and, before the final cadence, open fifths in the bass, tremolo-like bowing, and thematic fragments in the winds.	▲ Coda with open fifths in the bass, tremolo-like bowing, and thematic fragments in the winds.

[a] In the original version of this movement, two returns of the theme (at bars 322 and 332) were at first mere motivic developments; the effect of the rondo form was thus less apparent.

"law of unity"—which is in fact the law of symmetrical architecture, the law of circularity, the law of return to the beginning.

What I wish to demonstrate, then, is not that Berlioz's Adagio is literally modeled on Beethoven's, but that a number of elaborative musical procedures in the *Scène d'amour* seem to have been motivated by the composer's penetrating reading of Beethoven's score—above and beyond the narrative requirements of the Shakespearean drama, which conditioned the musical discourse of his movement; that Berlioz joined the symphonic properties invented by Beethoven to a musical restructuring of Shakespeare's dramatic narrative. Having sensed unsuspected relationships between the two artists, Berlioz illuminates the English poet's play with a new sort of expressive efficacy drawn from the German composer's symphonic paradigm.

Example 8.5a. Beethoven, Ninth Symphony, Adagio, mm. 150–155; pedal in fifths.

Example 8.5b. Berlioz, *Scène d'amour*, mm. 381–389; pedal in fifths.

Just as Shakespeare's plays proved to Victor Hugo that the hallowed "three unities" were an impediment to his own creative genius, so, too, did Beethoven's Ninth prove to Berlioz that formal rigidity could restrict his own development of a new aesthetics of musical craftsmanship. Abandoning the initial configurations by the procedure of variation allowed Berlioz to deploy materials in such a way as to suggest constant renewal, to foster expressive properties of exceptional freshness. It is by his "singular disposition of materials," as Berlioz puts it, that Beethoven succeeded in saying what no poet had been able to say. Berlioz attempts to achieve a Beethoven-like transcendence by revitalizing his forbear's symphonic procedures and applying them to Shakespeare's text. Guided by Shakespeare's scenic dramaturgy, Berlioz expands upon the musical experience offered by Beethoven by refining the variation procedure, by modifying the structure of the principal theme, and by accentuating a number of the effects realized by the German master.

A more detailed analysis of Berlioz's movement reveals to what extent Berlioz exploited a musical discourse that refuses to return to earlier materials—an idea that he surely took from Beethoven. Examples 8.6a to 8.6h illustrate this kind of linear discursiveness.[18] All of these lines, descending by fifth, correspond either to the presentation of the principal theme in its two aspects or to the theme of "Juliet's monologue." This underlines the communality of the two themes.[19] On the other hand, the diversity of thematic presentation, which these reductions display, has been noticed by a number of critics, in particular by Charles Rosen.[20] The first appearance of the main theme (at bar 146; ex. 8.6a) presents a complete line in the principal key sustained by a harmony in parallel sixths. There is no arpeggiation of the bass (in the Shenkerian sense), or no perfect cadence, and the fifth degree ($\hat{5}$) appears in the region of iii (C-sharp Minor). The second appearance presents a complete line sustained by a complete perfect cadence, but in the key of flat-III (C Major, bar 172; ex. 8.6b). According to Kemp's narratological analysis, the first appearance underlines the words that Romeo speaks to himself, while the second corresponds to his first open declaration of love. The three following appearances of the descending fifth belong to Juliet's central monologue (bars 250–256; 256–261; 261–274; ex. 8.6c). The second and third of these occur for the first time wholly in the principal key, with an arpeggiation in the bass, but the upper voice is an octave higher than the initial register. Furthermore, at the surface level of the score, this line does not support the principal theme but rather a melody more or less derived from it. Immediately after these lines, which comprise "Juliet's reply" to "Romeo's declaration of love," and which remain in the tonic, we have two complete linear descents from the fifth degree, with perfect cadence, and in the original register, i.e., the "fundamental structure" (bars 274 and 286; ex. 8.6d). This is the opening of Part II of the movement. The theme has changed its external appearance and all the parameters mentioned now come together to express the serene, nocturnal miracle of shared love.

After this double presentation, the theme will never be the same, even if new occurrences of its thematic substance will almost always be in the tonic. The

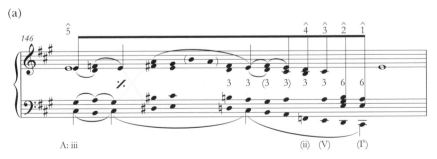

Example 8.6a–h. Reductive graphs of the *Scène d'amour.*

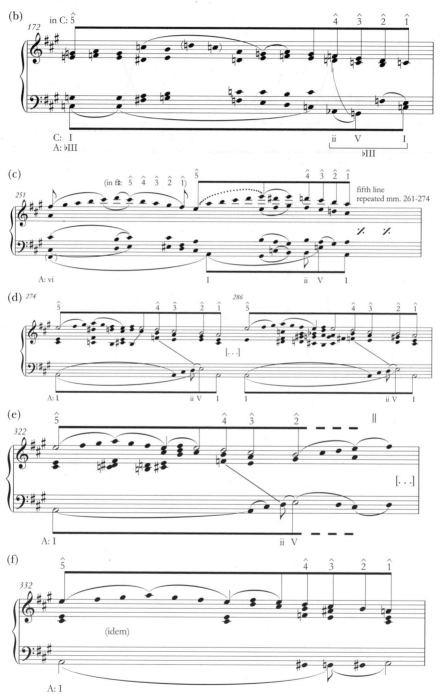

Example 8.6a–h (*continued*).

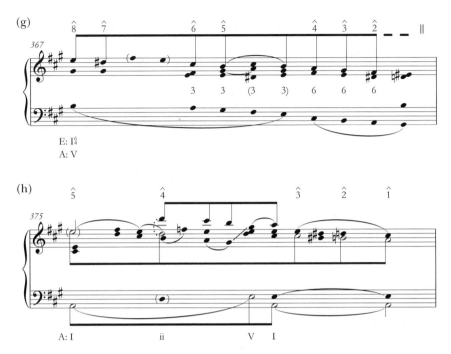

Example 8.6a–h (*continued*).

appearance of the theme in bars 322–328 is interrupted (after $\hat{2}$; ex. 8.6e); the next appearance, at bars 332–338, is perturbed by interventions from the strings, and its harmonization is exempted from a full cadence (ex. 8.6f). Bars 367–372 momentarily recover the theme in its original, richly embellished guise: we are in the key of the dominant and, with a full orchestral tutti, at the most intensely passionate moment of the movement. What is more, the bass moves forward in parallel thirds and sixths until the structure is dramatically interrupted (ex. 8.6g). The ultimate presentation of the principal melody (after the downbeat of bar 375; ex. 8.6h), realized by only suggestive thematic fragments, and hiding in its inner voices the fifth-descent in the initial register, dissolves in the nocturnal mist as it brings us to the final cadence.

Shakespeare according to Berlioz

Berlioz's formal strategy, for the period of its conception in the eighteen-thirties, is entirely unexpected. Listeners to symphonic music at the time would surely anticipate some sort of recapitulation or reprise; they would surely experience what Michel Imberty has referred to as the pleasure of waiting for an element that one is certain will return in a manner identical to its earlier appearance.[21] Berlioz, however, very subtly practices a "dérégulation" or curtailment of this process of gratifying expectation. The principal theme evolves constantly, as much in its orchestration and melodic behavior as in its harmonic and polyphonic dress. Its fully completed and realized structure (in the Shenkerian sense of the fifth-descent with arpeggiation of the bass) is announced first, because the first and second appearances of the theme seem to cause in the listener a feeling of expectation (each time the fundamental structure is left incomplete or set forth in a key other than the tonic). This expectation is satisfied first, at the center of the movement, by the two presentations in octaves of the fundamental melodic structure (the "acceptance of Juliet"); it is then more fully satisfied by the two nearly successive presentations of the fundamental melodic structure that support the "love theme" and that correspond precisely to the point in the Shakespearean drama at which the two protagonists proclaim and share their love. But henceforth the expectation that the fundamental melodic structure will return is thwarted: the hoped-for regularity does not occur. The development of the first part of the movement thus symbolizes anticipation. This finds fulfillment at the midpoint. But the action of the second part of the movement engenders a muted frustration, a feeling of anguish, which is appropriate to the course of the drama.

Berlioz's musical reading of Shakespeare's scene, with its elements in perpetual variation, is nothing short of stupefying. The moment of absolute happiness no sooner arrives than it is immediately superseded by a foreshadowing of the drama that is about to unfold, an expression of the evanescence of time, of a love that takes flight as soon as it is born. It speaks to us simultaneously of union and separation, of love and death—a notion that we might wish to see illustrated by the presentation, in the coda, of two *topics*: the open fifths representing absence, the thirds representing union. Berlioz's music seems to echo Shakespeare's melancholy discourse on time, insensible to the lovers' eternal aspirations:

> JULIET.
> [. . .] Although I joy in thee,
> I have no joy of this contract to-night.
> It is too rash, too unadvised, too sudden;
> Too like the lightning, which doth cease to be
> Ere one can say "It lightens." Sweet, goodnight!
> [. . .]
>
> ROMEO
> O, wilt thou leave me so unsatisfied
>
> JULIET
> What satisfaction canst thou have to-night?

ROMEO
Th' exchange of thy love's faithful vow for mine.

JULIET
I gave thee mine before thou didst request it:
And yet I would it were to give again.[22]

The formal logic of the piece may thus be said to follow Shakespeare's drama not only because it is possible to find in it the various episodes of the action as set down by the poet, but also because it may be seen as proposing a directed analytical reading, an interpretation, which reveals hidden senses of the action and of the avowals of the actors.

Berlioz Himself

It is with this creatively analytical intuition that Berlioz found a unique logic for his musical structure—one that may be described independently of the literary context. It is composed of two principal parts united by a central section. The first is articulated by two main thematic elements; the second abandons one of these and develops the other in a singular manner. This breaking down of the "unity" of the piece may be seen, when the Adagio of the Ninth Symphony is viewed in the light we attempt to cast here, as having been suggested by Beethoven. The musical continuity of the first part consists in the partial or "incomplete" presentation of fundamental material: that is, presentation not (entirely) in the tonic, or in the minor mode, or with unstable harmonic support, or without full cadences. The transitional section employs certain materials common to opera—recitative, dramatic arioso, aria—that try literally to dramatize the musical text; it eschews entirely the principal thematic material. Taken together these first two episodes create a formal dynamic (comparable in some ways to the development section of a classic sonata form) of anticipation—anticipation, that is, of a complete return of the principal materials in the tonic key. The end of the central section (comparable in some ways to the retransition of the sonata form) seems to prepare for such a structural and expressive resolution. When the next major section arrives, we do indeed hear the main theme fully realized—presented *for the first time* in the tonic and in a harmonically and melodically stable manner. This is the crucial formal and expressive point, for it corresponds to the moment of fulfillment of the anticipation developed in the two earlier sections. What follows is the presentation of a simulacrum of a rondo that alternates episodes of motivic development with the return, reshaped and retailored, of the principal theme—a configuration that results, again, from an interpretation (this time more free) of the slow movement of Beethoven's Ninth Symphony. But the principal theme never recurs in the way it is presented at the center of the movement. Various factors subvert each of its new occurrences: unstable harmonization, incongruous "commentary" from the strings, presentation in the dominant, interruption before the final cadence.[23] In the final measures the movement dissolves in the tonic harmonies with which it opened. Table 8.3 summarizes what has just been said.

Table 8.3. The Structure of the *Scène d'amour*

Part I	Transition		Part II	
Bars 124–181	181–246	246–274	274–389	
Engendering of the effect of anticipation	Intensification of the effect of anticipation	Announcement of resolution (retransition)	Brief resolution (two of citations of the theme in the tonic)	Simulacrum of a rondo with frustration of the desire for literal repetition

Thus may one describe the discursive logic of the movement in "absolute" musical terms. If its elucidation is facilitated via reference to the text of the play, it is no less authentically discernable and analyzable in purely musical terminology, and no less perceptible without reference to the text. Much as knowledge of Shakespeare's "pre-text" may enhance the pleasure, that knowledge is no way indispensable to the appreciation of the dramatic allure of this music—which in the end turns on the *evolution* of a principal theme, a formal principle employed by many composers of the romantic era and one that is particularly evident in the *Ballades* of Chopin, for example, and in *Vallée d'Obermann* of Liszt.

Consciously or not, Berlioz seems to have composed the Adagio of the symphony in the aftermath of two analytical efforts: one that explicitly tackled the Adagio of the Ninth Symphony, as we have seen, and another that took on Shakespeare's *Romeo and Juliet.* Clearly the action of the *Scène d'amour* seems to follow the action of the balcony scene in the play, but Beethoven's formal model allowed Berlioz otherwise to illuminate that action—to do so, that is, by constructing an abstract formal architecture ideally adapted to the situation. It would furthermore seem that a close reading of the sentiments expressed by Shakespeare's characters allowed Berlioz to refine the musical discourse and to strengthen what was propounded by Beethoven, which is a constant renewal of musical material and a refusal to turn back—something that became one of the fundamental principles of Berlioz's symphonic style, if not an obsession that inhabited almost all of his œuvre.[24] This explains the belittlement, in his article on the Ninth, of the "law of unity." Thus, by freely interpreting two preexistent discursive structures—one musical, the other literary, by comparing them and fusing them with his own subtle alchemy, Berlioz was able to forge the *Scène d'amour*. That fusion guaranteed the movement's autonomy vis-à-vis its two models, as well as its everlasting and inalterable beauty.

(Translated by Peter Bloom)

Notes

This article is a revision and expansion of a paper originally given in Montpellier, in 1995, at the Congrès européen d'analyse musicale, and published in *Analyse et création musicale* (Paris: L'Harmattan, 2001), pp. 485–518. I am grateful to Peter Bloom for offering helpful suggestions for revision in the course of preparing his translation.

1. Jacques Chailley, "Berlioz, *Roméo et Juliette*: Scène d'amour," in *Florilège d'analyses musicales*, vol. 2 (Paris: Leduc, 1984), p. 46. The article originally appeared in the *Revue de musicologie*, 63 (1975), pp. 115–122.

2. Ian Kemp, "*Romeo and Juliet* and *Roméo et Juliette*," in *Berlioz Studies*, ed. Peter Bloom (Cambridge: Cambridge University Press, 1992), pp. 37–79. The table appears on pp. 65–67.

3. Chailley, "Berlioz, *Roméo et Juliette*," p. 50. The polemical tone of this citation is due to Chailley's outspoken opposition, at the time, to the partisans of serial and post-serial music who advocated a total independence of music from text and a highly formalist musical aesthetics.

4. Kemp, "*Romeo and Juliet*," p. 68.

5. Julian Rushton, *Berlioz: Roméo et Juliette* (Cambridge: Cambridge University Press, 1994), pp. 35–42.

6. See Rudolph Reti, *The Thematic Process in Music* (London: Faber & Faber, 1961), esp. pp. 286–294.

7. Vera Micznik, "Of Ways of Telling, Intertextuality, and Historical Evidence in Berlioz's *Roméo et Juliette*," *19th-Century Music*, 24 (Summer 2000), pp. 21–61.

8. Wilhelm von Lenz, *Beethoven: Eine Kunst-Studie* (Hamburg, 1855–1860); cited in Micznik, "Of Ways of Telling," p. 54, note 69.

9. On might wish totally to deny any possibility that Berlioz's symphony might have been consciously imitative of Beethoven's quartet and still find similarities between them, as both could be based on the same Shakespearean model.

10. See Berlioz's biography of Beethoven in *Le Correspondant* of 4 and 11 August and 8 October 1829 (*CM* 1, pp. 47–61); and the first edition of Fétis's *Biographie universelle des musiciens* (Paris: Fournier, 1835), vol. 2, pp. 100–112.

11. The main theme of the *Scène aux champs* in example 8.4b would seem to derive from the *Gratias* of Berlioz's *Messe solennelle* of 1824–1827 (see *NBE* 23, p. x), although the chronology of this self-borrowing is complex. The *Gratias* as we have it does not exhibit the variation by heterophony that we speak of here. In his famous analysis of the *Fantastique*, Robert Schumann, speaking of this variation of the main theme of the *Scène aux champs*, writes: "Beethoven could hardly have given it more careful treatment." See Schumann's analysis in Berlioz, *Fantastic Symphony*, ed. Edward T. Cone (New York: Norton, 1971), p. 239.

12. On the relationship between these two works (and these two composers), see Mark Evan Bonds, *After Beethoven* (Cambridge, MA: Harvard University Press, 1996), pp. 28–72.

13. *À travers chants*, p. 74. The last sentence is not found in the original article (cf. *CM* 3, p. 406). [I have slightly modified the translation that appears in *The Art of Music and Other Essays* (*À travers chants*), trans. and ed. Elizabeth Csicsery-Rónay (Bloomington: Indiana University Press, 1994), pp. 33–34. —*Ed.*]

14. See for example the remarkable analysis of the Adagio by Heinrich Schenker, *Beethovens Neunte Sinfonie, eine Darstellung des musikalischen Inhalts unter fortlaufender Berücksichtigung auch des Vertrages und Literatur* (Vienna: Universal Edition, 1912), pp. 375ff.

15. Ibid., p. 194.

16. See, for example, Basil Deane, "The Symphonies and Overtures," in *The Beethoven Companion*, ed. Denis Arnold and Nigel Fortune (London: Faber & Faber, 1986), pp. 281–317, here, pp. 309–310. Sir George Grove's analysis resembles Berlioz's in considering the Adagio "absolutely original in form." See Grove, *Beethoven and His Nine Symphonies* (1898; New York: Dover, 1962), pp. 362–370.

17. See also the formal analysis proposed by Donald Francis Tovey (identical to that of Schenker), who likewise notes the origins of the form in the works of Haydn, in Tovey, *Essays in Musical Analysis* (London: Oxford University Press, 1935), vol. 1, pp. 74–77; vol. 2, pp. 28–35. It is Tovey who uses the expression "alternative theme" for what Schenker calls a "Zwischenthema."

18. In order to further the comparison, I have also compared the background layers of the two movements as revealed by Schenkerian analysis. The results are no more revealing than those suggested in table 8.2.

19. Note that in this movement there are no other fifth-descents.

20. See Charles Rosen, *The Romantic Generation* (Cambridge, MA: Harvard University Press, 1995), pp. 556–568.

21. Michel Imberty, "Psychanalyse de la création musicale ou psychanalyse de l'œuvre musicale? Essai sur la répétition," in *Analyse et création musicales* (Paris: L'Harmattan, 2001), pp. 33–55.

22. Act II, scene ii, lines 116–129. A moment later Romeo declaims, "O blessed, blessed night! I am afeard, / Being in night, all this is but a dream, / Too flattering-sweet to be substantial" (lines 139–141).

23. Unable to describe this section in classical terms of "organic development," Julian Rushton, borrowing a phrase from Herbert Eimert, jokes that what applies here is "inorganic vegetable inexactness." See Rushton, *Berlioz: Roméo et Juliette*, pp. 40 and 107, note 10.

24. I have developed this idea in "Forme narrative et principes du développement musical dans la *Symphonie fantastique* de Berlioz," *Musurgia*, II/1 (1995), pp. 26–50; in "La 'Technique de la cigale': La construction périodique et motivique des thèmes de Berlioz," *Musurgia*, IV/2 (1997), pp. 59–76; in "Les Ouvertures de Berlioz et la dramatisation du style symphonique," *Les Cahiers de l'Herne*, 77 [numéro Berlioz] (2003), pp. 96–104; and in "Forme symphonique," in the *Dictionnaire Berlioz*, ed. Pierre Citron, Cécile Reynaud, Jean-Pierre Bartoli, and Peter Bloom (Paris: Fayard, 2003), pp. 199–201.

Part Five

In Foreign Lands

Chapter Nine

Germany at First

PEPIJN VAN DOESBURG

"Germany at Last"
      —David Cairns, *Berlioz: Servitude and Greatness*, chapter 11

Berlioz's long-anticipated first major trip to Germany—he left Paris on 12 December 1842 and traveled by way of Belgium—did not begin auspiciously. After fruitless attempts in Brussels, Mainz, and Frankfurt, he finally succeeded in giving concerts in Stuttgart on 29 December 1842, and in Hechingen on 2 January 1843. When he returned to Stuttgart on 3 January, he received a much-awaited letter from his friend Johann Christian Lobe inviting him to come to Weimar.[1] Abandoning or postponing plans to visit Munich, Vienna, and Berlin, Berlioz replied to Lobe on the 6th: "I am leaving tomorrow, Saturday, the 7th, for Karlsruhe, where I hope to give a concert while passing through [on my way to Weimar, via Frankfurt]."[2] The next day he set out for Karlsruhe—eighty kilometers from Stuttgart—with his traveling companion, Marie Récio. Presenting some specific dates and other little-known details concerning the beginning of Berlioz's Weimar-bound odyssey—which consisted of one day in Karlsruhe and five days in Mannheim—is the primary purpose of this brief study.

To Mannheim

Karlsruhe, with its approximately twenty-three thousand inhabitants, was the capital of the Grand Duchy of Baden, and boasted an excellent orchestra of eight first and eight second violins, four violas, three cellos, and four basses, all under the direction of Kapellmeister Joseph Strauss.[3] Strauss informed Berlioz that he would not be able to give a concert in Karlsruhe for another eight to ten days because of the prior engagement of "un flûtiste piémontais," as Berlioz has it in chapter [LI-3] of the *Mémoires* and as most subsequent biographers have repeated.

    We learn more from the Karlsruhe correspondent of the *Mannheimer Journal*, who expresses his regret that Berlioz, "who in France is considered the equal of Beethoven," would be unable to give a concert because the stage was at the moment occupied by the Italian flute virtuoso Giulio Briccialdi, "the Paganini of the flute,"[4] and would soon be occupied by the Italian violin virtuoso Antonio Bazzini, whose performance had already been announced for the 14th. Berlioz, "plein de respect pour la grande flûte"—"full of wholesome respect for the great man and his flute," as David Cairns renders Berlioz's play on words—but unwilling to wait, decided then to try his luck in Mannheim. Necessarily making the sixty-five kilometer trip by horse-drawn coach, Berlioz and Marie arrived in Mannheim on Monday, 9 January 1843, at noon: the date is confirmed by the listing in the *Mannheimer Journal* of the 11th of all arrivals in the city on the 9th.

Mannheim in 1843 was a provincial town of the same size as Karlsruhe; it had belonged to the Grand Duchy of Baden since 1803. Then (as now) it was largely known as a commercial and industrial city, although it had of course been an important center of musical activity when the elector Carl Theodore resided there (1742–1778), and when the musical establishment attracted the attention and admiration of, among others, a certain Wolfgang Amadeus Mozart. The spirit of efficiency that prevailed in the city was reflected in the sensible chessboard layout that offered not street names but numbered city blocks: in July 1843 the Dutch music journalist Cornelis Kist found Mannheim to be "spacious, regularly built, prosperous, but not very cheerful";[5] six months earlier, Berlioz, as he later reported in chapter [LI-3] of the *Mémoires*, called it "very placid, very cold, very flat, very rectilinear," and doubted that its inhabitants were kept awake by their passion for music!

Berlioz and Marie took lodgings, we discover, in block D 1, number 5, at the Pfälzer Hof, where Mozart had lived in 1777. This was the most renowned hotel in the city at the time, although it now had competition from the newly built Europäischer Hof located near the banks of the Rhine. On the same day the Frankfurt Kapellmeister Karl Guhr, whom Berlioz had met in Frankfurt in October and again in December 1842,[6] also checked in at the Pfälzer Hof, while the famous soprano Sabine Heinefetter, due to perform in Mannheim on the 11th, arrived at the nearby Russischer Hof, in block O 3. Berlioz had dinner with Guhr that very evening, and they discussed arrangements for a concert in Frankfurt. Guhr's assurances of helping Berlioz to produce his works there had several times come to naught; this time his offer included the promise of no fewer than twenty-four violins. But the concert would have to take place after Berlioz's visit to Weimar, because Guhr was now going to be occupied in Frankfurt with producing a series of appearances for Sabine Heinefetter. Indeed, Guhr seems to have come to Mannheim not to meet with Berlioz, but, rather, specifically to engage Madame Heinefetter.[7]

On his first day in Mannheim, Berlioz would also have met Kapellmeister Vinzenz Lachner, the conductor and composer who in 1836 had succeeded his more famous brother Franz Lachner and who would stay in that post until 1872. During these years, opera performances in Mannheim were highly regarded, and the Mannheim Court Theater was said to have the most extensive repertory of all the theaters in Germany. In addition to conducting operas, Lachner gave four annual concerts or *musikalische Akademie* with the theater orchestra, some-times joined by a chorus. Later in his career Lachner became a somewhat closed-minded conductor, objecting to the mature works of Wagner, for example, but in his earlier years he seems to have been more adventurous. Lachner, "a gentle and unassuming artist endowed with both modesty and talent," Berlioz tells us, was perfectly willing to help his French visitor organize a concert, and they immediately scheduled one for the following Friday, 13 January, at the Court Theater. According to the printed program of the concert, the orchestra was going to be "positioned on the stage," which means that the concert took place in the theater hall itself, and not in the Redoutensaal in the same building, where the orchestra's *musikalische Akademie* were regularly held.

The building, situated in block B 3, was a warehouse that had been converted into a theater in 1775–1777 by the Italian architect Lorenzo Quaglio. It was here that, thanks to the legendary theater manager Wolfgang Heribert von Dalberg, the famous première of Schiller's tragedy *Die Räuber* took place in 1782. Mozart con-ducted *The Marriage of Figaro* at the Court Theater in 1790, and in 1810 Weber tried to obtain the post of Kapellmeister. Traveling virtuosi who had performed here include Paganini, in 1829, and Liszt, in 1840. According to Kist, the theater hall was large, and featured four levels of projecting, angularly shaped galleries. For Berlioz, however, the hall was only "the size of a hat," and the orchestra simply "embryonic."[8]

The next day, Tuesday, 10 January, anxious for news from Weimar, Berlioz wrote impatiently to Lobe, complaining that in rainy Mannheim he was "horribly bored" and "dreadfully sad."[9] From this we may presumably conclude that rehearsals for his concert had not yet begun. More generally—because the tone of this letter is unusually negative—one wonders if Berlioz was on the verge of losing faith in the whole undertaking and asking himself what he was doing in Germany at all. (On the same day, Berlioz wrote to Johann Joseph Schott, the sleepy "patriarch of music publishers" of chapter [LI-3] of the *Mémoires*, proposing to sell him the German rights of the *Traité d'instrumentation* for two thousand francs.)[10]

Berlioz kept a kind of musical diary during his German tour in which he noted fragments from works that were closely related to the cities he visited.[11] On the second day of his visit to Mannheim he set down a long fragment (the oboe solo, bars 151–197) from the overture *Le Roi Lear*. Does this reflect his melancholic mood? Or does it simply indicate that the concert program had now been drawn up? The draft of the program in Berlioz's hand, preserved in reproduction (see fig. 9.1),[12] lists the following works:

Berlioz	*Ouverture des Francs-Juges*
Berlioz	*Le Jeune Pâtre breton*, Romance avec orchestre (Marie Récio)
Francesco Masini	Romance (Marie Récio)
Berlioz	*Harold en Italie*
Meyerbeer	Air de *Robert le diable* (Marie Récio)[13]
Berlioz	*Ouverture du Roi Lear*

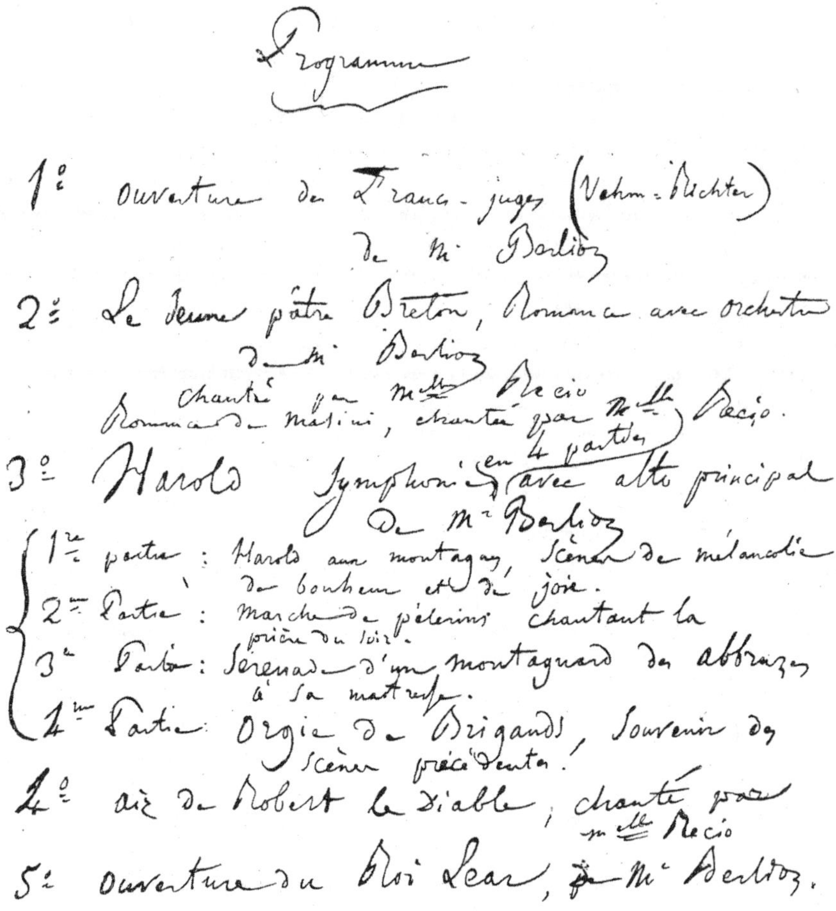

Figure 9.1. Berlioz's draft of the program for his concert in Mannheim on 13 January 1843. From a reproduction in the *Mannheimer Geschichtsblätter* of 1903. Present location unknown.

On the evening of the 10th, Berlioz attended the 6 p.m. vocal rehearsal of *The Creation*, conducted by Lachner, probably at the Court Theater.[14] Haydn's work would figure in Mannheim's regular series of *musikalische Akademie* on 14 February, with the forces of the theater chorus augmented by the amateur singers from the Musikverein. That group, directed by Simon Anton Zimmermann, consisted of a chorus of fifty-five and an orchestra of thirty-five; they rehearsed and gave concerts in the hall (Aula) of the former Jesuit school in block A 4, near the theater. For Berlioz, the singers "had reasonably good voices but were by no means all good musicians or sight-readers."

The next evening, Wednesday, 11 January, Berlioz attended the 6 p.m. performance of Bellini's *Norma* at the Court Theater, with Sabine Heinefetter making a single guest appearance in the title role.[15] Berlioz says he had last heard her at the Théâtre-Italien, in Paris, where she was occasionally employed after 1829. Of her performance in Mannheim he wrote: "Her voice is still powerful and fairly agile, but she is a little inclined to force it, and her high notes are now often difficult to bear. For all that, Mademoiselle Heinefetter has few rivals among German sopranos: she is a real singer." His opinion is reflected in a review of the same evening in the *Rheinische Blätter*, which reports a declining vocal quality, a tendency to sing sharp, a harsh sound in the upper register, but an excellent middle voice, a sound and tasteful performance, and unrivalled acting.[16] Others in the cast included the soprano Maria Lehmann-Rauch as Adalgisa, the tenor Heinrich Kreuzer as Pollione, and the bass Karl Ditt as Oroveso. Directly after her Mannheim engagement, Sabine Heinefetter would indeed make a series of highly successful guest appearances in Frankfurt, as we have noted, where she opened in *Norma* on 16 January 1843.[17]

By 12 January at the latest, Berlioz must have begun rehearsing his own concert, scheduled for the next day. (The number of rehearsals was unpredictable. In Stuttgart Berlioz would have two; in Hechingen, five.) The Mannheim orchestra seems to have had no previous experience with Berlioz's music; none of his works had been performed in the series of *musikalische Akademie*. A few months earlier, on 21 September 1842, Vinzenz Lachner and the orchestra of the Court Theater had been engaged to perform at a music festival in Mainz, where the program was to contain the *Francs-Juges* Overture, but in the event no work by Berlioz was performed.[18]

During the first rehearsal it became clear that the trombone players were not up to the fourth movement of *Harold en Italie*. Much to the disappointment of Lachner, the movement had to be cancelled (and duly excised from the printed program). Furthermore, the strings, led by Musikdirektor Joseph Leppen, were not strong in number (six or seven firsts, six seconds, four violas, four cellos, four basses),[19] and Lachner, having no ophicleide, replaced this instrument with a low valve trombone made, Berlioz tells us, specifically for the occasion. "It would have been simpler," he remarks, "to have had an ophicleide brought over; musically speaking this would have been much better, since the two instruments are hardly alike." The theater orchestra did employ players of other instruments then rare, including a "rather good" harpist and "an excellent oboist who was however rather mediocre when he played the English horn." In general, Berlioz thought the orchestra "very intelligent," praising the trumpet players, the cellist Jakob Heinefetter (the singer's cousin), and the modest violist who took the solo part in *Harold*.[20]

Ten months after Berlioz's visit, in November 1843, Vinzenz Lachner himself drew up a report on the court orchestra, in which he finds Leppen outstanding, the strings generally good, the winds rather poor, and the ensemble acceptable because, essentially, of his own efficient efforts.[21] Like Berlioz, Lachner, too, praises the cellist Heinefetter ("who sings so well on the cello that singers can learn from him") and criticizes the trombones: the alto trombone (Anton Mohr) is weak; there is no tenor trombone; and the bass trombone (Joseph Seitz) is feeble and often ill.[22] Carl Oberthür, usually a violist in Mannheim, played the harp: Lachner tells us he was more skilled on the latter instrument.[23] Berlioz calls the trumpets "intrepid," while Lachner's view of them (Carl Weiss and Michael Lippert) is mixed. And the man whom Berlioz speaks of as "un hautbois excellent," Eduard Frech, plays out of tune, in Lachner's estimation, and has a faulty technique.

Which member of the orchestra took the solo part in *Harold en Italie?* With Oberthür playing the harp, the candidates remaining would be Anton Schmidt, an "experienced musician," in Lachner's view, but not an extraordinary one; Heinrich Eckart, a better luthier than performer; and Blasius Janson, who plays the viola only because he has too few teeth to play second oboe. Perhaps the soloist was thus Gottfried Neher, "after Leppen the most intelligent player of the violin section," for Neher was also an excellent violist.[24]

Berlioz's concert on 13 January, which was not included in the regular subscription series, was briefly announced in Mannheim's three newspapers: the *Mannheimer Abendzeitung,* the *Mannheimer Journal,* and the *Mannheimer Morgenblatt.* The first two papers also published more specific advertisements for Berlioz's concert, on 11 and 12 January, stressing the "romantic, adventurous, and enormously grotesque" character of his compositions, which could be correctly rendered only by the master himself, and the honor bestowed upon the Mannheim orchestra, which was privileged to perform such difficult works. Playbills announcing the program were printed and put up around the town.[25] As was the custom in Mannheim at the time, the concert was preceded by a theatrical *hors d'œuvre*, in this case a German translation of the three-act comedy *Le Jeune Mari* (1826) by the French playwright Édouard Mazères.

Despite all these efforts, despite having to pay only the usual entrance fees, the public did not turn out in great numbers. Mannheim's city chronicler, Friedrich Walter, was able to calculate from the theater's box office reports that out of forty-four boxes only six, with a total of thirty-three seats, were sold, and that all in all some three hundred people may have attended the 6 p.m. performance. Berlioz received three-eighths of the gross receipts, which, after deduction of the pension fund tax, amounted to 63 guilders and 48 kreuzer.[26] This amount, roughly equal to 135 French francs, was more than Berlioz was paid for an article in the *Journal des débats* (100 francs) and more than he was paid as Bibliothécaire du Conservatoire (118 francs per month), but less than he typically earned from giving a concert in Paris.[27]

Among those present at the concert in Mannheim was the Grand Duchess Stéphanie (and not Amélie, as Berlioz originally wrote in the *Mémoires*). Stéphanie de Beauharnais had been married by order of Napoleon to the hereditary prince Karl of Baden, who resided in Karlsruhe, in order to bring Baden under his imperial sphere of influence. After Karl's death in 1818, Stéphanie went to live in the deserted Mannheim palace and kept a small court there, which became a modest center of cultural life. The day before Berlioz's arrival in Mannheim, for example, she visited, together with her guest the Grand Duchess Sophie,[28] the studio of court painter Jakob Götzenberger, a pupil of the Nazarene painter Peter von Cornelius, and she attended a performance of *The Magic Flute* at the Court Theater. After his concert on the 13th, Berlioz was told that Stéphanie had particularly liked the evocative colors of the two inner movements of *Harold en Italie* and that the *Sérénade d'un montagnard des Abruzzes* had reminded her of "the beauty and serenity of the Italian night."

In the *Mémoires* Berlioz writes that the three movements of the symphony were well executed and produced a "lively impression" on the audience; in a notice to the Paris papers he or one of his emissaries wrote: "Monsieur Berlioz continues his successful tour in Germany. In Mannheim his symphonies and his overture to *Les Francs-Juges* created a furor."[29] We have little evidence to confirm this perception: Stéphanie's approval of the inner movements of *Harold* could imply disapproval of the rest;[30] and had Lachner been enthusiastic, Berlioz would surely have said as much. The chorus master, Stephan Grua, in his repertory of performances at the Court Theater, does leave us a comment on Berlioz's concert: "The Parisians are said to call him their Beethoven, but only a lunatic could make such a comparison, because the music of Berliotz [*sic*], while highly original, is also highly deranged ['verrückt']."[31] But the strictly musical magazines in Germany paid no attention to the event. Nor did reviews appear in the *Mannheimer Journal*, the *Mannheimer Abendzeitung*, or the *Mannheimer Morgenblatt*. It is possible that the concert was reviewed in the *Belletristische Beilage*, a supplement to the *Journal*, but I have been unable to locate issues from 1843.

However, the *Rheinische Blätter*, a supplement to the *Mannheimer Abendzeitung*, did publish an anonymous critique that appeared on 17 January 1843. This was preceded by a short review of the evening (the play and the concert) in which the author admits he was left as cold by Berlioz's music, "which fails to move one's innermost feelings," as he was by "the singing of the weak, thin, uncertain voice of Monsieur Berlioz's companion."[32] A few days after the concert, Berlioz himself complained about Marie's singing to his friend Auguste Morel, in Paris: "Pity me, my dear Morel; Marie wanted to sing in Mannheim, in Stuttgart, and in Hechingen. The first two times, it was bearable, but the last! . . . and yet she couldn't stand the idea that I might employ another singer [. . . .]."[33] It would seem that Marie's presence during the concert tour had become agonizing to him. Unfortunately we have only a tiny fragment of Berlioz's letter to Morel, and no autograph. The full letter might help us to better understand the comment about Marie as well as the context of his stay in Mannheim.

The second, elaborate critique in the *Rheinische Blätter* itself is written in the form of a satirical essay that reveals not only the author's vivid imagination but also his somewhat capricious preconceptions about Beethoven and Bach. The listener, under the influence of Berlioz's music, is overwhelmed by fantastical visions. He imagines himself on a ship wrecked by a storm and eventually engulfed by the sea. He then pictures himself on an island, surrounded by frightening cannibals whose intentions towards him are unclear. Finally he finds himself driven literally mad by Berlioz's music. The listener then goes on to cite the opinion of a "friend," who declares that at first he laughed at the music, that he then became bored and finally irritated by it, wondering if the composer's aim was to perpetrate a hoax upon the world or if the composer himself was simply a fool. He finds that *even* a symphony by Beethoven seems heavenly compared to Berlioz's incessant muddle of sound, just as a violin duet by Pleyel seems divine compared to a fugue by the barbaric J. S. Bach. He literally hears the madness of Lear in the madness of Berlioz's music, and finds that only the *Marche de pèlerins* of *Harold en Italie* is comprehensible, original, and not tortuous to the ear. What could have driven Berlioz to write like this? The only intention he could have had was entirely to avoid writing eight measures the way someone else might have written them.

When Kist visited Mannheim, he was hosted by the music publisher Karl Ferdinand Heckel, the one prominent musical personality not mentioned in Berlioz's account. Berlioz himself was welcomed by the former cavalry officer Désiré Le Mire, whom he had known in Paris in the mid-eighteen-thirties.[34] But despite Le Mire's efforts, Berlioz did not enjoy his stay in Mannheim. The atmosphere of the industrial city simply did not appeal to him. "The fact is," he wrote in the *Mémoires*, "that one need only look at the inhabitants, or indeed at the town itself, to see that all real artistic interest is foreign to them and that music is regarded only as an agreeable pastime to which one is happy to resort in the moments of leisure left by business." The city's commercial symbol par excellence, the eighteenth-century Kaufhaus building, was located in the Paradeplatz, the same central square in which the Pfälzer Hof was situated. The impressive tower of the Kaufhaus was doubly vexatious to Berlioz: its bell sounded a sad minor third, and its inhabitants included "un méchant épervier"—an "evil sparrow hawk" or kestrel, whose discordant cries drove the composer mad. Finally—Berlioz insists on the point—the weather was miserable. In France a storm caused severe flooding and damaged one of the great stained-glass windows of the cathedral at Chartres, and in Mannheim, between 10 and 15 January, there were nearly two and a half inches of rain.

From Mannheim

We see, from this glance at Berlioz in Mannheim, that the composer was as yet not popular in Germany and not able to draw a crowd to the theater; in some quarters, he was seen as a grotesque and abnormal composer who was not to be taken seriously. Nor would the Mannheim concert have advanced Berlioz's quest for recognition abroad. One gets the impression, from the various documents examined here, of an experience that gave Berlioz practice in organizing a concert in a foreign city but that was otherwise disappointing. On 14 January Berlioz and Marie left Mannheim on the twelve-noon departure of the Rhine steamer and headed towards Frankfurt, the next stop on their eventual journey to Weimar, "the city of poets," which Berlioz was anxious to see.[35]

Shortly after Berlioz left the unpoetical city of Mannheim, Briccialdi, the "grande flûte" whose presence had prevented the French composer from giving a concert in Karlsruhe, gave a first concert in Mannheim, on 21 January, in the Aula hall. Unable to secure the cooperation of the court orchestra, however, he had to cancel a second concert, announced for 31 January. The next day, 1 February 1843, the ten- and fifteen-year old Milanollo sisters, the phenomenal violinists who had stood in Berlioz's way in Frankfurt the previous December, made their debut in Mannheim: they were so successful that they were able to give five concerts in a row.

Notes

1. *CG* III, p. 37. Johann Christian Lobe (1797–1881), composer, conductor, critic, had been a friend of Goethe's in Weimar and would befriend Liszt as well. He became one of Berlioz's earliest and staunchest admirers in Germany.

2. *CG* VIII, p. 212.

3. The figures are given in Florentius Cornelis Kist, "Reize door Duitschland in het jaar 1843: Een onpartijdig onderzoek naar den toestand der Muzijk aldaar," *Cæcilia* (15 August 1846), p. 165. Kist visited Karlsruhe in July 1843. Joseph Strauss (1793–1866) was Kapellmeister there from 1824 to 1863.

4. *Mannheimer Journal* (11 January 1843; the notice is dated 8 January). Briccialdi (1818–1881), not from Piedmont but from Umbria, is best known for his technical improvements to the flute, in particular his promotion of Böhm's B-flat thumb key. From the *Karlsruher Zeitung* (6 and 8 January 1843) and the *Karlsruher Tagblatt* (8 January 1843) we know that he was to give concerts on the 7th and 9th, but that only the one on the 9th took place. The reference to chapter [LI-3] of the *Mémoires* is to the third letter of that book's *Premier Voyage en Allemagne*.

5. See Kist, "Reize door Duitschland," *Cæcilia* (1 June 1846), p. 122.

6. *CG* VIII, p. 207, where Berlioz, with Guhr in Frankfurt on 19 December 1842, refers to his earlier "first" trip, which must mean that of mid-October. The portrait of Guhr (1787–1848) in the *Mémoires* is exceptionally humorous.

7. *CG* III, p. 54. It is likely that Guhr did not stay in Mannheim to hear Berlioz's concert. In the *Mémoires* Berlioz writes that he met Guhr again *after* leaving Mannheim.

8. *CG* III, p. 54. [The slightly vulgar expression Berlioz uses here, "un petit avorton d'orchestra," was changed in the *Mémoires* to "un petit orchestre très intelligent." — *Ed.*] Berlioz visited the theater on his first day in Mannheim, when Lachner presumably introduced him to the orchestra. Some ten years after Berlioz's visit, the theater was

rebuilt and enlarged by the architect and stage designer Joseph Mühldorfer (1800–1863).

9. *CG* III, p. 54. Here Berlioz writes "Je m'ennuie horriblement"; in the *Mémoires* he writes "Je me suis beaucoup ennuyé à Mannheim"; in the original version of this letter from Germany, in the *Journal des débats* of 28 August 1843, he wrote, "Je me suis splendidement ennuyé à Mannheim," that configuration having slightly less depressing overtones. That it was raining heavily is true: on the day before Berlioz's arrival in Mannheim, 8 January, one inch of rain fell in Karlsruhe, as per the statistics in the *Karlsruher Zeitung.*

10. This letter, unpublished, is preserved in the collections of the Herzog August Bibliothek, in Wolffenbüttel.

11. *Souvenirs—Bêtises—Improvisations* (*NBE* 25, pp. 251–252). The album is reproduced in *Hector Berlioz in Deutschland: Texte und Dokumente zur deutschen Berlioz-Rezeption (1829–1843),* ed. Gunther Braam and Arnold Jacobshagen (Göttingen: Hainholz, 2002), pp. 580–603 (henceforth Braam/Jacobshagen).

12. A reproduction of the draft appears in Friedrich Walter, "Berlioz' Besuch in Mannheim," in *Mannheimer Geschichtsblätter,* IV (1903), cols. 270–273. Its present location is unknown. Ms. Liselotte Homering of the Reiß-Engelhorn-Museen in Mannheim kindly informs me that it may well have been destroyed during World War II. Next to "Francs-Juges" Berlioz has set down the German word "Vehm-Richter." The draft suggests that the Masini was a last-minute addition.

13. Presumably the same aria that Marie performed in Brussels on 9 October and in Stuttgart on 29 December: Alice's Act III *couplets* "Quand je quittai la Normandie."

14. *Mannheimer Journal* (10 January 1843). The subsequent rehearsals, one vocal, one orchestral, took place on 14 and 15 January, by which time Berlioz, who notes in chapter [LI-3] of the *Mémoires* that he had been able to attend only one rehearsal of the "Académie de chant," had probably left Mannheim.

15. *Mannheimer Journal* (11 January 1843); theater playbill preserved in the Reiß-Engelhorn-Museen.

16. *Rheinische Blätter* (14 January 1843), pp. 46–47.

17. *Mannheimer Journal* (19 January 1843). This corrects all earlier accounts, including those in D. Kern Holoman, *Berlioz* (Cambridge, MA: Harvard University Press, 1989), p. 293; and in Braam/Jacobshagen, p. 611, which suggest that on 16 January Berlioz attended a performance of *Fidelio* in Frankfurt. In fact Berlioz must have seen *Fidelio* when he was in Frankfurt on 16 October 1842: the Fidelio was Elisa Capitain; the Pizarro was Johann Baptist Pischek; the Florestan (whose name Berlioz could not remember in chapter [LI-1] of the *Mémoires*) was Friedrich Caspari.

18. *Les Francs-Juges* was included in the notice dated 5 September in the *Revue et Gazette musicale* (18 September 1842).

19. See Kist, "Reize door Duitschland" (1 June 1846), p. 122. Kist praises the orchestra, which he heard in *Don Giovanni.*

20. In the *Biographie universelle des musiciens* Fétis identifies Heinfetter as the singer's brother, but it is Berlioz who is correct.

21. The autograph manuscript of this document is preserved in the Reiß-Engelhorn-Museen.

22. It was presumably the missing tenor trombone (and not the lack of an ophicleide) that caused Lachner to have a valve trombone made for the occasion. This instrument was "probably pitched in F like a bass trombone." See *Berlioz's Orchestration Treatise: A Translation and Commentary* [by] Hugh Macdonald

(Cambridge: Cambridge University Press, 2002), p. 229. In the *Traité d'instrumentation* Berlioz notes that the ophicleide can replace the tenor trombone (see *NBE* 24, p. 302). The first movement of *Harold en Italie* calls for three trombones (of flexible designation; see *NBE* 17, p. x); the ophicleide figures only in the finale, which was not given in Mannheim.

23. Following a dispute with Lachner, Oberthür left Mannheim, eventually settling in London as a harpist and teacher.

24. Neher was the violist in a string quartet, with Leppen, Hugo Hildebrand, and Heinefetter, and he was director of the Musikverein chorus before Zimmermann took over in 1840.

25. A copy is preserved in the Reiß-Engelhorn-Museen.

26. See Walter, "Berlioz' Besuch in Mannheim." The box office records have since disappeared.

27. See Peter Bloom, "Episodes in the Livelihood of an Artist: Berlioz's Contacts and Contracts with Publishers," *Journal of Musicological Research*, 15 (1995), pp. 219–273.

28. Sophie (1801–1865) was the wife of Leopold of Baden, Grand Duke from 1830 to 1852.

29. See *La Sylphide*, 6 (ca. 4 February 1843), p. 164. Such *bulletins de la grande armée*, as Berlioz called them (*CG* III, p. 85), authored or prompted by the composer, would appear regularly during Berlioz's trips abroad.

30. In his letter to d'Ortigue of 28 February 1843, Berlioz notes again that in Mannheim the two middle movements of *Harold* "ont eu les honneurs" (*CG* III, p. 74).

31. The repertory is preserved in the Reiß-Engelhorn-Museen.

32. *Rheinische Blätter* (17 January 1843), pp. 54–55. These critiques, mentioned by Walter in the *Mannheimer Geschichtsblätter*, V (1904), col. 20, are not cited in Braam/Jacobshagen. The editor of the *Rheinische Blätter*, and thus perhaps the author of the first notice, was Friedrich Moritz Hähner.

33. *CG* III, p. 55. Marie would sing in all but one of Berlioz's remaining concerts in Germany.

34. Désiré Le Mire (or Lemire, mentioned in chapter [LI-3]), chevalier de la Légion d'Honneur, was born in Rouen in 1796 or 1797, and lived in Mannheim, next to the theater, from 1839 to 1844.

35. There is no proof for the assertion, repeated in the literature since Boschot and Walter, that Berlioz and Marie left Mannheim on 14 January, other than the fact that Berlioz seems to have attended the performance of Spohr's *Faust* in Frankfurt, which was given on the 15th, at 6 p.m.: it is here that he came particularly to appreciate the talents of the Bohemian baritone Johann Baptist Pischek, as he reports in chapter [LI-3] of the *Mémoires* (although he had apparently heard him earlier; see note 17). By my calculations, Berlioz could have arrived in Frankfurt by 6 p.m. on either the 14th or the 15th, but the hour makes the latter date highly unlikely.

Chapter Ten

England and Berlioz

LORD ABERDARE (ALASTAIR BRUCE)

London is a roost for every bird.
—Benjamin Disraeli, *Lothair*

England seems to have a special affinity with Berlioz. Many leading conductors of Berlioz have been English, from Sir Thomas Beecham to a trio of present-day conductor-knights, Sir Colin Davis, Sir Roger Norrington, and Sir John Eliot Gardiner. So have many scholars and critics, with the result that Berlioz's standing in England seems higher than in almost any other country. Performances of his works, and not just the best-known ones, have been frequent in England and complemented by an impressive range of publications and events.

Did this "special relationship" take shape during Berlioz's lifetime, in the period of his five visits to England in the eighteen-forties and eighteen-fifties? What was special about England for Berlioz? Extensive accounts of Berlioz's time in London have already been given, particularly by A. W. Ganz, in his *Berlioz in London* of 1950, and most recently by David Cairns in his magisterial biography of Berlioz.[1] What I seek to do here is to review what we know, to fill some small gaps, and to offer some thoughts on what Berlioz's time in England meant to him.

Berlioz in England

Berlioz spent a total of just over seventy-five weeks in London, as shown in table 10.1—longer than anywhere else except Paris and his childhood home at La Côte-Saint-André.

The First Visit

Berlioz's first visit, in 1847–1848, was easily the longest, accounting for almost half the total time he spent in London. He arrived initially on his own, having managed through "not just one but a succession of coups d'état" to prevent his mistress Marie Récio from accompanying him.[2] She joined him a month later on 6 December, but appears to have returned to Paris around Christmas time, before coming back to London on 24 April 1848. Berlioz's relationship with

Table 10.1. Berlioz's Visits to London

Visit	Arrival in London[a]	Departure from London	Duration	Principal purpose
1	Thursday 4 November 1847	Wednesday 12 July 1848	36 weeks	To conduct Jullien's English Grand Opera at the Theatre Royal, Drury Lane
2	Saturday 10 May 1851	Monday 28 July 1851	11 weeks 3 days	To judge musical instruments at the Great Exhibition
3	Thursday 4 March 1852	Sunday 20 June 1852	15 weeks 4 days	To conduct the first concert series of the New Philharmonic Society
4	Saturday 14 May 1853	Saturday 9 July 1853	8 weeks 1 day	To conduct *Benvenuto Cellini* at Covent Garden
5	Friday 8 June 1855	Saturday 7 July 1855	4 weeks 2 days	To conduct two New Philharmonic Society concerts

[a] Arrival dates for 1847, 1852, and 1855 are based on the assumption that Berlioz reached London one day after leaving Paris. From 1843, when the cross-channel steam packet service opened between Boulogne and Folkestone, it was possible to make the journey between Paris and London in fourteen hours (the Calais-Dover crossing took longer). This was reduced to twelve and a half hours in 1848, when the railway reached Boulogne, and to eleven hours by the time of the Great Exhibition in 1851.

Marie may have cooled following his infatuation with a young Russian chorister in St. Petersburg during the spring of 1847, but he seems to have missed her company when she was not with him.

Berlioz was brought to London by the flamboyant impresario Louis-Antoine Jullien to conduct his English Grand Opera company at the Theatre Royal, Drury Lane.[3] The season opened with Gaetano Donizetti's *The Bride of Lammermoor* on Monday, 6 December, the very day that Marie arrived from Paris: Berlioz had to take her straight to the theater in a cab after meeting her off the train. Throughout the rest of the season, up to the end of February 1848, Berlioz was largely immersed in rehearsing and conducting. In total, there were forty-nine performances of four operas, recorded in table 10.2, as well as a number of "juvenile nights" and other special events.

Berlioz had hoped to stage Gluck's *Iphigénie en Tauride*, the opera that more than any other had inspired him to become a composer. It was announced several times in January, but no performance materialized. The first five performances of Michael Balfe's *The Maid of Honour*, to the end of December, were conducted by Balfe himself, after which Berlioz took over. Until 22 December

Table 10.2. Operas Performed by the Grand Opera at Drury Lane

Opera	Performances	First night	Last night
The Bride of Lammermoor (Donizetti)	15	6 December 1847	14 February 1848
The Maid of Honour (Balfe)	22	20 December 1847	16 February 1848
Linda di Chamounix (Donizetti)	7	12 January 1848	3 February 1848
The Marriage of Figaro (Mozart)	5	11 February 1848	25 February 1848

performances took place on Monday, Wednesday, and Friday of each week. Then, from Monday, 27 December 1847, to Saturday, 5 February 1848, there were six performances a week, every day except Sunday. Berlioz did not conduct each and every performance; he missed several nights through illness, especially in January, when his place was taken by colleagues, among them the violinist Auguste-Joseph Tolbecque.[4] He was not disappointed to skip Donizetti's *Linda di Chamounix*: "I have the good fortune to be ill," he quipped to an acquaintance.[5] Even so, he conducted some forty opera performances over eighty-two days, not to mention almost daily rehearsals in the afternoons—a grueling schedule.[6]

On 7 February 1848 Berlioz conducted a concert of his own works. Four of his overtures had been played in London during 1840 and 1841,[7] but this was the first real opportunity for Londoners to hear his compositions. The overture *Le Carnaval romain* was played again two days later, as a curtain-raiser before the performance of *The Bride of Lammermoor*. By this time Jullien was on the verge of bankruptcy: his company muddled on to the end of its season on 25 February, but only by dint of not paying its principal artists. Jullien was formally declared bankrupt on 19 April 1848, putting an end to Berlioz's hopes of a long-term remunerative post in London.

He nonetheless stayed on, believing that the February revolution in France would make it even harder for him to earn a living in Paris. He was able to give a second London concert of his own works on 29 June, with the soloists donating their services to help him make ends meet—but without percussion, because of noise regulations at the Hanover Square Rooms. He began work on his *Mémoires*, completed the version for choir and orchestra of *La Mort d'Ophélie*, and may also have composed *La Menace des Francs*. An English translation of his short story *Euphonia* appeared in *The Mirror* during June and July 1848, in a version that curiously enough excludes a complimentary remark about music in England ("England with a heart and an arm of steel, is an artist-nation in comparison with modern Italy") from the original 1844 French text; it was again omitted from the republication of the tale, in 1852, in *Les Soirées de l'orchestre*.[8]

The English version must represent an intermediate stage: the name of the singer, originally "Ellimac" and lastly "Mina," is here "Camilla." Perhaps Berlioz in London wished to make clearer the allusion to his former fiancée, the pianist Madame Pleyel née Camille Moke.

The Second Visit

He made his second visit almost two years later, in 1851, having been appointed the French representative on the musical instruments judging panel for the Great Exhibition at the Crystal Palace in Hyde Park. He wrote a series of articles about this visit for the *Journal des débats*, and reused the first two of these in the twenty-first evening of *Les Soirées de l'orchestre*.[9] Fully occupied by the task of assessing some eighteen hundred musical instruments, Berlioz had no time for conducting or composing, although he did manage to attend some opera performances and concerts. Among these was the Charity Children's Concert at St. Paul's Cathedral on the morning of 5 June, which made an enormous impact on him and led him to add a chorus of six hundred children to his *Te Deum*.

During this visit, Berlioz was asked by the Commissioners of the Great Exhibition to submit a plan for a music festival in the Crystal Palace.[10] He therefore produced, by early June, a "Plan pour l'organisation du Festival de l'Exposition universelle de Londres": the document, which has not previously been published in full, is written in dark blue ink on two light blue folded sheets preserved in the collections of the Département de la Musique of the Bibliothèque nationale de France.[11]

Plan for the Organization of the Festival for the Universal Exhibition in London
Plan for the Organization of a Grand Festival in the Crystal Palace

This festival would be organized with the aim of crowning the success of the Great Exhibition in London by means of a demonstration of the art of music on a grand, almost ritualistic, scale. Its *execution* should be entrusted to English musicians and music-lovers; but to retain the cosmopolitan character that is such an attractive feature of every aspect of the showcase that the English nation is currently providing for the industrial products of the entire world, it would be generous as well as beneficial for artists from neighboring nations to be invited to take part.

Here is how one might proceed:

1) An auditorium with straight (*not curved*) tiers of seating would be constructed at the end of the East gallery, in the United States zone, with capacity for fifteen hundred performers.

2) Within these musical forces there should be at least a thousand chorus members and five hundred instrumentalists. The thousand chorus members would come from the various musical institutions in London, Liverpool, and Manchester. The two Sacred Harmonic Societies would provide five hundred singers for a start, Her Majesty's Theatre would supply eighty, Covent Garden eighty, Liverpool and Manchester two hundred. The total of one thousand would be achieved through an appeal to the enthusiasm of all music-lovers of known musical ability and to a number of artists from the continent.

3) The combined orchestras of the two main opera houses and of Jullien's concerts and [those of] Vauxhall [Gardens] would produce a total of two hundred fifty musicians or more. So it would be necessary to invite all the foreign virtuosos passing through London to take part and to seek deputations of players from Paris, Manchester, Brussels, Cologne, Frankfurt, and even Lille.

3) [*sic*] A great organ would be set up right at the top of the auditorium in the center of the choral and orchestral body.

4) An entire month would be devoted to the preparations and rehearsals for this gigantic concert, which should be repeated weekly each *Saturday at 11 a.m.* for at least a month.

5) The organizing director of the concert would be Monsieur Hector Berlioz, who in 1844 organized the Festival of Industry in Paris, at the end of the French exhibition, on his own and without any support from the government or any other institution.

6) Monsieur Berlioz would be given complete freedom to choose the members of the executive committee needed to help him in the realization of his plan.

7) For the initial rehearsals of the chorus in London he would need to have at his disposal the concert halls of the Princess's Theatre, Willis's Rooms, the Hanover Square Room, and three other venues for *four days*, and after that the Hanover Square Room for two half-days.

8) Since the chorus rehearsals would be extremely important in order to achieve the goal of properly learning a new and difficult work, they would be managed as follows: The *sopranos* would rehearse *on their own* four times at Willis's Rooms at 8 a.m.; the *contraltos on their own* in the Princess's Theatre Concert Room at 8 a.m.; the *first tenors on their own* at the Hanover Square Room at 8 a.m.; the *second tenors on their own* at another venue at 8 a.m.; the *first basses on their own* at another venue at 8 a.m.; the *second basses on their own* at another venue at 8 a.m.

When each of the six choral parts had been rehearsed in this way *four times* separately in various locations, all of the London chorus members would be brought together for the first time at Hanover Square.

The overseas chorus members would have had to undertake the same work in their own locations before coming to London, and would then finally be brought together with those from the capital for a general chorus rehearsal at Hanover Square, still at 8 a.m. so as not to encroach upon rehearsals at the opera houses.

9) The orchestra would need to have a rehearsal on its own initially, *at the Hanover Square Room*; then two general rehearsals with the chorus in the Exhibition palace.

10) The ticket price for each concert would need to be no less than half a guinea or *half a pound*. Admittance to the final general rehearsal would be available on payment of *two guineas*.

11) The estimated costs of the first concert would be *£3,700* (92,500 francs). Those for each of the other three concerts would be *£1,500* (37,500 francs)—only a guinea each for the fifteen hundred performers for each concert after the first. Total cost for all four concerts: *£8,200* (205,000 francs).

12) The *seating* area set aside for the public should hold *twenty thousand* people, downstairs and in the upper side galleries. So the receipts for each concert could amount to *£10,000* (250,000 francs), which would make a total of *£40,000* (or one million francs) if *four* such concerts were given. Even supposing that the receipts reached only half of this sum there would still be a profit of *397,500 francs*, without counting the takings from the general rehearsal.[12]

Details of anticipated expenses for the first concert:

One thousand chorus members at £2 each	£2,000
Five hundred musicians at £2 each	£1,000
Costs of music engraving and copying	£200
Construction of the auditorium, desks, sound reflectors, and instruments	£400
Travel and accommodation expenses for overseas musicians	£800
Press announcements, posters, tickets, etc.	£200
Administrative director of the Festival and composer of the *Tè Deum*	£800

 (This individual would expect a share of the profits in addition to this sum.)

Details of expenses for each of the other three concerts:

Fifteen hundred musicians at less than £1 each plus £100 guaranteed for the director	£1,500

The program would be made up as follows:

1) Grand *Tè Deum* for two choirs, with orchestra and organ obbligato, composed by Monsieur H. Berlioz and performed for the first time.

2) Excerpts from Gluck's *Armide* (choruses and dances).

3) An aria sung by Mario.

4) An orchestral excerpt (*La Fête chez Capulet*) from the Symphony *Roméo et Juliette* by Monsieur H. Berlioz, performed by the orchestra and *forty harps*.

5) An aria sung by Mademoiselle Cruvelli.

6) The *Prière* from Rossini's *Moïse* (the solos sung by eighty voices) accompanied by the orchestra and the forty harps.

7) The *Marche hongroise* by Monsieur Berlioz (orchestra alone).

8) Bortnianski's *Chant des chérubins* (unaccompanied chorus).

9) The Triumphal Chorus from Handel's *Judas Maccabaeus*.

The director would require *one month* to have the music engraved and copied and to make contact with the continental artists and put arrangements in place with those in London, *before the month devoted to rehearsals*. This would put the Festival itself in the month of August. He would also need some funds in advance for initial expenses.

This document demonstrates Berlioz's longstanding concern with the architecture of musical performance; his attention to detail; his insistence on having personal responsibility for all aspects of the enterprise; his understanding of the need for sectional rehearsals to accomplish grandiose musical ends; his desire to make a commercial success of the festival; and his hopes of mounting the first performance of the *Tè Deum* (hopes that would remain unfulfilled for four more years).

The French government somewhat precipitately terminated his appointment as a juror on 15 July, but Berlioz stayed on in London, for two weeks, to complete his duties. Back in Paris, having told his friend Duchêne de Vère that he had no intention of writing his official report because of "brutal" treatment by the Minister of Commerce, who refused to reimburse the expenses of his extended stay in London,[13] Berlioz finally did prepare such a document, in which he claimed that "France, today, occupies the highest rank in the art of instrumental manufacture in general," citing the preeminence of the French manufacturers Érard (pianos), Sax (brass and wind instruments), Vuillaume (strings), and Ducroquet (organs) in their respective fields.[14]

The Third Visit

His third visit, in 1852, was to conduct the six concerts of the first season of the New Philharmonic Society. (Details of all Berlioz's concerts in London are set out below, in table 10.3.) Through this series Berlioz established himself in London as one of the finest conductors of his time, not least in the works of Beethoven, which figured in all six concerts. The impact of the Ninth Symphony at the fourth concert was such that it was repeated at the last. Berlioz as conductor evidently succeeded in revealing the greatness of Beethoven's final symphony to an extent that Londoners had not experienced before. In contrast to the usual custom in London of having a minimum of rehearsals and relying on superior sight-reading skills, Berlioz insisted on several rehearsals—at least six for the Choral Symphony[15]—including sectional rehearsals, even for the percussion.[16]

Table 10.3. Concerts Conducted by Berlioz (in Whole or in Part) in London

No.	Date	Description and venue	Works performed
First Visit: November 1847 to July 1848			
—	Monday 6 December 1847 to Friday 25 February 1848	English Grand Opera season at Theatre Royal, Drury Lane	Forty-nine performances of four operas, most conducted by Berlioz. The overture *Le Carnaval romain* was also played at the tenor Sims Reeves's benefit night on 9 February before the fourteenth performance of *The Bride of Lammermoor*.
1	Monday 7 February 1848	Berlioz's first concert of his own works in London, at the Theatre Royal, Drury Lane	Overture *Le Carnaval romain*; *Le Jeune Pâtre breton*; *Harold en Italie*; *La Damnation de Faust* (first two parts); excerpts from *Benvenuto Cellini*, from the *Requiem*, and from the *Symphonie funèbre et triomphale*.
2	Friday 7 April 1848	Amateur Musical Society concert at Willis's Rooms	The *Marche hongroise* from *La Damnation de Faust*.
3	Friday 16 June 1848	The pianist Madame Dulcken's Covent Garden concert	The *Marche hongroise*.
4	Thursday 29 June 1848	Berlioz's second concert of his own works, at the Hanover Square Rooms; soloists give their services free	Overture *Le Carnaval romain*; *Le Chasseur danois*; *Harold en Italie* (first three movements); *Zaïde*; *La Damnation de Faust* (four excerpts); *La Captive*; *L'Invitation*

Table 10.3. (*continued*)

No.	Date	Description and venue	Works performed
			à la valse; Mendelssohn (Piano Concerto in D Minor, last two movements); etc.

Second Visit: May to July 1851
Berlioz gave no concerts during this "official" visit

Third Visit: March to June 1852

No.	Date	Description and venue	Works performed
5	Wednesday 24 March 1852	First New Philharmonic Society concert at Exeter Hall	Mozart (*Jupiter* Symphony); Gluck (excerpts from *Iphigénie en Tauride*); Beethoven (Triple Concerto); Weber (*Oberon* Overture); Berlioz (*Roméo et Juliette*, first four movements); Bottesini (*Fantasy* for double bass); Rossini (*William Tell* Overture).
6	Wednesday 14 April 1852	Second New Philharmonic Society concert at Exeter Hall[a]	Cherubini (*Anacréon* Overture); Bortnianski (*Chant des chérubins*); Beethoven (Fifth Symphony); Mozart (*Magic Flute* Overture); Loder (*The Island of Calypso*); Gluck; Wylde; Gumbert.
7	Wednesday 28 April 1852	Third New Philharmonic Society concert at Exeter Hall	Mendelssohn (*Fingal's Cave* Overture); Berlioz (*Roméo et Juliette*, first four movements); Gluck (excerpts from *Armide*); Weber (*Conzertstück*, with Madame Pleyel as soloist; *Euryanthe* Overture); Spontini (excerpts from *La Vestale*); Beethoven (*Egmont* Overture).
8	Thursday 29 April 1852	Concert for Émile Prudent at Hanover Square Rooms	Berlioz (*Absence*, from *Les Nuits d'été*); Beethoven (*Prometheus* Overture); Auber (*Zanetta* Overture); Mendelssohn (Wedding March).
9	Wednesday 12 May 1852	Fourth New Philharmonic Society concert at Exeter Hall	Beethoven (Ninth Symphony); Mendelssohn (Piano Concerto in G Minor; Wedding March); Weber (*Der Freischütz* Overture); Wylde; Handel.

Table 10.3. (*continued*)

No.	Date	Description and venue	Works performed
10	Friday 28 May 1852	Fifth New Philharmonic Society concert at Exeter Hall	Mendelssohn (*Italian* Symphony; Violin Concerto); Berlioz (*Les Francs-Juges* Overture; *Invitation à la valse*); Beethoven (*Leonore* Overture No. 2); Mercadante; Silas; Smart; Handel.
11	Wednesday 9 June 1852	Sixth New Philharmonic Society concert at Exeter Hall	Beethoven (Ninth Symphony); Berlioz (excerpts from *La Damnation de Faust*); Liszt (works for solo piano, performed by Madame Pleyel); Wylde; Benedict; Weber.

Fourth Visit: May to July 1853

12	Monday 30 May 1853	(Old) Philharmonic Society concert—the sixth in their series—at Hanover Square Rooms, conducted by Berlioz (first half) and Costa (second half)	First half: Berlioz (*Harold en Italie, Le Repos de la Sainte Famille* from *L'Enfance du Christ*, first performance; *Le Carnaval romain*). Second half: Beethoven; Spohr; Bottesini; Donizetti; Weber.
—	Saturday 25 June 1853	First (and only) performance of *Benvenuto Cellini* at the Royal Italian Opera, Covent Garden, in the presence of Queen Victoria and Prince Albert	Cast: Tamberlik (Cellini); Mme Julienne-Dejean (Teresa); Mme Nantier-Didiée (Ascanio); Tagliafico (Fieramosca); Zelger (Balducci); Formes (Cardinal).

Fifth and Final Visit: June to July 1855

13	Wednesday 13 June 1855	New Philharmonic Society concert at Exeter Hall (the fifth in their series; originally planned for 23 May); attended by Wagner	Mozart (G-Minor Symphony, No. 40; *Magic Flute* Overture; etc.); Berlioz (excerpts from *Roméo et Juliette*); Beethoven (Piano Concerto No. 5); Leslie; Rossini; Venzano.
14	Wednesday 4 July 1855	Second New Philharmonic Society concert at Exeter Hall (the sixth in their series); attended by Meyerbeer	Mendelssohn (Symphony No. 1; etc.); Beethoven (*Fidelio* Overture); Berlioz (*Harold en Italie*); Benedict; Henselt; Glover; Mozart; Meyerbeer; Rossini; Praeger.

Table 10.3. (*continued*)

No.	Date	Description and venue	Works performed
15	Friday 6 July 1855	Final London concert conducted by Berlioz, at Covent Garden, with the New Philharmonic Society: "Mrs Anderson's Annual Grand Morning Concert"	Weber (*Euryanthe* Overture); Mozart (quintet from *Così fan tutte*); Berlioz (*La Captive*, Pauline Viardot; Ascanio's air, "Mais qu'ai-je donc?"); Beethoven (Choral Fantasy); Ernst (*Carnaval de Venise*); Rossini (*Stabat mater*).

[a] Some items at this and subsequent New Philharmonic Society concerts were conducted by Berlioz's deputy, Dr. Henry Wylde.

The same concert included Weber's *Conzertstück* with Madame Pleyel as the solo pianist. Relations between the former lovers clearly remained strained. Madame Pleyel complained to the committee that Berlioz had accompanied her poorly, and at the final concert she chose to play only solo piano pieces. Reviewers were divided on the merits of her claim.[17] Willert Beale, the son of Berlioz's friend and promoter Frederick Beale, says that "there is no doubt Weber's *Conzertstück* [. . .] was very clumsily accompanied by the band under the direction of the rejected suitor."[18] "Chorley may say spitefully that my conduct-ing of the Weber concerto played by Madame Pleyel was poor," wrote Berlioz himself on 12 May 1852, but "there are two thousand people who could attest to the exactitude, verve, and finesse of the performance of this masterpiece at our third concert."[19]

Despite the success of the concerts, Beale, who had arranged Berlioz's appointment and scrupulously paid his salary,[20] was unable to get him reap-pointed for the following season, largely as a result of the machinations of Dr. Henry Wylde, supposedly Berlioz's deputy, but also a key figure in raising funds, who seems to have wanted to use the New Philharmonic Society as a vehicle for his own conducting ambitions.[21]

The Fourth Visit

Nonetheless Berlioz was back in London again the following spring for his fourth visit. On 30 May he conducted the (old) Philharmonic Society for the first (and only) time. The original idea of giving the first London performance of the *Symphonie fantastique* at the concert was abandoned because only one rehearsal was allowed. The main purpose of this visit was to mount his opera *Benvenuto Cellini* at Covent Garden in June. Like all works at the Royal Italian Opera, it was to be sung in Italian: Berlioz had edited and corrected the translation in Paris in February.[22] He was looking forward to the opportunity to rehabilitate his opera after its disappointing run in Paris in 1838–1839 and its more recent success in Weimar under Liszt's direction in 1852.

The first London performance of *Cellini*, on 25 June 1853, was also the last. The work was booed off the stage, apparently by the preplanned efforts of a group of Italian opera supporters in the audience. Even the presence of Queen Victoria and Prince Albert in the royal box failed to calm the storm. In any case, Victoria herself was evidently "not amused" by Berlioz's opera. Her diary entry for that day reads:

> Dined as yesterday and then went to the Opera, where we saw and heard produced one of the most unattractive and absurd operas I suppose anyone could ever have composed, *Benvenuto Cellini* by Berlioz, who conducted himself. There was not a particle of melody, merely disjointed and most confused sounds, producing a fearful noise. It could only be compared to the noise of dogs and cats! The two first acts kept us in fits of laughter, owing to their extreme foolishness.[23]

She and Prince Albert had had previous opportunities to hear Berlioz's music. The *Waverley* Overture (twice), the March from the *Symphonie funèbre et triomphale*, and the *Marche hongroise* had all been played at royal occasions in Windsor Castle and Buckingham Palace by military bands between November 1844 and June 1851.[24]

The next morning, no doubt deeply wounded, and believing that subsequent performances would be subject to similar disruption, Berlioz wrote to Frederick Gye (the director of Covent Garden) to withdraw the work. Some two hundred friends and colleagues from the New Philharmonic Society and Covent Garden subscribed to a testimonial concert for him, to take place in Exeter Hall on 14 July, as consolation for the fate of his opera. When this concert proved impossible, the sum raised (approaching two hundred guineas, the equivalent of five thousand francs) was allocated instead to fund an English edition of *The Damnation of Faust*—although it eventually went towards the publication of *The Childhood of Christ*. Berlioz left London on 9 July. Later that year he apparently received "a proposal from London so brilliant that I don't believe it. If it actually happened I would think I had dreamt it." Whatever it was—possibly the conductorship of the Philharmonic Society, which he was indeed offered the following year, but had to decline—his skepticism proved justified.[25]

The Fifth Visit

Berlioz's fifth and, as it turned out, final visit to London came almost two years later, in 1855. In December 1854, following the sudden retirement of Michael Costa as conductor of the Philharmonic Society, Berlioz was invited to conduct all eight of its concerts in the coming season. But he was already committed to conduct two concerts of the New Philharmonic, and was unable to persuade Dr. Wylde to release him. He therefore had to decline the Philharmonic Society's offer, and the post eventually went to Wagner.[26] So the two composers found themselves in London together, Wagner to conduct the (old) Philharmonic Society and Berlioz, accompanied by Marie, who was now his second wife, to conduct the New.

Berlioz had two long meetings with Wagner during June, one of them after attending Wagner's final London concert.[27] Neither composer was a great admirer of the conducting abilities of the other, but the British public, or at least the critics, seem to have preferred Berlioz's style to Wagner's.

During this stay Berlioz and Marie visited the Crystal Palace in its new location at Sydenham. He was apparently offered the post of music director of the Crystal Palace concerts, which were to start the following year.[28] This offer would have been made by George Grove, then Secretary of the Crystal Palace Company, who also had hopes of persuading Tennyson to write an Ode to mark the opening of the concerts in Sydenham, and getting Berlioz to set it to music.[29]

Berlioz made his last appearance in London as a conductor at a Covent Garden morning concert organized by Queen Victoria's piano teacher, Mrs. (Lucy) Anderson. The next day, Saturday, 7 July 1855, he and Marie left for Paris, never to return to England. This was clearly a matter of chance rather than intention. Only two weeks after leaving, he was telling his friend Auguste Morel that he planned to return to London that very winter. Beale was negotiating for him to bring *L'Enfance du Christ* and the *Te Deum* over to St. Martin's Hall, and was also keen for him to inaugurate the new St. James's Hall in Piccadilly when it was completed in 1857. But the hall was not ready in time, and none of these plans came to fruition. Berlioz's contacts with England were limited during the remainder of his life—although he continued to correspond with some of his friends there (J. W. Davison, Charles Hallé, George Hogarth), and to see them on their visits to Paris.

In February 1859 Berlioz, along with D. F. E. Auber, Heinrich Ernst, Giacomo Meyerbeer, Gioacchino Rossini, and Louis Spohr, was made an honorary fellow of the new Musical Society of London. Shortly afterwards he wrote to George Osborne to discourage the Society from trying to play the *Symphonie fantastique*: "[T]o perform it after just one rehearsal, following the normal London practice, would be a complete massacre. I beg you, therefore, to dissuade the committee from this project, if it exists."[30] (The overture *Le Roi Lear* was played instead.) Later that year he was also made an honorary member of the Philharmonic Society—somewhat ironically in view of the consistent failure of that institution to support him in more practical ways.

England and Berlioz

"England" really means London, the capital of the world's then largest empire. Berlioz never ventured beyond London suburbs such as Chelsea, Greenwich, Hampstead, and Richmond. He based himself within quite a limited geographic area: all of his lodgings, and most of the venues he attended for concerts, operas, and other performances, were within a half-hour walk of Oxford Circus.

Berlioz describes his life in London during his first visit in a letter of 15 March 1848 to his friend Joseph d'Ortigue:

> London life is even more absorbing than that of Paris; everything is in proportion to the immensity of the city. I get up at midday, and at one o'clock the visitors arrive: friends, new acquaintances, artists with introductions; willy-nilly I lose three good hours like this. From four to six I work; if I haven't received any invitations I go out then to eat, a little way away from my apartment, and I read the papers, after which it's time for the theater and concerts: I go on listening to music of some sort until 11:30; then finally three or four of us artists go together for supper at a pub and smoke until 2 a.m. That's my daily life.[31]

In 1855 his London life was equally hectic, as he told his young friend the pianist Théodore Ritter on 3 July:

> [L]ots of visits, lots of dinners, lots of piano trios, correspondence in the *Musical World* with the amateur choristers I didn't allow to sing in *Roméo et Juliette,* lunch with Beale, piano rehearsals at Glover's house, riots in Regent's Park, a hundred men arrested, the workmen [in English] wanting to free their comrades, my wife arriving home terrified, a headache, reading Handel's *Samson,* return of the headache, a frightful rehearsal at Exeter Hall yesterday [. . .], an evening with Glover [. . .], moonlight wanderings in the streets of London, then going to rejoin my wife at Ernst's . . .[32]

where musical discussions continued until 3 a.m.

In London, as elsewhere, Berlioz was almost totally absorbed in musical life and activities. No doubt it fell to Marie to manage everyday practicalities: in a letter of 15 March 1855 Berlioz refers to her as his "*homme* d'affaires."[33] She accompanied him during every visit (with the possible exception of the second, funded by the French government), may have had a hand in managing his bank account at Coutts in 1847,[34] and perhaps procured the English tea that Berlioz apparently enjoyed.[35]

How well did Berlioz speak English? Writing in 1889, the critic Francis Hueffer (who had lived in London since 1869) says that "he had by this time [1847] become tolerably familiar with our language, and could communicate with his orchestra without an interpreter. I have been assured by various competent witnesses, that although Berlioz preferred to speak French, he could speak English fluently and even eloquently when it came to the point."[36] In a letter to his father, as early as November 1847, Berlioz himself writes, "I'm quite surprised to know so much English; I can say almost everything I need to say, and without much of an accent, but I don't understand anything like half of what's said to me. I've got some serious studying to do."[37]

The accuracy of this statement can be gauged from a number of letters in which Berlioz includes some English. In 1849, referring to Jullien in a letter to his friend Morris Barnett, he says, "If you see him touch a little this question."[38]

Later that year, a letter to Ernst includes a note in English to Stephen Heller, which starts:

> Oh! To blow! To blow! What a profound satisfaction! But alas! To blow is not for me. My dear Heller, I am a very suffering man. Aye! And I cannot to be a blowing man. Don't forget me! I will be to morrow, I *shall* be to morrow, as poor Mercutio, a very *grave* man. I am dead, dear, receive my soul—or perhaps—I am not sure of it.[39]

Berlioz presumably means "breathe" rather than "blow," and is joking about the difficulty in breathing caused by his suffering from abdominal pain; his pun on "grave" is more successful. He tended to assume that similar French and English words have similar meanings and to translate French phrases word-for-word into English. Recommending Adolphe Sax in April 1851, again to Morris Barnett, he writes, "Be kind for him as you are, and any thing more, for every one; as you are for me."[40] In 1852 he asks the *Times* critic J. W. Davison, "Can you have two places for us in your Box for the Wagner's Début? If I have not an answer to-morrow, I will understand an impossibility. Thousand friendships."[41] Berlioz's need to use English was apparently too occasional for him to become truly fluent.

The majority of his acquaintances and friends in London, almost all connected with music, would anyway have spoken French themselves. They included the violinists Heinrich Ernst, Bernhard Molique, Émile Prudent, Prosper Sainton, and Auguste-Joseph Tolbecque; the pianists Louise Dulcken, Théodore Ritter, and Sigismond Thalberg; the singers Julie Dorus Gras and Enrico Tamberlik; the critics Henry Chorley (of the *Athenaeum*), J. W. Davison (of the *Musical World* and the *Times*), Morris Barnett and Howard Glover (of the *Morning Post*), Charles Lewis Gruneisen (of the *Illustrated London News*), Edward Holmes (of the *Atlas*), and Charles Rosenberg; the composers George Osborne and William Wallace (as well as Wagner, and possibly, in 1848, Chopin); the conductors Julius Benedict and Charles Hallé; and the impresarios Frederick Beale, John Ella (of the London Musical Union), and Scipion Rousselot (of the Beethoven Quartet Society). The number of non-English names in this list is striking.

Berlioz does seem to have felt at home in London, although he was not always happy there, especially during 1848, when he was desperately short of money, trapped in London by the revolution in Paris, and feeling "superfluous in the world."[42] But despite frustrations and disappointments, he was at least able to live in London as a practicing musician, with only an occasional need to engage in the criticism he professed to dislike so much. Furthermore, despite his occasional mentions of Chartist riots and other disturbances, he does not seem to have found his musical activities constrained by English politics (apart from the strictly musical politics that brought about the failure of *Benvenuto Cellini*): to that extent the English system of government must have seemed close to his ideal.

He did not share certain English musical tastes. He makes clear his lack of empathy for Handel and Purcell, whose approach could hardly be further removed from his own pursuit of dramatic expression in music. But he was delighted with the quality of orchestral musicians in England, as well as of some of the singers and choirs (especially the women). He found himself in a cosmopolitan society of musicians, with the opportunity to hear and perform much stimulating music. As he says in a letter, "the desire to love music is at least real and persistent" in England.[43] And "the London public is one of very attentive and serious music-lovers, and I cannot deny its excellent qualities."[44]

During most of his London visits his musical life revolved around conducting: "Berlioz forthwith proved himself a conductor of the first class: among his contemporaries Michael Costa only was comparable with him."[45] In Charles Hallé's words, "[W]hat a picture he was at the head of his orchestra, with his eagle face, his bushy hair, his air of command, and glowing with enthusiasm. He was the most perfect conductor that I ever set eyes upon, one who held absolute sway over his troops, and played upon them as a pianist upon the keyboard."[46] Berlioz's enjoyment of his conducting was no doubt enhanced by the quality of his orchestras, containing many leading players from across Europe. His one constant complaint was over their reluctance to rehearse: "I have only one fear, the precipitate approach of the English to all things musical and the hatred of their artists for rehearsing. This love that they have for the *so-so*, for rough-and-ready performance, can ruin everything."[47]

He was perhaps less fully appreciated as a composer. He gave complete performances of only two of his large-scale works in London: *Harold en Italie* (three times in full, and once without the final movement) and *Benvenuto Cellini* for its one ill-fated night at Covent Garden. But all except two of the fifteen concerts (other than opera performances) that he conducted in London included one or more of his own works, as shown in table 10.3 (pp. 180–183). These works represent an extensive cross-section of Berlioz's compositions up to that time. The most notable omission is the *Symphonie fantastique*, which had to wait until January 1879 for its first English performance, in Manchester, under Sir Charles Hallé.[48]

In the end, Berlioz's hopes of a permanent musical post in England, like similar hopes elsewhere, were disappointed, not least as a result of the maneuverings of people hostile to him, such as Costa and Wylde. Over the years there had been many unrealized ideas and opportunities, summarized in table 10.4.

After 1855 Berlioz's music was performed in England by a number of conductors, notably August Manns at Crystal Palace, but also Charles Hallé in Manchester, Jules (later Sir Julius) Benedict, Alfred Mellon, and even Jullien himself in his Promenade concerts. There were some twenty-six performances of works by Berlioz between 1856 and March 1869 (the month of his death), almost half of them conducted by Manns; but these were nearly all of overtures or marches. Not one of the large-scale works was performed during this period.

Table 10.4. Unrealized Opportunities for Berlioz in England

Date	Description	Outcome	References
June 1843	HB sent two invitations from the (old) Philharmonic Society to "superintend" a performance of the *Symphonie funèbre et triomphale.*	HB's reply is received too late to be acted upon.	*CG* III, p. 100 & n.
November 1847	At Jullien's suggestion, HB considers writing a piece based on *God Save the Queen.*	Idea abandoned; HB decides he would be unable to repeat the success of the *Marche hongroise* in Hungary.	*CG* III, p. 459.
November 1847	HB hopes to write an opera, *Méphistophélès,* on a libretto by Scribe, to be performed in 1848 at Drury Lane.	Abandoned following Jullien's bankruptcy.	*CG* III, pp. 466–467, 473–475, 484–485.
January 1848	HB plans to approach Lumley about giving concerts at Her Majesty's Theatre if not paid by Jullien; he hopes to fill the position in London left vacant by Mendelssohn's death.	Max Maretzek, chorus master at Drury Lane, sounds out Lumley on HB's behalf, but with no result.	*CG* III, p. 503; Max Maretzek, *Sharps and Flats,* pp. 40–41, 71–81
January 1848	HB hopes to direct Gluck's *Iphigénie en Tauride* at Drury Lane.	*Iphigénie* is announced several times during January 1848, but never rehearsed or performed.	The *Times* (15, 21, 22 January 1848); *CG* III, p. 507; *Mémoires,* chap. LVII.
February 1848	HB prepares to conduct works based on Shakespeare (*Roméo et Juliette, Le Roi Lear, Fantaisie sur La Tempête, La Mort d'Ophélie*) at a "Musical Shakespeare Night" at Covent Garden.	The concert does not take place.	*CG* III, p. 522.

Table 10.4. (*continued*)

Date	Description	Outcome	References
March 1848	HB plans to make his future career in either England or Russia: "sooner or later a solid position will come up for me here."	—	*CG* III, p. 528.
April 1848	An article by Charles Rosenberg (plus an editorial) in the *Musical World* appeals to the Philharmonic Society to perform works by Berlioz.	The appeal is ignored.	The *Musical World* (8 and 15 April 1848).
April 1848	HB is invited to conduct at the Norwich Festival in September.	HB does not conduct at Norwich.	*CG* III, pp. 534–535.
May 1850	The *Times* laments HB's absence from London as conductor.	—	The *Times* (21 May 1850).
September 1850	HB is approached by Frederick Beale about conducting some of his works at Hanover Square Rooms in May 1851.	No performance materializes, although Beale has a hand in some of HB's subsequent visits to London.	*CG* III, p. 735.
October 1850	An announcement appears of forthcoming "Grand National Theatre" concerts at Her Majesty's Theatre, to include compositions by HB.	—	The *Times* (8 October 1850).
May/June 1851	HB proposes a "gigantic musical enterprise," a festival of four concerts over four weeks in the Crystal Palace, "to crown the success" of the Great Exhibition; this	The proposal is submitted to the Commission (see the translation above and the Appendix); the response is	*CG* IV, pp. 62–63, 71.

Table 10.4. (*continued*)

Date	Description	Outcome	References
	would include the first performances of HB's *Te Deum*.	unknown, but the festival does not take place.	
February/ March 1852	HB hopes for a position in London following his appointment to conduct the New Philharmonic Society.	No position is secured, partly because of the opposition of "la Vieille Angleterre."	*CG* IV, pp. 116, 122–123.
June 1852	HB is sought after to conduct at a Festival in Birmingham; he is reluctant to return to Paris with so many opportunities in England.	—	*CG* IV, p. 172.
December 1852	Frederick Beale seeks to have HB reengaged as conductor for the second season of the New Philharmonic Society, in 1853.	HB is not reappointed, largely because of maneuvering by Henry Wylde; Beale resigns; Spohr is engaged.	*CG* IV, pp. 240, 274–275.
March 1853	At the start of the New Philharmonic Society's second season, the *Times* asks: "Where is Berlioz?"	—	The *Times* (17 and 23 March 1853).
April/May 1853	HB hopes to get (at least part of) the *Requiem* performed in London.	The *Offertory* is suggested to the Philharmonic Society for its 30 May 1853 concert, but is declined.	*CG* IV, pp. 307–308, 318.
July 1853	Supporters of HB propose a concert in Exeter Hall on 14 July 1853, following the failure of *Benvenuto Cellini* at Covent Garden.	The concert does not take place because of the Covent Garden orchestra's	*CG* IV, pp. 336–340, 343, 347.

Table 10.4. (*continued*)

Date	Description	Outcome	References
		commitments at the Norwich Festival. The funds are reassigned to publication of *The Damnation of Faust.*	
July 1853	HB hopes sooner or later to find a good position in England.	—	*CG* IV, p. 347.
October 1853– January 1854	HB receives a "brilliant proposition" (unspecified) for England.	The proposition comes to nothing (as anticipated by HB).	*CG* IV, pp. 368, 371, 425, 445.
December 1854	HB suggests to Chorley a performance in London, in 1856, of *L'Enfance du Christ.*	—	*CG* IV, p. 651.
December 1854	HB is invited to conduct all eight concerts of the Philharmonic Society season (March–June 1855) following Costa's resignation. (This could be the "brilliant proposition" mentioned above.)	HB is unable to accept because of his prior commitment to conduct two New Philharmonic Society concerts; Wagner is appointed instead.	*CG* IV, pp. 661, 665, 672, 686.
June 1855	HB is invited (presumably by George Grove) to be conductor of the proposed Crystal Palace concerts at Sydenham; he indicates to his sister Adèle the likelihood of his staying in England.	HB apparently declines the offer.	*CG* V, pp. 113n, 117 & n., 123–124.
July/ September 1855	HB mentions plans to return to London "this winter" in a letter to Morel, and speaks to William Pole of "my next visit."	—	*CG* V, pp. 131, 159.

Table 10.4. (*continued*)

Date	Description	Outcome	References
October 1855	HB describes to Adolphe Duchêne de Vère the requirements for a monster concert at the Crystal Palace in Sydenham during 1856.	The concert does not take place.	*CG* V, pp. 174–176.
November 1855	Beale plans for HB to conduct two concerts at St. Martin's Hall in 1856; the programs would include *L'Enfance du Christ* and the *Te Deum*.	The concerts do not take place, partly because of "Jenny Lind fever" in London.	*CG* V, pp. 197–198, 229, 235, 237.
June 1856	John Ella, perhaps at Beale's instigation, proposes that HB conduct the opening concert of the new St. James's Hall in 1857.	St. James's Hall is not ready in time.	*CG* V, pp. 324, 433.
June 1861	For a planned second visit to London of the French *orphéonistes* HB completes *Le Temple universel* for French and English choruses of 4,000–5,000 men's voices, each singing in its own language.	The visit does not take place. (HB had not planned to attend himself.)	*CG* VI, pp. 200–201; Julien Tiersot, *Berlioziana*, in *Le Ménestrel* (28 January 1906).

Berlioz did grow to feel genuine affinity and affection for London and, as table 10.4 demonstrates, had enduring hopes of planting deeper roots in England. There he was able to live the life of a musician and conductor, to absent himself from his role as reluctant music critic in Paris, to immerse himself in a cosmopolitan circle of musical friends and acquaintances, and to enjoy a varied and stimulating life largely free from Parisian politics. But there is little evidence that the English themselves felt any more strongly drawn to his music than peoples of other nations, and little foreshadowing during his lifetime of the remarkable acceptance and admiration which Berlioz and his music have enjoyed in England during more recent times, and which have been exported elsewhere through the efforts of English conductors, scholars, and critics.

Appendix

The original text of Berlioz's "Plan pour l'organisation du Festival de l'Exposition universelle de Londres" (*F-Pn* L.a. Berlioz [vol. VIII], fol. 231).

[p. 1:] Plan pour l'organisation du Festival de l'Exposition universelle de Londres
[p. 2:] [blank]
[p. 3:] Plan pour l'organisation d'un Grand Festival dans le Cristal Palace.

Ce festival organisé dans le but de couronner, par une manifestation grandiose et presque religieuse de l'art musical, le succès de l'exposition universelle de Londres, devrait être confié pour l'exécution aux artistes et amateurs anglais; cependant pour conserver le caractère de cosmopolitanisme que l'on se plaît à remarquer dans tout ce qui touche à la fête que le peuple anglais donne en ce moment à l'industrie du monde entier, il serait beau et utile que des artistes des nations voisines fussent appelés à y prendre part.

Voici comment on pourrait procéder:

1° Un amphithéâtre en gradins droits (*non circulaires*) serait élevé au fond de la galerie de l'Est, quartier des États-Unis, capable de contenir quinze cents exécutants.

2° Sur cette masse harmonique, il faudrait compter mille choristes au moins, et cinq cents instrumentistes. Ces mille choristes seraient pris dans leurs diverses institutions musicales de Londres, de Liverpool et de Manchester. Les deux *Sacred Harmonic Societys* [*sic*] fourniraient d'abord 500 chanteurs, Her Majesty's Theatre en donnerait 80, Covent Garden 80, Liverpool et Manchester 200, et un appel fait au zèle de tous les amateurs connus pour savoir la musique et à quelques artistes du continent complèterait le nombre de 1000.

3° Les orchestres réunis des deux grands théâtres lyriques, du concert [p. 4:] Jullien et du Vauxhall produiraient un total de 250 musiciens ou plus. Il faudrait donc adresser une invitation à tous les virtuoses étrangers de passage à Londres et demander des députations de Paris, de Manchester, de Bruxelles, de Cologne, de Francfort et même de Lille.

3° [*sic*] Un grand orgue serait établi tout en haut de l'amphithéâtre au centre de la masse des chœurs et de l'orchestre.

4° Un mois entier serait consacré aux préparatifs et répétitions de ce concert gigantesque, qui devrait se reproduire chaque semaine *le samedi à 11 h: du matin* pendant au moins un mois.

5° Le directeur organisateur de ce concert serait M. Hector Berlioz, qui en 1844 organisa, seul et sans appui du gouvernement ni d'une société quelconque, le Festival de l'Industrie à Paris, à la fin de l'exposition française.

6° M. Berlioz serait laissé entièrement libre de choisir les membres du comité exécutif nécessaire pour l'aider à la réalisation de son plan.

7° Il devrait avoir à sa disposition pour les études préparatoires du chœur à Londres, les salles de concert du Princess's Theatre, les Willis's Rooms, Hanovre Square Room et trois autres salles, pour *quatre jours*, et ensuite Hanovre Square Room pour deux demi-journées.

8° Les répétitions du chœur étant très importantes et ayant pour objet de bien apprendre un ouvrage nouveau et difficile, seraient ainsi réglées: *Les soprani* répéteraient *seuls* quatre fois dans Willis Room à 8 h: du matin. *Les contralti seuls* dans le Concert Room du Princess's Theatre à 8 h: du matin. *Les 1ers ténors seuls* dans Hanovre Square Room à 8 h: du matin. Les *2èmes ténors seuls* dans une autre salle à 8 h: du matin. [p. 5:] *Les 1ères basses seules* dans une autre salle à 8 h: du matin. *Les 2èmes basses seules* dans une autre salle à 8 h: du matin.

Quand chacune des six parties du chœur aurait été ainsi exercée *quatre fois* isolément dans divers locaux, on réunirait une 1ère fois tous les choristes de Londres à Hanovre Square.

Les choristes étrangers ayant dû faire chez eux le même travail avant de venir à Londres, seraient enfin réunis à ceux de la capitale, dans une répétition générale des chœurs à Hanovre Square toujours à 8 h: du matin pour ne pas entraver les études des théâtres lyriques.

9° L'orchestre aurait à faire une répétition pour lui seul d'abord, *dans Hanovre Square Room*; puis deux répétitions générales avec le chœur dans le palais de l'Exposition.

10° Le prix du billet pour chaque concert ne pourrait pas être moindre qu'une demi-guinée ou *une demi-Livre*. À la dernière répétition générale on admettrait des auditeurs payant *deux guinées*.

11° Les frais présumés du 1er concert seraient de: *3700 £ St.* (92,500 fr). Ceux de chacun des trois autres concerts seraient de: *1500 £ St.* (37,500 fr) (les 1500 exécutants ne coûtant qu'une guinée par concert après le premier). Somme totale pour les 4 concerts en tout: *8200 £ St.* (205,000 fr).

12° La place destinée au public *assis* devrait contenir, en bas et dans les galeries latérales supérieures, *20,000 personnes*. Chaque recette pourrait ainsi s'élever à *10,000 £ St.* (250,000 fr), ce qui, si l'on en faisait *quatre* semblables, donnerait *40,000 £ St.*: ou (un million de francs). En supposant que les recettes ne s'élevassent qu'à la moitié de cette somme il y aurait encore *397,500* fr de bénéfice; sans compter le produit de la répétition générale.

[p. 6:] Détail des frais présumés pour le premier concert:

1000 choristes à 2 £ St. chacun	2000 £
500 musiciens à 2 £ chacun	1000 £
Frais de gravure et de copie de musique	200 £
Construction de l'amphithéâtre, pupitres et réflecteurs et instruments	400 £
Frais de voyage et de séjour des étrangers	800 £
Annonces dans les journaux, affiches, billets, etc.	200 £
Le directeur organisateur du Festival et auteur du *Te Deum*	200 £

(Ce dernier demanderait, en outre de cette somme, un intérêt dans les bénéfices.)

Détail des frais pour chacun des trois autres concerts [:]
1,500 musiciens à moins d'une £ St. chacun
    et le directeur ayant 100 £ assurées   1,500 £ St.

[p. 7:] Le programme serait ainsi composé:
    1° Grand *Te Deum* à 2 chœurs, avec orchestre et orgue obligé composé par M.
H. Berlioz et exécuté pour la 1ère fois.
    2° Fragments de l'*Armide* de Gluck (chœurs et airs de danse).
    3° Air chanté par Mario.
    4° Fragment instrumental (*La Fête chez Capulet*) de la Symphonie de *Roméo et
Juliette* de M. H. Berlioz, exécuté par l'orchestre et *40 harpes*.
    5° Air chanté par Melle. Cruvelli.
    6° *Prière de Moïse* de Rossini (les solos chantés par 80 voix) accompagnée de
l'orchestre et les 40 harpes.
    7° *Marche hongroise* de M. Berlioz (orchestre seul).
    8° Le *Chant des chérubins* de Bortnianski (le chœur seul).
    9° Chœur du Triomphe de *Judas Macchabée* de Handel.

Le directeur demanderait *un mois*, pour faire graver et copier la musique et
correspondre avec les artistes du continent et prendre ses arrangements avec
ceux de Londres *avant le mois consacré aux études*. Ce qui remettrait au mois
d'août l'exécution du Festival. Il lui faudrait aussi une avance de fond pour les
premiers frais.

Notes

1. See A. W. Ganz, *Berlioz in London* (London: Quality Press, 1950); and *Cairns 2*,
passim.
2. *CG* III, p. 462.
3. From the contract Berlioz signed with Jullien on 19 August 1847 and from
correspondence we learn that he was to conduct at Drury Lane for at least three
months per year for a period of six years at a salary in the first year of 400 pounds
(10,000 francs) and in later years of 133 pounds 6 shillings (3,333 francs) per
month. Two further contracts included supplementary remuneration of 400
pounds for four concerts of Berlioz's own music and of considerably more for
the composition (for the 1849 season) of a successful three-act opera (*CG* III,
pp. 446–455; 765–767).
4. *CG* VIII, p. 277, where Auguste-Joseph is misidentified as Jean-Baptiste-Joseph.
5. *CG* III, p. 514.
6. The dates of the various performances over the period are recorded in the
Times.
7. *Les Francs-Juges* twice, *Waverley*, *Le Roi Lear*, and *Le Carnaval romain* (the last
sometimes wrongly named as the overture to *Benvenuto Cellini*). See F. G. Edwards,
"Berlioz in England," *The Musical Times*, 44 (July–December 1903), p. 442.

8. See *The Mirror* (June 1848), pp. 365–374; (July 1848), pp. 37–48; and *Les Soirées de l'orchestre*, p. 619. The original text appeared in eight numbers of the *Revue et Gazette musicale* from 18 February to 28 July 1844.

9. The original articles appeared in the *Débats* on 31 May 1851, 20 June 1851, 1 July 1851, 29 July 1851, 12 August 1851, and 30 December 1851.

10. *CG* IV, p. 71.

11. *F-Pn* L.a. Berlioz (vol. VIII), fol. 231. The original text will be found in the Appendix to this article. One page of the document is reproduced in *Berlioz: La Voix du romantisme*, ed. Catherine Massip and Cécile Reynaud (Paris: Bibliothèque nationale de France/Fayard, 2003), p. 206.

12. Berlioz has halved the costs as well as the receipts to reach this figure. If all four concerts were given, the profit on takings of 500,000 francs would be only 295,000 francs.

13. *CG* IV, p. 111.

14. The report itself, not published until 1854 (by the Imprimerie impériale), was sketched in December 1851, as we learn from an unpublished letter from Berlioz to Érard of 2 December [1851]: "Le ministre du commerce me demande mon rapport sur l'Exposition universelle" (*Arts et Autographes*, Catalogue No. 34, p. 73). The text of the complete report may be found at Monir Tayeb and Michel Austin's web site: www.hberlioz.com.

15. The *Times* (13 May 1852).

16. Ganz, *Berlioz in London*, p. 124.

17. *Cairns* 2, p. 483.

18. Willert Beale, *The Light of Other Days* (London: Richard Bentley, 1890), pp. 183–184.

19. *CG* IV, pp. 154–155.

20. *CG* IV, p. 182.

21. *CG* IV, p. 240.

22. *CG* IV, p. 275. The Italian translation of Berlioz's opera was by J. Nicodemo di Santo Mango.

23. Quoted in George Rowell, *Queen Victoria Goes to the Theatre* (London: Paul Elek, 1978), p. 37, from Queen Victoria's *Journal*, 25 June 1853 (Royal Archives, Windsor Castle). Nineteen reviews of the opera are printed in *The Musical Voyager: Berlioz in Europe*, ed. David Charlton and Katharine Ellis (Frankfurt: Peter Lang, 2007), pp. 265–310. This volume also contains four articles on Berlioz and *Benvenuto Cellini* in London.

24. As noted in the *Times* of 28 November 1844, 12 February 1848, 27 December 1848, and 24 June 1851.

25. *CG* IV, p. 368.

26. In fact George Hogarth, for the directors of the Philharmonic Society, officially offered engagements to Berlioz and Wagner on the same day, 24 December 1854. See [Stewart Spencer], "Wagner in London," *Wagner*, 3 (October 1982), pp. 98–123, here, pp. 100–101.

27. On what the two men might have discussed, see Peter Bloom, "Berlioz and Wagner," in *The Cambridge Companion to Berlioz*, ed. Bloom (Cambridge: Cambridge University Press, 2000), pp. 235–250, here, pp. 243–245.

28. *CG* V, pp. 123–124 (a letter from Marie Récio to Mme Duchêne de Vère dated 2 July 1855).

29. Michael Musgrave, *The Musical Life of the Crystal Palace* (Cambridge: Cambridge University Press, 1995), p. 19; Charles L. Graves, *The Life and Letters of Sir George Grove CB* (London: Macmillan, 1903), p. 10n.

30. *CG* V, p. 662.

31. *CG* III, p. 527.

32. *CG* V, pp. 124–126.

33. *CG* V, p. 32.

34. See Alastair Bruce, "Hector Berlioz's Bank Account at Coutts," *Berlioz Society Bulletin,* 146 (Autumn/Winter 1992), pp. 8–11.

35. Francis Hueffer, *Half a Century of Music in England, 1837–1887* (London: Chapman & Hall, 1889), p. 168.

36. Ibid., pp. 183–184.

37. *CG* III, p. 459.

38. *CG* III, p. 628.

39. *CG* III, pp. 661–662.

40. *CG* IV, p. 57.

41. *CG* IV, p. 144. The reference is to Johanna Wagner, the composer's niece.

42. *CG* III, p. 543. Several contemporaries refer to Berlioz's perennial air of unhappiness in London: Max Maretzek, *Sharps and Flats* (New York: American Musicians Publishing, 1890), pp. 73–74; Willert Beale, *The Light of Other Days,* pp. 182–183; and J. Sims Reeves, *My Jubilee, or Fifty Years of Artistic Life* (London: London Music Publishing, 1889), pp. 71–73.

43. *CG* IV, p. 104.

44. *CG* III, p. 547. He was also impressed by the use of miniature scores ("petites partitions-diamant") by some members of the London audience—although not convinced that they could actually read the music—and by the distribution of program notes in advance by Ella for his London Musical Union concerts. See the *Journal des débats* (31 May 1851), reused in the twenty-first evening of *Les Soirées de l'orchestre.*

45. Dutton Cook, "Jullien and Berlioz," *Belgravia,* 41 (March–June 1880), pp. 285–296, here, p. 290.

46. Sir Charles Hallé, *Life and Letters of Sir Charles Hallé,* ed. C. E. Hallé and M. Hallé (London: Smith Elder, 1896), p. 64. The analogy of the conductor as keyboard artist comes directly from chapter 66 of Berlioz's *Traité d'instrumentation* (*NBE* 26, p. 480).

47. *CG* IV, p. 116.

48. Edwards, "Berlioz in England," p. 787, lists first performances of Berlioz in England.

Part Six

An Artist's Life

Chapter Eleven

Berlioz Writing the Life of Berlioz

PETER BLOOM

Fiction is the higher autobiography.
—Saul Bellow

What we might have liked to discover is sex. What we do discover is love. And humor. And truthfulness, elegance, magnanimity, modesty, perceptiveness about himself and others, and countless further virtues that Jacques Barzun well catalogued in his great book of many years ago.[1] But is it not curious that the *Mémoires*—of a man born in the same year as the creator of Carmen, of a man friendly with such connoisseurs of women as Victor Hugo, Théophile Gautier, and Alexandre Dumas *père et fils*, of a man on intimate terms with the great *séducteur* who was Franz Liszt—should remain almost speechless in the theaters of eroticism and lust?

Missing

That Berlioz was a man of passion there is no doubt. That he chose to portray himself absent the tones of the flesh speaks to . . . Chastity? Diffidence? Discomfiture? The right word, I think, is Discretion. Like his music, which can be tempestuous, asymmetrical, unpredictable, but never unpremeditated, Berlioz's *Mémoires*—enthusiastic, selective, heterogeneous—always remain *composed*. They are a counterpoint of sound and silence. "I have nothing to say, and I am saying it," quipped John Cage in a poem Berlioz might have liked. True, he refers to "the wild enthusiasm of the whores" in his famous description of Paris in the immediate aftermath of the July Revolution.[2] True, he gives a recipe to awaken the desires of Italian chamber maids—"a melancholy expression and white trousers"—in a comment on the life of the prize winner in Rome.[3] True, he mentions his wife's virginity, to Liszt, in the immediate aftermath of his long-delayed wedding to Harriet Smithson.[4] But of Berlioz's indulgence with an inamorata in Nice, which put an end to an unnecessary fidelity to an unworthy fiancée, and of his affairs with chorus girls—one whom fate had thrown into his arms, he told Humbert Ferrand, when, in frustration over Harriet Smithson's hesitancy to marry, he was going abruptly to leave for Berlin; one whom he took as a mistress sometime after the first performance of the *Requiem* in 1837 (if my suspicion is correct about the identity of the "Mademoiselle Martin" in the chorus); one whom he pursued in St. Petersburg, in the spring of 1847, when his love of love got the better of him—of these women, in the *Mémoires*, we hear nothing at all.[5]

Much more of importance—to the life, to the work—is simply left out. A recent scholarly biography of Beethoven *opens* with "The Death of Beethoven's Mother," taking the event as one of far-reaching consequence.[6] The death of Berlioz's mother, and for that matter the death at nineteen of his younger brother, must have affected the mature composer, but the former is mentioned only in passing in the *Mémoires*, the latter is mentioned nowhere. What Berlioz does offer in the book that ensures his lasting literary reputation is a series of episodes and anecdotes, observations and assessments, that he knew would act to shape the future's memory and knowledge of the man he was and hoped to be. This objective, usually unspoken, is one most autobiographers share. Berlioz went so far as to articulate it, at least indirectly, by seeing to it that the book was printed—precisely as he had written it—before and not after his death.

The *Mémoires* have been much written about, but certain facts need amplification, certain questions and themes more air. Such are the goals of this brief study.

Particulars

Writing to his sister of his arduous work on *Les Troyens*, Berlioz explains that his musical identity is quite different from his identity as her brother: "Le *moi* musicien est bien différent du *moi* que tu connais."[7] My title attemps to put distance between the author of the *Mémoires d'Hector Berlioz*, his "*moi* écrivain," and the subject of that book. Serving as it has for almost one hundred forty years as a primary source for the particulars of his life, Berlioz's final masterpiece is more work of art than exposition of actuality. Facts it contains, of course, most of them accurate. But more essential truths emerge from the means he employs to spin the tale he wishes to tell. Memories (and thus *mémoires*) transform reality, as Berlioz knew and did not fear. He trusted his fallible if quite remarkable memory because the reality he was after did not really depend on particular numbers and particular dates.

The particulars of the printing of the book, generally known for years, have never been set down with the kind of precision that modern scholarship requires. To do so is one of the purposes of the new critical edition that is, as I write, in its early stages.[8] As most people know it, this is the work of which we speak:

MÉMOIRES / DE / HECTOR BERLIOZ / MEMBRE DE L'INSTITUT DE FRANCE / COMPRENANT / SES VOYAGES EN ITALIE, EN ALLEMAGNE, EN RUSSIE / ET EN ANGLETERRE / 1803–1865 / Avec un beau portrait de l'Auteur / M. L. / PARIS / MICHEL LÉVY FRÈRES, ÉDITEURS / RUE VIVIENNE, 2 BIS, ET BOULEVARD DES ITALIENS, 15 / A LA LIBRARIE NOUVELLE / MDCCCLXX.

This is the title of the book as it was issued approximately twelve months after the composer's death, in March 1870, at a price of twelve francs, by the firm of Michel Lévy frères, the still prominent Parisian publishers now styled *Calmann-Lévy*.[9] Michel Lévy, Calmann's younger brother, with whom Berlioz had had cordial business relations since 1852, when he brought out *Les Soirées de l'orchestre*, had in fact proposed to Berlioz, in 1855, when he learned of their existence, that his firm be charged with the publication of the *Mémoires*.[10]

What is emphasized in Lévy's title is, first, Berlioz's identity as a member of the Institut de France—an institution he had often mocked but much appreciated when he finally joined its ranks in 1856; second, the importance of his travels abroad—which, representative of the literary genre of the *voyage* or travel narrative, provide the content of at least thirty-five of the book's seventy-nine chapters (the latter number arrived at by the present writer, not by the author, who was unfussy about such things); and third, the portrait of the artist—the work of François-Marie-Louis-Alexandre Godinet de Villecholle, a photographer of some importance in the early era of photographic portraiture, who was known simply as Franck. Berlioz sat for this portrait at some point after 15 August 1864—as we gather from the rosette of Officier de la Légion d'honneur in his lapel, awarded to him on that date, an honor, as correspondence recently published suggests, of which he was sincerely proud—and before the book was actually produced, in the spring of 1865.[11]

When the book was first advertised, in *Le Ménestrel* of 27 March 1870, Lévy added a phrase to the title: *Mémoires d'Hector Berlioz / comprenant: / ses voyages en Italie, en Allemagne, en Russie / et en Angleterre (1803–1865) / Souvenirs, Impressions, Anecdotes / Un beau volume grand in-8°, 12 fr. (envoi franco) / avec portrait de l'auteur.* I cannot discover if "Souvenirs, Impressions, Anecdotes" helped early sales.

The front wrapper of the book as Berlioz sent it to the printers in 1865 reads as follows:

MÉMOIRES / D'HECTOR BERLIOZ / MEMBRE DE L'INSTITUT DE FRANCE / CORRES-PONDANT / DE L'ACADÉMIE DES BEAUX-ARTS DE BERLIN, DE CELLE DE SAINTE-CÉCILE DE ROME / OFFICIER DE LA LÉGION D'HONNEUR / CHEVALIER DE PLUSIEURS ORDRES ÉTRANGERS, ETC., ETC. / PARIS / CHEZ TOUS LES LIBRAIRES / MDCCCLXV

As half title in that 1865 publication we find:

MÉMOIRES / D'HECTOR BERLIOZ / DE 1803 A 1865 / ET SES VOYAGES EN ITALIE, EN ALLEMAGNE, EN RUSSIE ET EN ANGLETERRE / ÉCRITS PAR LUI-MÊME

Apart from "D'HECTOR"—which is correct (the H of Hector is *muet* like those of *hectare* and *hectique*, and requires elision), and which differs from the "DE HECTOR" that results uniquely from a later designer's time-honored decision to set the preposition on a separate line[12]—what we notice, what was removed from the publication in 1870, are the words "écrits par lui-même"—"written by himself." Berlioz was too careful a writer to set down a silly tautology; he presumably wished doubly to emphasize the fact that no other cook had spoiled the stew. The phrase was of course conventional: it was used by Alexandre Dumas when he edited the *Mémoires de Talma écrits par lui-même* in 1849–1850, and it was used by Jules Michelet when he published the *Mémoires de Luther, écrits par lui-même* in 1854; it is here conspicuous largely by its absence from the edition published by Michel Lévy frères in 1870.[13]

That "edition" is technically the first published issue of the volume which Berlioz himself had printed privately in 1865. In fact, as we learn from slight differences among the three copies of the 1865 book now preserved at the Bibliothèque nationale de France,[14] there was more than one *tirage* or impression of the original text, something that was of course perfectly normal, since first impressions sometimes served as proofs. (The same process may be observed in the early prints of the *Grand Traité d'instrumentation et d'orchestration modernes*: the first impressions were made in 1843, the definitive impressions in 1844. To which year should we assign the treatise?) It may be that what we call the half title above (found on p. [3] of the pristine copy in the private collection of Richard Macnutt) was originally set down for the outer wrapper and only later removed to an inner page. The title page of the same copy appears on p. [5]: the text is identical to that of the outer wrapper but the date is printed as "1865" and not as "MDCCCLXV."

The first printing, some twelve hundred copies, was set in type by compositors at the Imprimerie Valée in the rue Bréda—a short walk from the rue de Calais where Berlioz was living—at a cost, he told his son Louis on 18 July 1865, of forty-eight hundred francs.[15] It was the author's intention, we know, to keep all twelve hundred copies in his office in the library at the Conservatoire until his death. It was also his intention, we are entitled to presume, that they be published posthumously via arrangements to be concluded by his son.[16] But Louis Berlioz died, shortly before his thirty-third birthday, on 5 June 1867. Less than two months later, in the wake of that tragedy, Berlioz wrote out a last will and testament that asks his heirs and executors to bring out the *Mémoires*—by that time printed—"either by publishing only the first edition or by selling all the rights of the work to a bookseller such as M. Michel Lévy, or M. Hachette, or someone else."[17]

On 31 January 1870, a contract was signed by Michel Lévy frères and the representatives of Berlioz's family—Édouard Alexandre, the executor of the composer's estate, and Maurice-Edmond Masson, the notary acting in behalf of the heirs—that gives to those publishers the rights to the *Mémoires*. In fact the contract, for six thousand francs, gives to Michel Lévy frères the rights to *all* of Berlioz's published writings ("tous les volumes et feuilletons publiés par Hector Berlioz"), demonstrating the publishers' plan to enjoy the benefits of Berlioz's *œuvres [littéraires] complètes*. In 1870 however, Michel Lévy frères contented themselves with issuing only the *Mémoires*: this they did by taking possession of the copies of the *Mémoires* Berlioz had left in his office at the Conservatoire,[18] by canceling Berlioz's title page and replacing it with one of their own, and by putting the book on sale in March, an entire year after the composer's death—a delay that for some was unconscionable.[19] Oddly enough, Lévy included at the back the same printed *errata* that Berlioz had had inserted in the summer of 1865. Only in 1878, when they reset the text in two volumes, did Michel Lévy frères incorporate into the main text the *errata* already noted by Berlioz. The two-volume set became the standard edition of the *Mémoires* until a one-volume publication of the text appeared, in 1991, edited by Pierre Citron.[20]

In his will Berlioz further stipulated that a German translation be negotiated with the Leipzig publishers Gustave Heinze, who in 1863–1864 had brought out Richard Pohl's long-delayed translations of Berlioz's three earlier books, *Les Soirées de l'orchestre*, *Les Grotesques de la musique*, and *À travers chants* in a four-volume *Gesammelte Schriften*.[21] In keeping with his lifelong desire to publish what he wrote *as he wrote it*, Berlioz insists that the translation of the *Mémoires* be undertaken by Susanne Cornelius (1828–1917), the sister of the man who had been his most faithful German translator, Peter Cornelius,[22] and specifically not by Pohl, whose volumes "fourmillent de contre-sens"—"crawl with absurdities"—as Berlioz, who did not speak German, seems to have learned shortly after their publication. Already in 1855 Pohl had told Berlioz that he hoped to make a translation of the *Mémoires*, but apart from bringing out excerpts in translation, he never completed the work. Berlioz was fearful of Pohl's limitations, telling Liszt that the *Mémoires* were saturated with words, allusions, and locutions that would be utterly unintelligible to his German friend, and asking Liszt kindly to explain these to him.[23]

The prepublication story of the *Mémoires*, the composition and recomposition of texts old and new, is equally complex and (to those who feed on such facts) fascinating. Dating the pieces of the puzzle is no easy matter: some chapters are dated with precision, but others were written and revised at moments we cannot specify. Only for chapters II, IV–XXXI, LIV, LVII, and [LXII], in whole or in part, do we have autograph manuscripts. The number in square brackets represents my editorial numbering of the last three parts of the book: the *Post-Scriptum* [LX], *Postface* [LXI], and *Voyage en Dauphiné* [LXII]. For ease of reference the new edition will also number the separate letters that comprise Berlioz's *voyages musicaux:* in today's world, Berlioz's charming habit of numbering some sections and only naming others, as I have noted, is disconcerting.[24] One wonders if this is an overblown reaction to the maniacal orderliness of his nemesis, Cherubini, who even numbered his *handkerchiefs*.[25]

For many chapters of the *Mémoires* we have versions printed in the daily, weekly, and monthly press. These sources, in addition to the publication of the *Voyage musical en Allemagne et en Italie* as a book, in 1844, invite the gathering of significant variants. A missing source—a *copy* of the manuscript that Berlioz seems to have had made before he sent the original to Franz Liszt[26]—would, with the variants we have, help to provide the answer to the question of What was written When.

When reusing previously published material, Berlioz's usual procedure—with the important exception of parts of the *Voyage musical en Allemagne et en Italie*—was to copy the text into the autograph manuscript of the *Mémoires*, revising as he completed what was otherwise a mechanical process. This may be seen in a striking way in chapter XXIV where, in the autograph manuscript, we find the text of the anecdote he first published in the *Journal des débats* of 7 October 1846: "Le Droit de jouer en *fa* dans une symphonie en *ré*." Readers familiar with Berlioz's books will recognize this as the title of the first regular chapter of *Les Grotesques de la musique*. Berlioz originally intended to include the anecdote in the *Mémoires;* he changed his mind in late 1858 or early 1859, while assembling materials for *Les Grotesques*, which appeared in March 1859. We cannot be certain, because we do not possess autographs for all chapters of the *Mémoires*, but it is reasonable to assume that other chapters of *Les Grotesques* were likewise selected from texts at first designed for inclusion in what became Berlioz's final book publication.

Recopying is always inexact; the "scribal errors" that mesmerize musicologists are not limited to the lapses of medieval monks. When reusing material from his *voyages musicaux*, however, Berlioz tried to minimize the problem by pasting pages from the earlier publication onto the larger pages of the manuscript, and by making marginal *corrections et perfectionnements* by hand.

Secrets

We know that Berlioz wished to cast a veil of secrecy over the existence of his *Mémoires*. When he sent the text to Liszt in May 1855, he told his friend to acknowledge receipt of only the *package*, not the *manuscript*: "I will know what that means."[27] Three years later, in May 1858, he told his sister, with whom both he and his second wife were in frequent contact, that in her letters she should *never* speak of the *Mémoires*.[28] And yet excerpts from the book had already begun to appear in *Le Monde illustré*: the first of thirty-five selections came out on 13 February 1858, the last, on 10 September 1859. The existence of Berlioz's *Mémoires* was known to all with an interest in music.

Earlier, excerpts from what in the *Mémoires* became the *Voyage musical en Russie* were published in the monthly *Magasin des demoiselles*, from 25 November 1855 to 25 April 1856, but these passages (which I shall mention below) were not identified as constituting parts of the author's autobiography. Years before, however, when *Les Soirées de l'orchestre* went on sale, in late November 1852, the publishers included an explanatory note at the foot of the first page of *Le Premier Opéra*, the tale recounted in the first *soirée*. Here we learn that that story was originally published in the *Voyage musical en Allemagne et en Italie* (of 1844), that that book was out of print, and that the author had refused to permit a second edition because "all of the *autobiographical* material of this *voyage* is to be used and completed by him in another, more important book, at which he is currently at work."[29] It would not have taken a genius to figure out that the "more important book" was an autobiography. Furthermore, when Berlioz's even earlier communication to John Ella of 15 May 1852, regarding the mysterious composition of *La Fuite en Égypte*, was published in the *Musical Union* on 18 May 1852, and reprinted in *Le Ménestrel* on 30 May 1852, the editor announced that that boutade was "a page torn from his previous life, a page borrowed from his future *Mémoires*."[30] Already in the spring of 1852, the secret existence of the *Mémoires* was not really secret at all.

In chapter [LI–5], the fifth letter of the first *Voyage musical en Allemagne* that bisects the *Mémoires*, Berlioz speaks in detail of the concert he gave in Dresden on 10 February 1843. After praising the accomplished singing of Joseph Tichatschek, Berlioz tells of the difficulties he had in finding a proper singer for "Entre l'amour et le devoir," Teresa's cavatina from the *premier tableau* of *Benvenuto Cellini*: Maschinka Schubert came to the rescue and performed admirably. In the original version of this chapter, which appeared in the *Journal des débats* on 12 September 1843, we read—between the comment on Tichatschek and the comment on *Cellini*—another sentence: "Mademoiselle Récio, who happened to be in Dresden at the time, very graciously also consented to sing two *romances* with orchestra, for which the public galantly paid her tribute."[31] This sentence also appears in Berlioz's 1844 book, the *Voyage musical en Allemagne et en Italie*. It is not immediately obvious why he removed it from the manuscript of the *Mémoires*.

The "secrecy" mentioned above is usually seen as designed to prevent Marie from learning of the existence of the book. In my view this secrecy—which we also find in the letters that encompass the gestation of *Les Troyens*, and which is a natural product of any artist's fear that the creative spark might be snuffed out by the light of day—was designed rather more to prevent Marie from becoming desirous of *reading* it: the female protagonists whose stories structure so much of the text—Estelle Dubœuf, who inspired the tales of his youth and old age; Harriet Smithson, who inflamed his passion for Shakespeare—left no place for Marie. Récio was practical—she became Berlioz's "homme d'affaires" at a time when it was important that he have one; and she was professional—the Dresden audience's "galant" applause rewarded singing that was probably unexceptional but also unobjectionable. I have elsewhere defended Marie Récio against the negative press she has had for generations.[32] She was present at the creation of

Les Nuits d'été but she never became the composer's muse;[33] her faithful companionship never elicited from Berlioz the poetic prose with which he composed the tales of love and adventure that make up the *Mémoires*. Marie would have resented not the book's emotional pages regarding Estelle in her teens and Harriet in her twenties, but rather the absence of any such page devoted to her.

Politics

Milan Kundera, in his recent book of essays called *Le Rideau*, writes that there are now so many writers at work that literature itself is committing a kind of suicide. Only literature that is essential should be published. He goes on:

> But there are not only authors, hundreds, thousands of authors, there are also scholars, armies of scholars, who, guided by some opposite principle, accumulate everything they can possibly find in order to present the Totality, their supreme goal. The Totality, that is, an additional mountain of drafts, of crossed-out paragraphs, of chapters rejected by the author but published by the scholars in editions called "critical" under the perfidious name of "variants"—which means, if words still have meaning, that everything written by the author would be valuable and would be equally approved by him.[34]

Here Kundera, almost always right, is wrong. Few scholars, I think, take the list of readings for *das Ding an sich*. And if space is not an issue—it is in *this* book but not in *every* book—then why not show what we can of the compositional process?

In chapter [LI-5] of the *Mémoires*, mentioned above, we find Berlioz's account of his encounter in Dresden with Richard Wagner. The Frenchman admires the German composer who was ten years his junior, but reserves his keenest accolade for the King of Saxony, who has munificently ensured the existence of a deserving artist of "précieuses facultés." In the original version of this text, the following sentence occurs after those two words: "Richard Wagner, above and beyond his dual literary and musical talents, is also a gifted conductor; I saw him direct his operas with uncommon energy and precision."[35] For Berlioz, in 1843, Wagner was not yet *Wagner*. But in the eighteen-fifties and sixties, when Berlioz was revisiting and revising the *Mémoires*, Wagner's star was rising in ways that neither man could have predicted: Berlioz's deletion of that sentence—Milan Kundera to the contrary notwithstanding—suggests the heat of competition; it suggests the politics of art.

At the end of chapter VIII, Berlioz interrupts the narrative of his youth in order to express revulsion over the consequences of the 1848 revolution in Paris, which include the suicide of his once wealthy and lately ruined friend Augustin de Pons, the man who in July 1825 had lent him twenty-five hundred francs to cover the cost of the first public performance of the *Messe solennelle*. That sad turn of events leads Berlioz, writing in 1848, to lament: "Oh! malheureux! pauvres abandonnés artistes! République de crocheteurs et de chiffonniers! . . . "—"Oh, unhappy, wretched artists! [Damn this] republic of pickpockets and scandalmongers!"[36] Presumably because of their potentially inflammatory nature, Berlioz or his editor removed these words and other comments regarding Paris in the aftermath of the June days before the text appeared in *Le Monde illustré* on 6 November 1858. In fact the aftermath of the June days *fills* the pages of Berlioz's writings from 1848, especially the *Voyage musical en France*—which he might have included in the *Mémoires* but eventually reserved for *Les Grotesques de la musique*—and two lesser-known tirades on the *droit des pauvres* and on the impoverished state of the art of music in France.[37] The *Mémoires* might, in other words, have been a far more politically charged book.

In the excerpts that appeared in *Le Monde illustré*, we find a number of "political" suppressions, such as that of the final lines of chapter XXIV, where Berlioz sarcastically explains the delights of living in France: "How sparkling our ingenuity! How brilliant our way with words! How royally we poke fun, and how *republicanly* we do so (although the latter manner is the least amusing)."[38] The last sentence, its invented adverb seething with contempt, occurs only in the *Mémoires*.

Suggesting the opposite tendency—approval of the July Revolution—is the richly textured description, in chapter XXIX, of *Les Trois Glorieuses*:

> I shall never forget how Paris looked during those famous days: the fantastic bravery of the guttersnipes, the enthusiasm of the men, the wild excitement of the whores, the grim resignation of the Swiss and the Royal Guard, the strange pride of the working class in being, as they said, masters of Paris and stealing nothing; the young men bragging of preposterous exploits, based on feats of genuine courage but so thickly embellished and exaggerated in the telling as to sound ludicrous.[39]

In *Le Monde illustré* the text is far more sober: the passage from "the fantastic bravery" to "stealing nothing" along with the aforementioned remark about the whores is removed.

The publication in the *Magasin des demoiselles* in 1855–1856 of what in the *Mémoires* is the *Voyage en Russie* (chapters LV, LVI, and [LVI-1]) is a story in itself, for it raises questions of *genre*—what is this travelogue doing in a fashion magazine otherwise concerned with young women's conduct and personal hygiene?—as well as of politics: we are in the midst of the Crimean War, France is allied with England in a struggle against Russia, but of the "enemy" Berlioz has only good things to say. His introductory letter to the editor of the *Magasin des demoiselles* is to my knowledge all but unknown:

> To the Editor:
> Monsieur,
>   You have asked me for an article on the trip I made to Russia eight years ago, and you suppose that such a narration, different from the subjects you usually treat, might interest your gentle readers. God will that it be so! As for myself, I find it difficult to believe. If we are highly preoccupied by the Russians at this hour, interest in "harmony"

has absolutely nothing to do with that preoccupation. Indeed, it may even be inappro-priate for a Frenchman to speak of the Russians without revulsion. And yet far from wanting to speak ill of the Russians, something, you must admit, that would at this moment be crudely platitudinous, I must in fact express to them my gratitude for the cordial and heartwarming reception which they offered me during my sojourn.

But you wish to have my piece. . . . Thus, if I offend the patriotism of your youthful subscribers, if I fail and if I bore them to death, if my recitation is neither tasteful nor graceful nor in the least bit interesting, *you* will be the truly guilty party—and I will do my best to pardon you.[40]

By the time of the last installment of Berlioz's series, which appeared in the *Magasin des demoiselles* on 25 April 1856, the Treaty of Paris had concluded the business of a war that in fact, most historians agree, had never been popular in France.[41] Still, instead of concluding the series in the way it appears in chapter [LVI-1] of the *Memoires*, with a remark on the King of Prussia, Friedrich-Wilhelm IV—"The King of Prussia is no longer the sole European sovereign interested in music. There are two others: the young King of Hanover [George V], and the Grand Duke of Weimar [Carl Alexander]. In all, three"—Berlioz rather concluded with what we might regard as a profession of faith:

> There you have, Monsieur le Directeur, what I can say of my travels in Russia. And yet if, since my return to France, I have often reflected nostalgically upon that ardent and intel-ligent public, upon those splendid musical *soirées*, upon those grandiose performances in St. Petersburg, and upon the gracious hospitality of the Russian people, you must believe me when I say that I am no less a patriot than you, and that I am proud to be French.[42]

Discretion

If that outburst did not find its way into the *Memoires*, other differences between the serialized articles and the definitive text show the former as more discreet than the latter—not surprising, since the book was designed to appear only after Berlioz would no longer be susceptible to the reviews. In chapter II, for exam-ple, we read of his father's probity and independent spirit. We also read of his attempted suicide: "A few years ago, demoralized by excruciating pain, he swal-lowed at once thirty-two grains of opium. 'I assure you,' he later told me on recounting the story, 'that that was not designed to make me well.'" This para-graph never appeared in *Le Monde illustré*.

In chapter XIV Berlioz mentions the very serious case of tonsillitis he suffered as a student in Paris in 1827, when he would have liked his then roommate, Antoine Charbonnel, to bring him something to eat. Nothing doing, Charbonnel was chasing girls or, as Berlioz puts it, "Antoine courait les grisettes." The word *grisettes* was too risqué for the editors of *Le Monde illustré*—it refers to working class women with loose morals—so we read there that Charbonnel "courait les aventures."

In chapter XLV we come to Berlioz's post-Roman career as a composer in Paris: "To finish paying off my wife's debts I once more set about the laborious business of arranging a benefit, and after a great deal of exhausting effort succeeded in organizing a joint theatrical and musical evening at the Théâtre-Italien." Berlioz was forever worried about money, as is particularly evident in his private correspondence. Members of his family, who had objected to his marriage to Harriet Smithson in part because she was penniless, were embarrassed by the slightest public hint that he was in financial distress. It was doubly valorous of Berlioz to excise from *Le Monde illustré* the offending phrase concerning "les dettes de ma femme."

When Berlioz met the violinist and conductor Karl Wilhelm Ferdinand Guhr in Frankfurt in late 1842, he was amused by Guhr's constant habit of swearing: "sacré nom de Dieu!" As Guhr prounced the words, they became "sacré nom te Tieu," which appeared in the *Journal des débats*, and again in chapter [LI-1] of the *Mémoires*, as "S.N.T.T." However, when Berlioz was preparing his travel pieces for publication in book form, in 1844, he seems to have wished to intensify the joke by signing his *own* letter to Guhr not with "S.N.T.T.," but with "adieu, adieu, S.N.D.D." This sonorously sinful matter is complicated by Johann Christian Lobe's German translation of Guhr's expletive as S.N.Z.T., which, because it is repeated, cannot be a misprint. "Sackerment nochmal, zum Teuful!"[43]

Malice?

"The remarkable thing," wrote Cairns in 1968, is that Berlioz's volume "is not more bitter."[44] Those who shaped the Berlioz renaissance of the twentieth century have tended to see the composer's behavior, in extremely difficult circumstances, as having been admirable in the extreme. In general (Cairns in 1999), "he was courteous and conscientious to a fault."[45] Even lofty men have their lowlier attributes, of course, and some of these become magnified when we look closely at the texts of the *Mémoires*.

The famous portrait of Luigi Cherubini that emerges from Berlioz's last book is anything but complimentary. Here in particular the author succeeded in casting a long shadow upon the reputation of a man who, apart from his accomplishments as a composer, was of singular importance in establishing the Paris Conservatoire as the leading music school in Europe. When Berlioz first published chapter IX's hilarious if somewhat cruel description of being chased from the library by the director and the usher, in *Le Monde illustré* of 6 November 1858, he altered the autograph manuscript, before sending it to the editor of the magazine, such that all the words that he had bent in order to imitate Cherubini's stuttering and pronounced Italian accent now appeared in straightforward French. In the posthumous publication, of course, the imitation of the Italian accent is the crucial comedic element. From beyond the grave Berlioz had no compunctions about lampooning one of those who, he was certain, had inhibited his early success. In fact we find in the autograph that Berlioz's original intention was to address Cherubini as "vieux maniaque, vieux fou!" and to include at the end of that discourteous outburst the following sarcastic note:

> No, no, calm down, O ye respectful admirers of this Father of the Church of Music; it is the thrust of my narrative that made me set down such irreverent words. I slander myself. I never called Cherubini a fool or a lunatic, although it frankly surprises me that I didn't, because I was at that time, as Philip of Macedon dubs them, one of those foul-mouthed fellows who calls everything by its name.[46]

These remarks—confirming Cairns's observation—did not find their way into the 1865 printing.

The portrait of Camille Moke in the *Mémoires,* painted in chapter XXVIII, when we meet the passionate young woman, and in chapter XXXIV, when we learn of her betrayal of Berlioz, is also selective and skewed, partly because the young woman in question—who certainly earned the composer's animosity—became one of the finest pianists of her generation. Berlioz tells of yielding to her sexual advances by inventing a verb—"je finis par me laisser *Putipharder*"—that resists literal translation. "At the end of the day I allowed myself to be *Potifered*" would mean that he finally ceased to "play Joseph to her Potiphar's wife," as Cairns decorously has it. In the autograph manuscript, that biblical personage is also mentioned in chapter XXXI, where Berlioz explains in a note the reason for wanting to use his Prix-de-Rome stipend in Paris: "Mlle Putifar [*sic*] me rendait fort agréable le séjour de Paris"—"Mademoiselle Potiphar rendered my life in Paris highly satisfying." That note was never printed. It has been convincingly argued that Berlioz fictionalized his revenge upon Camille in such stories as *Le Suicide par enthousiasme* (1834), *Le Premier opéra* (1837), and especially *Euphonia* (1844).[47] The *Mémoires* did not need to go that far.

A less-celebrated figure whose portrait is darkened in the *Mémoires* is Narcisse Girard, who became Habeneck's successor as conductor at the Société des Concerts du Conservatoire in October 1848. A good friend of Berlioz's in the earlier eighteen-thirties, Girard seems to have fallen from grace for having on several occasions poorly conducted *Harold en Italie,* thus deciding the composer thereafter to conduct his works himself. In chapter LIX, speaking of one of the rare occasions on which his music was performed by the Société des Concerts, Berlioz writes that Girard had "very clumsily and very prosaically conducted the performance"—"fort maladroitement et fort platement dirigé l'exécution." Yet in a letter to his sister Nanci of 25 April 1849, ten days after that very concert, Berlioz said the opposite: Girard "had done a very good job"—"s'en est bien tiré."[48] Berlioz himself may have given us the reason for the sour public version when he spoke to an acquaintance about Wagner: "Wagner bitterly hates every one who has humiliated him by rendering him a service. *I know something about it myself.*"[49] The comment in the *Mémoires* simply continues the downward sweep of the book's account of Girard's talents.

Indeed, a downward sweep may be said to characterize much of Berlioz's narration. Most of the comical scenes occur in the earlier part of the book, while the original ending (at chapter LIX) was bitter indeed: "As for you, maniacs and dim-witted bulls and bulldogs, and you, my Guildensterns and Rosencrantzes, my Iagos, my little Osrics, snakes, and pests of every kind: *farewell,* my . . . friends; I curse you, and hope to forget you before I die." When we read such vitupera-tion today we smile: its intensity seems more literary than real. In its own day, however, such artifice produced little such cozy amusement. Philarète Chasles's commentary rings true: "It is specifically his ardent, violent, acid-tipped, venge-ful, and militant polemics, attacked and attacking in turn; it is his prejudice, his use of the newspaper as a weapon of attack and defense; his epigrams, satire, and irony—which diminished and weakened Berlioz."[50] "Everything hurt the great artist, poor fellow, everything irritated him," wrote another French reviewer. "At every turn, for the slightest wrong note, he called for the executioner or for the hitman!"[51] An English critic was even less sympathetic: Berlioz told his life "with such an agony of self-exaltation that it is impossible to withold pity, akin though that be to contempt."[52] Nor was his private behavior regarded as eternally scin-tillating. Describing Sainte-Beuve's efforts to engage Berlioz in conversation, Marie d'Agoult wrote to Liszt, on 18 November 1839, that this was "something difficult, something impossible! All you get out of him is a boar's growl."[53]

Is there the hint of a scowl in the photograph that Berlioz affixed to the first edition of the *Mémoires?* Had he wanted to present a softer image, would he not have used one of the pictures shot by Pierre Petit in 1863, where the pose, with his head resting on his hand, is the long traditional one of meditation-cum-melancholy? We find a logical explanation of Berlioz's bitterness in the portrait by Saint-Saëns: "Given his superior nature, he found it impossible to approve of the vulgarity, rudeness, ferociousness, and egoism that play such important roles in this world and by which he was so often victimized."[54] Reviews of the *Mémoires* have yet to be the object of special study, but their authors would perhaps char-itably accept the truth of an aphorism found in Théophile Gautier's *Mademoiselle de Maupin*: "Toute grande haine sert de contrepoids à un grand amour."—"all great hatred acts as a counterbalance to great love."

Love, etc.

In chapter XVIII Berlioz comes to the "supreme drama" of his life—the encounter with Shakespeare and Smithson. The plot is set down with supreme economy: "In the role of Ophelia I saw Harriet Smithson, who five years later became my wife. The impression made on my heart and mind by her extraor-dinary talent, nay her dramatic genius, was equalled only by the havoc wrought in me by the poet she so nobly interpreted. That is all I can say." These three sentences, which do not appear in the chapter as published in *Le Monde illustré* on 1 January 1859, are more rational than emotional. Only in the final addition to the book, the *Voyage en Dauphiné*, do we find a more effusive expression of affection. Indeed it is here, in the episode on Estelle, that we find the only "love letters" in all of Berlioz's preserved correspondence. "Mes adorations seront discrètes," he assured the object of his attentions. But in the autograph draft of this page, before the citation from Thomas Moore's *Irish Melodies* that captured for Berlioz the sentiments he felt for Madame Fornier, the composer let himself go: "I adore her! How bitter the laughter of fate! How immeasurable the caprices of this monster we call the human heart!"[55] This chapter reveals a side of the man's soul that he had in many ways explicitly attempted to conceal.[56] His usual mode was ironic. In London in 1847, he took a sincere line from *The Divine Comedy*—"There is no greater sorrow than to recall happiness in times of misery"—turned it around—"There is no greater pleasure than to recall misery in times of happiness"—and set it down, *lento et grazioso*, in G Major.[57]

Working closely with the texts and variants of the *Mémoires* leads to new appreciation of Berlioz's playfulness, erudition, and verbal craftsmanship. Pierre Citron, in the annotations he has provided for the *Mémoires*, the *Correspondance générale*, and the ongoing *Critique musicale*, has demonstrated that forging neologisms was not the least of Berlioz's pleasures as a writer.[58] But there is far more than that. "As for my literary style, to the extent that I have one," wrote Berlioz, "it is that of a writer who seeks but always fails to find the word capable of rendering precisely what he feels. I am too full of violence; I have tried to calm down but I have not succeeded. This causes the flow of my prose to be unbalanced, or *titubatious*, rather like the gait of a man who is drunk."[59] The word I italicize forces into English something from the Latin *titubare*, "to stagger," from which French gets the verb *tituber* and participle *titubant*—a word, now common, which Berlioz may have been one of the first to employ.[60] All of this to say that Berlioz has in a sense contradicted himself, because in *titubant* he found the word that renders precisely what he felt.[61]

Berlioz began his literary career, in retaliation to what he saw as others' stupidities, as a polemicist: the first article he published, in the issue of *Le Corsaire* of 23 August 1823, fell under the heading of *Polémique musicale*. A polemicist, it has been said, is happiest when he has an enemy. Berlioz had many: Cherubini, Fétis, Mainzer, Scudo, and more, as one learns from reading the reviews.[62] It may be fair to say that he needed enemies in order to motivate his mordant pen. We enjoy the results. But those enemies, who serve in the *Mémoires* to illuminate the portrait of a man not known for his smile, were not good for the composer's health. A part of his personal biography is his medical biography. "Berlioz," his doctor said to him, prescribing distractions and baths, "you are ill more from anger than from fatigue."[63]

Notes

1. Jacques Barzun, *Berlioz and the Romantic Century* [1950], 3rd ed. (New York: Columbia University Press, 1969), chapter 20, "Memoirs of Art and Life." Among others who have written on the *Mémoires* are Joseph-Marc Bailbé, *Berlioz, artiste et écrivain dans les "Mémoires"* (Paris: Presses universitaires de France, 1972); Pierre Citron and David Cairns in their introductions to the *Mémoires* and the *Memoirs* (see the list of Abbreviations); Béatrice Didier, "Les *Mémoires*: Berlioz et l'écriture de soi," in *Berlioz écrivain*, ed. Cécile Reynaud et al. (Paris: Ministère des Affaires étrangères/ADPF, 2001), pp. 6–16; and Richard Macnutt (who has unfailingly shared with me his boundless knowledge of Berlioz and the *Mémoires* and to whom I am very grateful), "Les Mémoires," in *Berlioz: La Voix du romantisme* (Paris: Bibliothèque nationale de France/Fayard, 2003), pp. 95–96.

2. *Mémoires*, chapter XXIX.

3. *Journal des débats* (15 August 1846).

4. *CG* II, p. 119.

5. See *CG* I, pp. 445; *CG* II, p. 112; *CG* III, pp. 462–464, 478–481, 497–498. A "Mlle Martin"—who could be the woman we know as Marie Récio—sang in the first performance of the *Requiem*, on 5 December 1837. Marie Geneviève Martin, the daughter of Joseph Martin, would at that time have used her father's admittedly very common surname.

6. Lewis Lockwood, *Beethoven: The Music and the Life* (New York: Norton, 2003).

7. *CG* V, p. 508.

8. The new edition of the *Mémoires* (in French) will be edited by Catherine Massip, Cécile Reynaud, and Peter Bloom.

9. For a history of the publishing house, see Jean-Yves Mollier, *Michel & Calmann Lévy ou la naissance de l'édition moderne, 1836–1891* (Paris: Calmann-Lévy, 1984).

10. On 10 May 1855, Berlioz wrote to Liszt that in the event of his death, Liszt (in possession of the manuscript) should arrange publication of the book with Michel Lévy, "who proposed it" (*CG* V, p. 87).

11. See *NBE* 26, pp. 100–101.

12. Maurice Grevisse (the French Fowler, Strunk, and White to the power of ten), in *Le Bon Usage*, ed. André Goosse, 13th ed. (Paris: Duculot, 2000), p. 62, states unequivocally that Latin proper names have a *mute* H—but recognizes that usage has sometimes varied. When there was a choice, Berlioz preferred the *H muet* to the *H aspiré*: he always referred to his wife, for example, as *Henriette*, never *Harriet*.

13. When Katharine Boult published her abridged English translation of the *Mémoires*, in 1903, she used the title *The Life of Hector Berlioz, as Written by Himself* (London: J. M. Dent).

14. Two copies of the 1865 *Mémoires* are in the Collection Macnutt; a third—the copy Berlioz sent to Estelle Fornier—is now in the collection of the *réserve*.

15. *CG* VII, p. 285.

16. On 10 May 1858, Berlioz explained to his sister Adèle that he would soon send the manuscript of the book to her husband, Marc Suat, for safekeeping, and that he would bequeath the manuscript to his son Louis with the request that he publish the three volumes "tels qu'ils sont," with no modification (*CG* V, p. 571).

17. Berlioz's last will and testament with its attendant documents may be consulted in Peter Bloom and Hervé Robert, "À propos de la vie matérielle et de la condition sociale d'Hector Berlioz: L'apport des actes authentiques," *Cahiers Berlioz*, 2

(1995), pp. 7–79, here, pp. 50–52. Berlioz had had no dealings with Louis Hachette, but books by friends of his were indeed published by that great competitor of Michel and Calmann Lévy.

18. The precise number of copies taken over by Lévy was not twelve hundred but rather eleven hundred seventy-five, as we learn from the inventory of Berlioz's possessions completed immediately after his death: "[A] package of twenty-five copies had been removed by Berlioz to be given to various persons." See Bloom and Robert, "À propos de la vie matérielle," p. 72.

19. See Ernest Reyer, for example, in *La France musicale* (27 February 1870).

20. In fact Calmann-Lévy did advertise the *one-volume* edition of the *Mémoires* as late as 1902, as may be seen from the listing of the *Ouvrages d'Hector Berlioz* on the inside title page of *Les Soirées de l'orchestre* reissued in that year. Also mentioned there, in addition to the works we know (including *Les Grotesques de la musique*, which Lévy purchased from Achille Bourdilliat in 1861), are volumes entitled *Historiettes et scènes musicales* and *Les Musiciens et la musique*, both said to be "sous presse." The former collection of Berlioz's *feuilletons* (advertised as early as 1871 in Lévy's edition of *Les Grotesques de la musique*) was never issued; the latter title was used for a collection introduced by André Hallays and published by Calmann-Lévy in 1903—from which book mention of the *Historiettes* was removed.

Citron's one-volume edition is now the only one currently available. It was first issued in by Flammarion in 1991 and then again, in 2000, in that publisher's series "Mille & Une Pages." In the Berlioz dossiers of the Calmann-Lévy archives, which I visited in 1994, we find the record of print runs of the two-volume set as follows: March 1878 (1,500); May 1881 (1,000); March 1887 (1,000); September 1896 (1,000); February 1904 (1,000); March 1919 (500); March 1919 (500); June 1921 (1,000); June 1926 (750); November 1930 (1,000). A note reads: "épuisé depuis 1938," although at the time of the centenary of Berlioz's death, in 1969, Garnier-Flammarion did bring the two-volume edition back into print. It is no longer in their catalogue—but the old two-volume text remains available on the web at gallica.bnf.fr/ark:/12148/bpt6k3621ow and gallica.bnf.fr/ark:/12148/ bpt6k362117.

21. In 1864 Heinze had furthermore brought out Alfred Dörffel's translation of the *Traité d'instrumentation*. And in 1866 he issued a piano-vocal score of Gluck's *Orphée* that conforms to the version Berlioz had prepared for the Théâtre-Lyrique in 1859.

22. See Herbert Schneider, "Cornelius, Peter," in *Dictionnaire Berlioz*, ed. Pierre Citron, Cécile Reynaud, Jean-Pierre Bartoli, and Peter Bloom (Paris: Fayard, 2003), pp. 122–123. In 1866 Cornelius was counting on fifteen hundred francs for the translation of *Les Troyens*, which seems not to have materialized (*CG* VII, p. 493).

23. See Berlioz's letter to Liszt of 10 May 1855 (*CG* V, p. 87). In the end, the first German translation of the *Mémoires*, by Elly Ellès, was published in Leipzig by Breitkopf & Härtel, in 1905, as a part of Berlioz's *Literarische Werke*. A second, by Hans Scholz, was published in Munich, by C. H. Beck, in 1914. A new translation by Dagmar Kreher, edited by Frank Heidlberger, will appear from Bärenreiter, in Kassel, in 2007. Hainholz, in Kassel, will reissue the Scholz translation, newly edited by Gunther Braam, also in 2007.

24. In the *Traité d'orchestration*, Berlioz numbered the first six chapters and left the numbers of the next sixty or so to us. See *NBE* 24. Furthermore, publishing excerpts from the *Mémoires* in *Le Monde illustré*, Berlioz included under "chapter LV" bits from four different chapters of the actual book.

25. As noted in a recollection of Cherubini by Ferdinand Hiller, *Macmillan's Magazine*, 32 (May–October 1875), p. 270.

26. On 24 January 1854, Berlioz told Liszt that he had not sent him the *Mémoires* because he "did not *yet* have a copy of this voluminous manuscript" (*CG* IV, p. 462; my emphasis).

27. The manuscript was sent on 9 May 1855; the letter to Liszt, the very next day (*CG* V, p. 87).

28. "*Ne me parle jamais de cela* dans tes lettres" (*CG* V, p. 571).

29. My emphasis. See *Les Soirées de l'orchestre*, p. 27.

30. Cited in *CG* IV, p. 156. In fact it turned out that this page would appear not in the *Mémoires* but in *Les Grotesques de la musique*. The metaphor of the page torn from the manuscript is apt, for more than one such page was surely torn from the manuscript of the *Mémoires* for use in *Les Grotesques*.

31. "Mlle Récio, qui se trouvait alors à Dresde, consentait très gracieusement aussi à chanter deux romances avec orchestre, et le public l'en récompensa galamment." The *romances* were Berlioz's *Le Jeune Pâtre breton* and *La Belle Voyageuse*.

32. In *The Life of Berlioz* (Cambridge: Cambridge University Press, 1998), passim, and in my review of David Cairns's magnificent two-volume biography of Berlioz, in *Music & Letters*, 81 (2000), pp. 455–460. Berlioz may have relied on Marie in the way Wagner depended on Minna, his first wife, another woman who, with stereotypical misogyny, has been portrayed as a hindrance to the "Master." See Chris Walton's review of Eva Rieger, *Minna und Richard Wagner* (Düsseldorf: Patmos, 2003), in the *Musical Times*, 146, no. 1891 (Summer 2005), pp. 98–99.

33. In his article elsewhere in this book, Julian Rushton argues that *Les Nuits d'été* was almost certainly conceived for the voice of Rosine Stolz (see p. 74).

34. "Mais il n'y a pas seulement les auteurs, les centaines, les milliers d'auteurs, il y a aussi les chercheurs, les armées de chercheurs qui, guidés par une morale opposée, accumulent tout ce qu'ils peuvent trouver pour embrasser le Tout, but suprême. Le Tout, à savoir aussi une montagne de brouillons, de paragraphes rayés, de chapitres rejetés par l'auteur mais publiés par les chercheurs dans des éditions dites 'critiques', sous le nom perfide de 'variantes', ce qui veut dire, si les mots ont encore un sens, que tout ce que l'auteur a écrit se vaudrait, serait pareillement approuvé par lui" (Milan Kundera, *Le Rideau* [Paris: Gallimard, 2005], p. 115).

35. "Richard Wagner, outré son double talent littéraire et musical, possède encore celui de chef d'orchestre; je l'ai vu diriger ses opéras avec une énergie et une précision peu communes" (*Journal des débats*, 12 September 1843).

36. In this often-quoted passage, Berlioz seems to use the word "chiffonniers" as employed by Chateaubriand in *La Liberté de la presse* (1822–1828): "Les folliculaires, les pamphlétaires, les chiffonniers et les académiciens" (*Trésor de la langue française*).

37. I refer to Berlioz's articles for the *Journal des débats* of 23 September and 5 December 1848.

38. "Comme l'esprit y pétille! Comme on y danse sur la phrase! Comme on y *blague* royalement et républicainement! . . . Cette dernière manière est la moins divertissante . . ." The passage is all but untranslatable because the adverb *royalement*, apart from its overtones of royalty, means *intensely*, and because in English one cannot, as one can in French, smoothly transform the adjective *républicain* into an adverb.

39. *Memoirs*, p. 109, which I have slightly modified.

40. The letter, undated, appeared in the *Magasin des demoiselles* of 25 November 1855:

À M. le Rédacteur en chef.

Monsieur,

Vous me demandez le récit d'un voyage que je fis en Russie, il y a huit ans. Vous supposez que cette narration, ainsi faite hors de propos, peut intéresser vos lectrices. Dieu le veuille! Quant à moi, j'ai peine à le croire. Si l'on se préoccupe fort des Russes à cette heure, les intérêts de l'harmonie ne sont pour rien dans cette préoccupation; un Français sera peut-être mal venu de parler d'eux sans haine. Et loin d'avoir du mal à dire des Russes, ce qui serait en tout cas, avouez-le, une assez vulgaire platitude en ce moment, je dois leur témoigner de la reconnaissance pour l'accueil flatteur et cordial que j'ai reçu d'eux.

Mais vous le voulez. . . . Alors si je choque le patriotisme de vos jeunes abonnées, si je les ennuie, si je fais fiasco, si mon récit n'a ni goût, ni grâce, ni intérêt quelconque, vous serez le vrai coupable, et je ferai mon possible pour vous pardonner.

41. See, among others, J. M. Thompson, *Louis Napoleon and the Second Empire* (New York: Noonday Press, 1955); D. W. Brogan, *The French Nation from Napoleon to Pétain* (New York: Harper, 1957); and Alfred Cobban, *A History of Modern France* (New York: Braziller, 1961).

42. "Voilà, monsieur le directeur, ce que je puis dire de mon voyage en Russie. Mais si, depuis mon retour en France, il m'est souvent arrivé de soupirer en songeant à cet ardent et intelligent public, à ces splendides soirées musicales, à ces exécutions grandioses de Saint-Pétersbourg, et à la gracieuse courtoisie des Russes, croyez-le bien, je n'en suis pas moins aussi patriote que vous, et très fier d'être Français. H. Berlioz" (*Magasin des demoiselles*, 25 April 1856). Berlioz's high regard for Russian musical life was obviously known to others, including Giacomo Meyerbeer, who in 1858 recommended him (along with François-Joseph Fétis and Fromental Halévy) as a potential director of the St. Petersburg Conservatory. See Meyerbeer, *Briefwechsel und Tagebücher*, vol. 7, ed. Sabine Henze-Döhring (Berlin: Walter de Gruyter, 2004), p. 339.

43. This solution—"Upon my bedevilled soul!" or "Damn it to hell"—was suggested to me by my distinguished colleague Hans Rudolf Vaget.

44. *Memoirs*, p. xvi.

45. *Cairns* 2, p. 585.

46. "Non, non, calmez-vous respectueux admirateurs de ce *père de l'Église* musicale; c'est l'entraînement de mon récit qui m'a fait écrire des paroles aussi irrévérencieuses. Je me calomnie. Je n'ai point traité Cherubini de fou ni de maniaque, mais je m'étonne de ne l'avoir pas fait, car j'étais alors de ces gens dont parle Philippe roi de Macédoine, gens grossiers qui appellent chaque chose par son nom." (The autograph manuscript of this chapter is preserved in a private collection.) Berlioz presumably read about Philip of Macedon, father of Alexander the Great, in Plutarch's *Vie d'Alexandre*, which he had found as a boy in his father's library.

47. See, for example, Katherine Kolb, "The Short Stories," in *The Cambridge Companion to Berlioz*, ed. Peter Bloom (Cambridge: Cambridge University Press, 2000), pp. 146–156; Katharine Ellis, "Berlioz, the Sublime, and the *Broderie* Problem," *Ad Parnassum Studies*, 1 (Bologna: Ut Orpheus Edizioni, 2005), pp. 29–59, esp. p. 38; and the article in the present volume by Joël-Marie Fauquet.

48. *CG* III, p. 625.

49. The acquaintance was Juliette Adam, née Lambert, who recorded that conversation in *Mes Souvenirs* (1904), cited in Michael Rose, *Berlioz Remembered* (London, Faber & Faber, 2001), p. 225.

50. He then added: "If his talent, or rather his genius, resisted this, it is because he had a great deal of it." Philarète Chasles, "Berlioz," *L'Art musical* (31 March 1870), p. 137; cited in Lesley Wright, "Berlioz's Impact in France," in *The Cambridge Companion to Berlioz*, pp. 253–268, here, p. 258. The number of early reviews of the *Mémoires* is not large: the book appeared in time of war; furthermore, the Catholic press might not have wished to publicize the work of one who announces at the opening his departure from the church.

51. "À chaque instant, pour une note fausse, il criait au bourreau, à l'assassin!" *Le Monde illustré* (2 April 1870; article by Philippe Dauriac).

52. From a review of the *Mémoires* in the *Edinburgh Review* (January 1871), p. 44.

53. "L'autre soir il [Sainte-Beuve] s'était mis en tête de faire causer Berlioz: chose difficile! chose impossible! Un grognement de sanglier est tout ce qu'on obtient de lui" (*Correspondance de Liszt et de Madame d'Agoult*, ed. Daniel Ollivier [Paris: Grasset, 1933–1934], vol. 1, p. 289). Berlioz dedicated the first version of *La Mort d'Ophélie* to the comtesse d'Agoult.

54. "Avec sa nature supérieure, il ne pouvait aimer la vulgarité, la grossièreté, la férocité, l'égoïsme qui joue un rôle si considérable dans le monde et dont il avait été si souvent victime." See *Portraits et Souvenirs* [1889], cited in Saint-Saëns, *Regards sur mes contemporains*, ed. Yves Gérard (Paris: Bernard Coutaz, 1990), pp. 108–109.

55. "Je l'adore. Ô amères railleries du sort! Ô caprices insensés de ce monstre qu'on nomme le cœur humain! . . ." This page is preserved in the collection of Hugh Macdonald.

56. On this point, with reference to the publication of *Une Page d'amour romantique*, see Lesley Wright, "Berlioz in 1903," in *Ad Parnassum Studies*, 1 (2005), p. 241.

57. See *NBE* 15, pp. xviii, 251. The musical setting may also be a parody of Rossini's setting of the original lines from Dante ("nessun maggior dolore") in the Canzone del Gondoliero, in G Minor, at the beginning of Act III of *Otello*.

58. Pierre Citron is explicitly the editor of the *Mémoires* and *CG*. He has furthermore been a member of the editorial board of the *Critique musicale* since the appearance of *CM* 4 in 2003.

59. "[. . .] cela donne aux allures de ma prose quelque chose d'inégal, de *titubant*, comme la marche d'un homme ivre" (*CG* VII, p. 102; my emphasis). In his essay for this volume, David Cairns offers a more felicitous translation of the same passage I cite here (see p. 230); for my purpose, a somewhat literal rendering is needed.

60. Using the University of Chicago ARTFL project database, we learn that "tituber" first occurs in Edmond About, *Le Nez d'un notaire*, published in 1862 by Berlioz's friend Michel Lévy.

61. On the literary aspects of Berlioz's denial of literary pretensions, see Guillaume Bordry, "'Je ne suis pas un homme de lettres': Berlioz, écrivain paradoxal," in *Hector Berlioz: Regards sur un dauphinois fantastique*, ed. Alban Ramaut (Saint-Étienne: Université de Saint-Étienne, 2005), pp. 95–108.

62. In this regard, *Benvenuto Cellini: Dossier de presse parisienne*, ed. Peter Bloom (Heilbron: Lucie Galland, 1995), and *Les Troyens: Dossier de presse parisienne*, ed. Frank Heidlberger (Heilbron: Lucie Galland, 1995) make interesting reading, as does the

section on critical reception in Julian Rushton, *Berlioz: Roméo et Juliette* (Cambridge: Cambridge University Press, 1994).

63. In the *Revue et Gazette musicale* of 10 September 1848, the composer cites Dr. Amussat: "Berlioz, vous êtes malade de colère plus que de fatigue." On the nature of the relationships between Berlioz's physical and mental states and his creative imagination, see Francesca Brittan, "Berlioz and the Pathological Fantastic: Melancholy, Monomania, and Romantic Autobiography," *19th-Century Music,* 29 (2006), pp. 211–239, where the emphasis on this much-discussed question is upon disease and medical infirmity.

Chapter Twelve

Berlioz: Autobiography, Biography

DAVID CAIRNS

We must not forget that our primary source for the story of his life is Berlioz himself.
—Peter Bloom, *Berlioz: Past, Present, Future*

S.N.T.T.
—Berlioz, *Mémoires, Premier Voyage en Allemagne*

It was the *Memoirs*, in the Everyman translation by Katharine Boult, together with the 78-rpm black-label recording by Jean Planel of *Le Repos de la Sainte Famille*, that first kindled my interest in the composer, after a predominantly Germanic musical upbringing which left no room for Berlioz, indeed made his music incomprehensible to me.

After that my education progressed rapidly. These were the years of *Les Troyens* at Covent Garden (1957, 1958, 1960)—the event which, with Jacques Barzun's equally epoch-making *Berlioz and the Romantic Century*, transformed Berlioz's fortunes and reputation—and of the annual performances by the Chelsea Opera Group, of which I was a founder-member and for which I wrote the program notes and played in the percussion section. I learned *La Damnation de Faust*, *Roméo et Juliette*, *Les Troyens*, and *Benvenuto Cellini* from the inside and, in doing so, discovered a composer rather different from the view of him still common among those who professed to know about such things. To put matters right and restore amends became the ruling passion of a group of young British musicians and writers, of whom I was one. In particular, our energies were devoted to getting *Les Troyens* published and recorded. Both aims were achieved in 1969, the centenary of the composer's death, when the *New Berlioz Edition* issued the opera in full score, edited by Hugh Macdonald, and Phonogram, using the new material, recorded the work under Colin Davis.

Berlioz's autobiography had commonly been regarded with a comparable skepticism. The more I worked on it the more I realized that here too was an attitude that cried out for correction. After it had first appeared, in 1870, the book, christened by Charles Villiers Stanford "Berlioz's masterly work (? of fiction)," was ready prey for commentators bent on proving its author at best a fantasist and at worst a liar.[1] But it became increasingly clear to me that here was a far more accurate account than I had been led to believe, and that—as I wrote in the commentary to my edition—"to an impartial critic" the *Memoirs*, with all its errors of fact and emphasis such as any human memory is prone to, "must none the less appear a largely and essentially truthful account of his life and of the feelings and thoughts that inspired it."[2] Cross-questioning an autobiography demands a care and judiciousness that Berlioz's inquisitors, prominent among them Edmond Hippeau, Adolphe Boschot, and Ernest Newman, were often guilty of forgetting.

They forgot, too, in their zeal for refutation, that it is unwise to make assumptions based merely on the absence of corroborating documents. From his premise of Berlioz the fantasist with a fatal weakness for tall stories, Hippeau assumed that the episode of the enthusiast at the performance of Sacchini's *Œdipe à Colonne* in chapter XV ("Deep Feelings of a Mathematician") was pure invention. Berlioz's veracity would be vindicated when a letter from him to the man in question, Le Texier or Le Tessier, came to light, in which he speaks of the ecstasy to which Sacchini and Dérivis (the Oedipus) had reduced them both.[3]

Certainly, Berlioz loves a good story, and he knows how to tell it. The dramatized dialogues which enliven the *Memoirs*—the conversations with Pingard the Institute usher, the argument with Cherubini over Berlioz's proposed use of the Salle du Conservatoire for his concert in May 1828, the exchange between Le Texier and the orange-eating billiards aficionado Léon de Boissieux during the trio "O doux moments" in *Œdipe*, the humorous account of Karl Guhr the Frankfurt Kapellmeister, with his "Sacré nom te Tieu" (S.N.T.T.)—may well have been touched up a little; but we no longer feel impelled to insist that they never took place. Berlioz was one of those people—we all know them—who attract bizarre events. Unusual things happened to him.

Some of the dialogues may even be more or less verbatim. There is no reason why we should doubt that Lázár Petrichevich Horváth, the Hungarian newspaper editor, on examining the score of the *Marche hongroise*, expressed anxiety about Berlioz's stating the Rákóczy theme *piano* at the opening of the piece and that Berlioz replied, "Don't worry, you shall have such a forte as you never heard in your life," or that, conducting the first performance, he "shot [Horváth] a glance as if to say, 'Well, are you still nervous, or are you satisfied with your forte?'"[4] In Berlioz's newspaper account of the concert's sequel, when an excited Hungarian bursts into the artists' room and, embracing him convulsively, blurts out his admiration in a Mr. Jingle–like staccato, the words "Allemands chiens" ("German dogs") found in the later *Memoirs* are missing. One can dismiss the phrase as an example of subsequent embroidery for greater effect, and this has been done. Or—I think, more reasonably and plausibly— one can interpret its omission from the original account as having been due to diplomacy and tact, given that that account described a tour of German lands and was aimed at a largely German readership.

These are random examples. The general process of exoneration has been long and arduous; but it has resulted in an autobiography that is worthy, as a whole, of respect and that can be used with confidence as a prime source for the composer's life. The *Memoirs* are a constant challenge and stimulus to the biographer, both in what they reveal and even more in what they don't. Every biographer of Berlioz is by definition locked into a close but critical relationship with them. Writing his biography is both helped by his own account of it and, in a sense, required by it. Once I had translated and annotated it and, in the process, had acquired some familiarity with the composer's life, I was more or less obliged to take the next step. The book does not set out to give the full story. It is no day-to-day record or anything like it (it is far less explicit than Chateaubriand's *Mémoires d'outre-tombe*, the detailed, intimate account of an artist's existence, whose impending publication may have spurred Berlioz to begin his own in 1848). He has, he says in his Preface, no desire to write confessions: he will tell only what he wants to tell about his personal life. He wishes simply to correct certain misstatements about his career, describe the influences that have shaped his art, and give an idea of the difficulties an aspiring composer faces in France, while at the same time offering "a few useful hints." It is, expressly, a tale with many gaps in it.

To fill them, while also testing and confirming, or not, its statements of fact, has been made far easier by a mass of documents and published studies that were not available to (or not consulted by) earlier biographers—publications prompted by, and in turn furthering, the modern revival and reappraisal of Berlioz's music. This new knowledge has been particularly useful in the mapping of the least well-known period of Berlioz's life, his childhood and his early years in Paris. There is now a whole intricate network of interrelated material for the biographer to work on. The letter to Le Texier cited above is one of hundreds that have appeared—letters revealing all kinds of insights and information that make possible a fuller picture of his life and personality. Taken in conjunction with his journalistic writings—now much more accessible than before and often containing autobiographical material—and with the large number of often revelatory papers in public archives or in private collections, they enable us to form a more rounded portrait of the man and of his struggles—what he called in the Postscript of the *Memoirs* his "Thirty Years War against the routineers, the professors and the deaf."

To take one example, the lists of orchestral musicians with their addresses and fees which have survived in the composer's hand for the year 1835 and which are preserved in the "Berlioz papiers divers" in the Département de la Musique of the Bibliothèque nationale de France illustrate in the most vivid way possible what it took to organize his Paris concerts in the eighteen-thirties, when he had to assemble his orchestra each time from scratch, player by player. In another library, the Bibliothèque municipale de Grenoble, an autograph document—a two-page sketch for one of the monologues in *Le Retour à la vie*—makes it clear that the work was conceived and begun before Berlioz left Paris for Italy and was originally associated with his love for Camille Moke: the "return to life" it celebrated was his Camille-inspired recovery from the Harriet Smithson obsession.[5]

Sometimes, of course, new knowledge creates new uncertainties. The baccalauréat records in Grenoble provide the pleasant information that one of the Latin passages Berlioz was asked to translate in March 1821 was the description in *Aeneid* Book 2 of Cassandra dragged captive from Minerva's sanctuary. But they also suggest that he failed his *bac* the first time he presented himself, in December 1820. An intriguing thought: but what exactly lay behind this surprising failure we have, unfortunately, no idea.

The family papers preserved by the descendants of Berlioz's sister Nancy have proved particularly rich, and it was for me a great stroke of fortune to be able to spend weeks searching through them in the apartment of Yvonne Reboul-Berlioz in the rue de Ranelagh, Paris XVI.[6] Its prize possession was the Livre de Raison of Dr. Louis Berlioz, the composer's father, who, for over twenty years, from 1815 to the late eighteen-thirties, entered in it a detailed record of his family and household and the running of his estate. The book gives the inventory of his extensive library (where his son first acquired his lifelong passion for reading) and of his surgical instruments, and, in addition, an account of the two occupations of La Côte-Saint-André by allied troops, in 1814 and 1815, which would be of interest to students of the Napoleonic Wars.

The Livre de Raison was known to earlier Berlioz specialists, but none of them before Pierre Citron, general editor of the *Correspondance générale d'Hector Berlioz*, seem to have grasped its importance for their work and realized what a mine of information it is. Boschot refers to it only in passing. If he had studied it in earnest and read Dr. Berlioz's homilies on politics and society he could never have portrayed him as a reactionary or made such an insistent point of Berlioz's being brought up the "fils d'un ultra."

Julien Tiersot quotes at length from it in the first volume of his edition of Berlioz's letters,[7] but it is by no means certain that he ever consulted it in person: the extracts he prints are jumbled about in the wrong order. In particular, Dr. Berlioz's father's antirepublican sentiments are systematically erased. Missing, too, are the statements that the family's seventeenth-century ancestor Claude Berlioz was illiterate and that Hector Berlioz married Harriet Smithson "malgré les parens." Expunging the antirepublican sentiments could conceivably be Tiersot's work, but the removal of the other two items suggests the bourgeois prejudices of the then owner, Marie Masclet-Reboul (Nancy's granddaughter), who—if my conjecture is right—transcribed selected paragraphs for Tiersot rather than letting him see the book for himself.

If Tiersot did see it, he failed to read far enough to understand that Dr. Berlioz recorded more than (in Tiersot's words) the list of "dépenses, recettes etc. de sa maison, pêle-mêle avec d'autres indications": in particular, precious information about the chronology of Berlioz's student years, including the dates of his departure for Paris after summer or autumn vacations at La Côte—entries that reveal, among other things, that chapter X of the *Memoirs*, which ostensibly describes a single return visit, is in fact a conflation of several visits, and that Berlioz went back in 1822, 1823, 1824, and 1825 (though not in 1826, to which biographers used to ascribe it). These simple dates show how protracted was the family dispute over the eldest son's career. Not till 1826, five years after he first went to Paris, did Berlioz feel sufficiently independent and sure of himself to resist the order to return home.

The Livre de Raison also tells us where and when the new flute which Berlioz says he set his heart on (*Memoirs*, chapter IV) was purchased and how it was made and constituted ("red ebony, with eight keys and a slide, both silver, and a foot joint in C"); when, too, Dr. Berlioz bought him his guitar. Over and above its value as a source of these and similar biographically fruitful details, the book is important in its totality, as illuminating the environment of the first sheltered but momentous years of Berlioz's life and the values and beliefs which led Dr. Berlioz to oppose his son's vocation so bitterly, though in the end to no avail.

Important as it is, however, it is far from being the only treasure of the Reboul Collection. For the first volume of the *Correspondance générale* alone—the period least rich in Berlioz letters—the collection produced nearly thirty that had been unknown till a few years before. Hidden away in drawers, too, were dozens of letters written by Berlioz's son Louis, from his childhood to within a few months of his death, which cast new light on their troubled but in the end close and loving relationship. There were others no less useful for the biographer, especially for the years when no or very few Berlioz letters existed: from Berlioz's uncle the music-loving cavalry captain Félix Marmion; from a former lover of his, a Madame Husson, which show that his seventeen-year-old nephew confided his secret ambitions to his uncle ("you must be finding it hard not to sympathize with your nephew in his enthusiasm for music"); from Dr. Berlioz himself, which reveal him to have been a more volatile and irrational creature than either his view of himself or his portrait in the *Memoirs* would have us believe, and which also correct the traditional view of his marriage; from Joséphine Berlioz; from her old school friend, Nancy's godmother Nancy Clappier, gossipy missives full of shrewd observations bearing on Berlioz's life and character; and many letters from Adèle Berlioz to her sister Nancy, with little tidbits like the remark, near the end of their brother's year in Italy, "Talking of noses, no news of Hector," or the information that in 1846 Berlioz seems to have been seriously thinking of splitting up with Marie Récio.

Not least, there are the diaries (*tableaux journaliers*) that Nancy kept off and on from 1822 to 1825 and the more sporadic *cahiers de souvenirs* from the late eighteen-twenties and early eighteen-thirties, the years first of Berlioz's most fraught relations with the family over his career, and then of his return as second prizewinner of the Prix de Rome (when Humbert Ferrand visits La Côte and comes under Nancy's sharp-eyed scrutiny), and of his love affair with Camille Moke. In addition to the valuable information they provide, they make much clearer her ambiguous, fluctuating relationship with her brother—at one period in their lives very close. They also illuminate the character of Nancy herself, "so like her brother in many respects, stirred by similar longings and idealisms, prey to similar despairs but, unlike him, without the means of escape."[8]

Apart from a brief and garbled reference by Boschot, I have found no sign that any Berlioz scholar before Citron realized what a vital source these diaries are or even knew of their existence. In them we read of the excitement at La Côte at the news of Hector's engagement to Camille (it is from Nancy that we learn that Camille called him "le fiancé de mon cœur"). Thanks to the eighteen-year-old Nancy's daily entries we experience at first hand the tumult of the household during the last days of his five-week visit in June–July 1824—a visit that had seemed to begin so well but that ended in anguish—and glimpse the intense emotional strain that Berlioz was subjected to, only twenty years old and in many ways young for his age.

> We were hardly back before Mama realized that Hector had sent his trunk off and would soon be following. On discovering it she broke down and wept a lot and berated him quite harshly, but justifiably. He took it with a most distressing air of unconcern. He can't wait to go.

> We talked of my brother this afternoon. My father is dreadfully affected by it all. "I have always been unfortunate," he said. "My childhood was not happy, my youth was very stormy, and now the son who was to have been my consolation is destroying the happiness I might have had."

> This evening Papa has just exhausted his remaining eloquence in an attempt to move my brother and bring him back to a more sensible line of conduct. He replies with the absurd argument that he was "born like this." He curses his existence.

Sadly, Nancy is not on hand either in August–November 1825, when Dr. Berlioz, angered by the success of the *Messe solennelle*, makes his last sustained attempt to dissuade his son—the diary had stopped in March "until such time as I can paint a less gloomy picture" (though we do have a letter in which Nancy speaks of the "wall of separation" between father and son)—or in autumn 1822, or in spring 1823 when, as I have argued, the confrontation with his mother described in chapter X of the *Memoirs* very probably took place.[9] For that crucial period of the conflict we can, however, to some extent fill the void by reading—again in the Reboul Collection—the letters of Félix Marmion, that shrewd observer and ambivalent go-between who always took a keen interest in his nephew's affairs.

Nancy's diary can also be frustrating by falling silent just when it has whetted your appetite. In April 1822, when Berlioz's cousin and fellow medical student

Alphonse Robert pays a surprise visit to La Côte, we read that he "told us a lot about their way of life [in Paris], Hector's in particular" and, a few days later, that "Monsieur Alphonse spoke to us a great deal about the theater." That is all. What wouldn't we give for a full account of those conversations!

Such frustrations are the common lot of biographers, especially if their subject lived a long time ago, when contemporary testimony is likely to be sparse. Even when there is testimony, too often there can be no certainty. But biographers are "hot for certainty." We fasten on passing witness and are prone to set it in stone.[10] Here is a tiny example. Replying to his mother's offer of some new clothes, Berlioz says, in a letter of 1836, that a few shirts would be welcome, but he doesn't need an overcoat: "I never wear one"—"Pour le manteau, je n'en porte jamais."[11] Evidently that was so in 1836; but does that mean we can state, as a fact, that Berlioz never wore an overcoat, *tout court*? We might conclude otherwise from the famous photograph taken by Nadar in 1857, where he is shown draped in an ample coat, were it not that the coat belonged not to him but to the studio, and figured in other Nadar portraits.[12] Yet would Berlioz have agreed to be portrayed in it if he "never" wore one?

Reminiscences of Berlioz by friends and acquaintances, of which there are many, are subject like any others to the natural uncertainties and distortions of the human memory, as well as being influenced by the nature and degree of closeness of the relationship in question.[13] Ernest Legouvé writes fascinatingly and at length about Berlioz in his *Soixante Ans de souvenirs* and one would not be without it. But many of the events he describes took place half a century earlier. How trustworthy is he? Certainly not when he says that Berlioz was not widely read and had only a very limited knowledge of literature. Berlioz's letters and published writings are peppered with allusions to Racine, Molière, Corneille, Boileau, La Fontaine—they are so much part of the furniture of his mind that they almost cease to be quotations—as well as to Shakespeare (he cites well over thirty of the plays), and he was a voracious reader of contemporary publications. The inescapable conclusion is that for whatever reason (diffidence in the presence of an eminent literary figure?) he did not choose to discuss the topic with Legouvé.[14]

For that matter, can we trust Legouvé's story of Marie Récio knocking on Harriet Smithson's door and saying triumphantly, "You're not Madame Berlioz, you're the old, rejected one, I am the real Madame Berlioz, the young and pretty one"? Could Marie have been so cruel, so odious? Yet could even a romancer as inveterate as Legouvé have invented it? We simply don't know. On the other hand his story of the six-year-old Louis woken in the night by the noise of his mother upbraiding his father, and running to her and crying "Mama! Don't be like Madame Lafarge"—the murderess whose trial in 1840 was the talk of France—has, it seems to me, the strong ring of truth. In the end, however, we can only go with what our judgment and our instinct tell us.

Equally, when one has a sudden hunch one should be prepared to back it— as I did when it occurred to me that the famous incident of Habeneck's "pinch of snuff," commonly pooh-poohed but attested by independent witnesses, may have taken place not at the première of the *Requiem* but at the public dress rehearsal. Hunches, needless to say, are not necessarily right. In trying to conceive Berlioz's increasingly anxious state of mind as he made his way to the rue de la Tour des Dames to call on the great Talma and ask him to include *Beverley* in his benefit performance at the Théâtre-Français in April 1824, I assumed that he went there from the rue Saint-Jacques, and I walked the distance myself to see how long it would have taken him (about forty-five minutes), his nervousness growing all the while. But supposing he went not from his lodgings but from the Bibliothèque du Conservatoire, or from Lesueur's house in the rue Sainte-Anne?

Sometimes the evidence is conflicting. On the question of Berlioz's piano-playing, or lack of it, are we to believe the witness who says that all he could do was pick out a tune with one finger or the one (Auguste Barbier) who says that, although no pianist in any conventional sense, he could give a remarkable impression of a piece of music?

Another biographical hazard is that the testimony we have, in the form of letters, may well contain allusions that we are unaware of. This is particularly so of family letters. Families have their private code, their jokes which do not have to be spelled out and which are necessarily lost on outsiders. When Mozart tells his father that he has written the symphony he is sending him (for a celebration by the Haffner family) in D "because it is your favorite key," there is surely more in the remark than meets the eye. Behind the correspondence of the Berlioz family, like any other's, must lie a whole world of shared experience, and of shared humor, that is largely denied to us. Communications between friends, too, may contain references which the two correspondents take for granted and which are therefore hidden from us. When Berlioz told Ferdinand Hiller that he was writing *La Belle Voyageuse* very slowly, "a few bars at a time, like a counterpoint lesson," we should surely not take it literally; he was, very likely, teasing Hiller—there was a lot of that in their relationship. Hiller may well have said Berlioz composed too quickly, and this was his (jesting) response.[15]

One asset a biographer needs but cannot of course rely on is luck—the serendipity, for instance, that led Richard Macnutt unsuspectingly to a particular shelf in the back room of a shop off the quai des Grands-Augustins in Paris, where he found a one-hundred-twenty-page manuscript containing arias from Gluck's two *Iphigénie* operas in a familiar hand, written out by Berlioz from the full scores in the Conservatoire Library in 1822, a discovery that made thrillingly alive and real the passage in chapter V of the *Memoirs* where Berlioz speaks of reading and re-reading Gluck's scores, copying them and learning them by heart, going without sleep because of them and forgetting to eat. When "I was at last able to hear *Iphigénie en Tauride* I vowed as I left the Opéra that in spite of father, mother, uncles, aunts, grandparents, and friends, I would be a musician."

Again and again, when working on the *Memoirs*, I found that the records of the time confirm this or that detail in the book, even when it seems exaggerated or purely fanciful. To take one example among many, Berlioz makes great comic play with the fact that the text of the Prix de Rome cantatas usually began with a sunrise, and that it is typical of him ("eternally at odds with life and with the Academy") that when he eventually wins the prize, in 1830, it should be with a sunset instead. Sure enough, the archives of the Institut de France record sunrises in 1822, 1823, and 1825: "Le jour a pénétré sous cet épais ombrage," "L'aube a doré les monts d'une clarté nouvelle," "La fraîcheur du matin ranime la nature."

Not that such accuracy is always the case. The *Memoirs'* emphasis on the crucial role of Gluck in Berlioz's apprenticeship is indeed borne out by all the evidence; but it led him, when recalling those heady events twenty-five years later, to shorten the period of his medical studies and represent his abandoning of them as more clear-cut than it was. Here other evidence can be drawn on—medical registers, Opéra archives, documents unearthed by the researches of Donnet and Moureaux—to correct the *Memoirs'* account.[16] The revival of *Iphigénie en Tauride* at the Opéra on 21 August 1822 recorded in the Opéra's archives and in the *Almanach des spectacles* was unquestionably decisive, but the medical and musical careers overlapped for several months—indeed until the providential closure of the École de Médecine in late November—as we can see from the school's registers, where Berlioz's signature at the beginning of each of the four terms shows that he completed the first-year course, undoubtedly passing the end-of-term exams and obtaining the *certificat d'assiduité* which every student had to present when signing on for the new term.

Although luck cannot be summoned, it can be encouraged. Opportunism seems to me an essential tool of a biographer. If your subject is ever-present in your mind, if you are constantly, even if half the time unconsciously, on the qui vive, unlooked-for pieces of information will seek you out. You never know when one isn't going to fall into your lap. Though F. R. Leavis used to deride the Sunday book reviews as worthless, I am grateful for them. It was happening to read a review of a biography of the famous German scientist and explorer Alexander von Humboldt (whom Berlioz knew) that put me in the way of solving a minor puzzle of the *Memoirs*: the identity of the "oiseau colossal" soaring above the snows of Chimborazo to which Berlioz likens the lonely, exalted spirit of Beethoven, after hearing Anton Bohrer and friends play the Adagio of one of the late quartets.[17] Newman liked to make fun of Berlioz and his "colossal bird." But the review, in describing Humboldt at twenty-three thousand feet in the Andes watching a solitary condor circling far above him, led me to the answer. I already knew, from the inventory in the Livre de Raison, that Humboldt's *Tableaux de la nature* was one of the books in Dr. Berlioz's library. The young Berlioz, with his interest in exploration and in science (which will persist all his life and be reflected in his writings), certainly read it and found there the solitary condor, as I did when I borrowed it from the London Library. After that, it was no surprise to find, in the same book, the South American boa constrictor that covers its victim with a mucous slaver before swallowing it, and which Berlioz remembers as he stands on the tilting deck of the Sardinian brig during the perilous crossing to Leghorn and watches the waves foaming over it, "comme les boas d'Amérique, qui couvrent leur victime de leur bave avant de la dévorer."[18]

To a Sunday review I also owe the less important but piquant discovery that William Hazlitt was in Paris in 1824, reporting on it for the *Morning Chronicle*, and went to the Opéra and heard Piccinni's *Didon*, very probably on a night when Berlioz (who never missed a performance if he could help it) was in the audience—though Berlioz would not have shared his opinion of Dérivis, the Iarbas, whom Berlioz and his friends admired greatly but whom Hazlitt, like Berlioz's hated *dilettanti*, thought a crude and overvehement singer: "Ten bulls could not bellow louder, nor a whole street-full of frozen-out gardeners at Christmas."[19]

It goes without saying that it is an advantage for biographers to like their subject—to feel drawn to the person in the first place and to continue to even after years spent in their intimate company.[20] Berlioz has been, for me, never a mere "subject"—to borrow the word used, in both French and English, to designate the corpses that he dissected at the Hospice de la Pitié while humming Salieri and Spontini—but a living person, whom, whatever his faults, I have never felt the desire to debunk or cut down to size. Besides, he could do it so well himself. One of the attractions of the *Memoirs* is his self-deflating irony, the way he will bring his most inspired flights of fancy down to earth.

This is a characteristic of his writing in general, as when, in a *feuilleton*, after imagining that if he "were rich, really rich, like those poor deluded souls who give a singer five hundred francs for a cavatina worth five sous," he would buy the plains of Troy from the Sultan and set sail with a choice orchestra to the Troiad, there to perform the *Eroica* in a specially constructed temple of music, he modulates abruptly to a performance of the same work at the Salle du Conservatoire in the rue Bergère, "a damp and grimy little hall where a few oily chandeliers define the murk, and you see pale women raising their eyes heavenward in studied poses and rubicund men struggling not to fall asleep or nodding their heads out of time with the music and smiling as the anguished orchestra utters its cries of pain."[21]

Berlioz, as Edward Cone remarked, may be his own best critic.[22] But we do not have to agree when he describes himself, in a letter, as a writer who "searches for the word that will convey what he feels, without ever finding it—I write with too much violence; I would like to calm down but can't. This lends the movement of my prose an uneven, lurching gait, like the steps of a drunken man."[23] We may note that the passage is an example of a characteristic found here and there in the *Memoirs*: the tendency, not unknown in autobiographers, to make himself out a more extreme, eccentric fellow than he really is ("I know nothing about art and have little feeling for conventional beauty"),[24] and to heighten his quirks and prejudices—what he himself calls in chapter XXXVIII of the *Memoirs* "the proneness of artists to write for effect." But we warm to someone so free from self-love or complacency, so alert to puncture any conceit in himself, so honest. He takes himself seriously—why not?—but he never takes himself too seriously. He is well aware of his cussedness, his black moods. The crotchety description of the Salle du Conservatoire and its audience quoted above is humorous in both senses of the word (as well as being necessary for the balance and irony of the piece). He knows perfectly well that the reader will accept it in that light, as the momentary spasm of irritation in one who has written so many rhapsodies about the hall and its memorable concerts that he will be forgiven this brief jeu d'esprit in another key.

Berlioz's playfulness rarely deserts him. In his writings, as in his music, there is scant danger of dullness. I remember Daniel Barenboim saying, of the music, at a time when he was conducting a good deal of it with the Orchestre de Paris: "It grows." That is true of Berlioz's achievement and personality as a whole. He does not let you down. During all the years I have spent immersing myself in them I have not once tired of him. Amid the traumas and vicissitudes of a tragic life, the acute sufferings physical and emotional—which, being the person he was, he lived to the top of his bent—he hardly ever lost his resilience, his humor, his quickness and energy of mind, his mordant sense of irony, his fertile imagination, his curiosity.

His last-but-one *feuilleton* in the *Journal des débats*, written in the midst of frequent bouts of severe pain and anxious preoccupation with the coming production of *Les Troyens à Carthage*, is a dazzling flight of fancy which uses the revival of Albert Grisar's *opéra comique Les Amours du diable* as the launchpad for a futuristic vision of the earth made one world by air travel, and himself issuing orders to his orchestral attendant as the next musical festivity draws near: "Where's Vieuxtemps? And Becker?" "They're in Sydney, sir." "Go and fetch them. And Sivori, and Bottesini, and Piatti?" "Sir, they're in Canton, Timor, and Mindanao." "All right, pick them up as you pass, they're on your route. [. . .] I want these virtuosos five days from now."[25]

To read Berlioz is a constant pleasure. He is irrepressible. "Où diable le bon Dieu avait-il la tête," he demands (in chapter XXV of the *Memoirs*) of the Good Lord's decision to make him a Frenchman. His enthusiasm refuses to be quenched. To the end he will proselytize his gods, never quite giving up hope. In the late, long essay on *Fidelio* (which Wagner admired), after analyzing the work number by number, in a style that, as is his wont, mingles the poetic and the technical, he concludes:

> [*Fidelio*] belongs to that powerful race of maligned works [. . .] whose vitality is so intense that nothing can prevail against them—like those sturdy beeches born among rocks and ruins, which end by splitting the stone and breaking through the walls, and

rise up proud and verdant, the more solidly rooted for the obstacles they have had to
overcome in order to force their way out; whereas the willows that grow without effort
on the banks of a river fall into the mud and rot, forgotten. [Its time will come.] Who
knows that light will not dawn sooner than one thinks, even for those whose spirits are
closed at the moment to this beautiful work, as they are to the marvels of the Ninth
Symphony and the last quartets and the great piano sonatas of that inspired, incompa-
rable being. Sometimes, when one looks at a particular part of the heaven of art, a veil
seems to cover "the mind's eye" and prevent it from seeing the stars that shine there.
Then all of a sudden, for no apparent reason, the veil is rent and one sees, and blushes
to have been blind so long.[26]

Beethoven is his god, and Gluck and Virgil, and Shakespeare ("thou art our
father, our father which art in heaven—if there is a heaven"), not le bon Dieu,
who has a rather rough ride in Berlioz's writings and letters:

Yet another of my friends is dead. [. . .] The Good Lord is gunning us down ["le bon
Dieu nous mitraille"]. I hope he's missing you all at Weimar.[27]

Five days ago [. . .] I was in a state of ecstasy—I had played my first act [of *Les Troyens*]
through mentally from beginning to end. There's nothing so absurd as an author who,
imitating the Good Lord, considers his work on the seventh day and "finds it good."
But imagine: apart from two or three pieces I had forgotten the whole thing—hence
my delight. [. . .] The only part I hadn't written was the mime scene for Andromache.
Its importance daunted me. Now it too is done, and of the whole act I think it's the
piece that comes off best. [. . .] I wept buckets over it. Imitating the Good Lord again,
you see—though a lively sensibility was not his strong point, if one is to believe that
appalling old rogue Moses.[28]

The letters written during the months of the composition of *Les Troyens*—April
1856 to March 1858—show Berlioz at the top of his form. The creative exuber-
ance released by the achieving of a lifetime's ambition overflows into his correspondence. It documents the making of the opera in exceptionally full and vivid
detail; with no other work of his can we follow the progress so closely. For that
reason, when I came to these years in my biography of Berlioz, I decided that
the whole section should consist simply of extracts from the letters: I would leave
him to speak for himself and tell the story of his "ardent existence" in those two
years in his own words.

   I did so, as well, in pursuance of a governing idea. In the same spirit, I per-
suaded the publisher to reproduce Claude's late Virgilian painting *Vue de
Carthage avec Didon et Énée* on the back of the dust jacket of the second volume.
Les Troyens, I argued, is the work that lends unity to Berlioz's life, that makes
sense of it. In the light of its greatness—so long denied—we see that he did ful-
fill himself. I chose the opera, perhaps at first only half-consciously, as the central motif of the book, beginning with the Latin lessons in his father's study, the
tears shed for Dido, and the Virgilian epiphany at Vespers in the church at La

Côte, continuing with the discovery of Gluck's "reconstructions of the ancient world" and the revelatory performances by Madame Branchu ("tragédie-lyrique incarnate") in *Iphigénie en Aulide, Alceste,* Piccinni's *Didon,* and Spontini's *Olympie,* then flowering under the sun of Italy with the guitar improvisations in the Campagna and the mirage of his Virgilian heroes swarming before him as he looks down on the coast of Naples from the heights of Posilippo. After that, as I wrote, "there is never a time when Virgil is not his companion and the work [*Les Troyens*] is not present by implication like an underground river running beneath the external reality of his life." In the early eighteen-fifties it rises to the surface. With the encouragement of the Princess he finally commits himself to it and writes the work which he knows to be the culmination of his existence.

The fate of the opera—sliced in two, the Carthage acts alone given, themselves mutilated—is all too well known. It was the crowning blow. The pages in the *Memoirs* recounting the opera's "damn'd defeat" are the bitterest in the whole book. In Gounod's phrase, like his namesake Hector he "died beneath the walls of Troy."[29]

Berlioz would not have agreed with Tolstoy, who entitled his tale of an innocent man sent to Siberia for a murder he did not commit and exonerated years later, at the point of death, "God sees the truth but waits." But he would surely have relished the poetic justice whereby it was his long-suffering opera that, nearly a century later, began the great upturn in his fortunes which has gone from strength to strength in the succeeding fifty years. His dying words, "They are finally going to play my music"—a prophecy that certainly meant France (it was already being played regularly in Germany and Russia)—were vindicated in 2003, two hundred years after his birth, when at the Théâtre du Châtelet, directly opposite the Théâtre-Lyrique where Berlioz had watched his visionary masterpiece brought low, Paris cheered *Les Troyens* to the echo.

Notes

1. Charles Villiers Stanford, *Pages from an Unwritten Diary* (London: E. Arnold, 1914), p. 68.

2. *The Memoirs of Hector Berlioz,* trans. and ed. David Cairns, Everyman's Library 231 (New York: Alfred A. Knopf, 2002), p. xx. My translation was first issued in London, by Victor Gollancz, in 1969, and in New York, in the same year, by Alfred A. Knopf. It appeared in the Norton Library, in New York, in 1975, and as a Cardinal Book, in London, in 1990.

3. *CG* I, pp. 80–82.

4. *Memoirs,* p. 416. Lázár Petrichevich Horváth (1807–1851) was editor of the newspaper *Honderü.* This account originally appeared in the *Journal des débats* on 19 October 1847.

5. See *Cairns 1,* p. 471; and *NBE* 7, p. xx.

6. See Cairns, "The Reboul-Berlioz Collection," in *Berlioz Studies*, ed. Peter Bloom (Cambridge: Cambridge University Press, 1992), pp. 1–17. Madame Reboul was the widow of Nancy's great grandson Admiral Georges Reboul, who took the name Reboul-Berlioz. Yvonne Reboul herself was descended directly from Henry Pal, brother of Nancy's husband Camille Pal. What we know as the Reboul Collection is now in the possession of Madame Reboul's three children: M. Guy Reboul-Berlioz, Mme Catherine Vercier née Reboul-Berlioz, and Mme Martine Perrin née Reboul-Berlioz. [Elsewhere I adopt Hector Berlioz's spelling of the name of his sister: Nanci. David Cairns prefers the spelling adopted by the name's possessor: Nancy. —*Ed.*]

7. Berlioz, *Les Années romantiques (1819–1842)*, ed. Julien Tiersot (Paris: Calmann-Lévy, 1904).

8. "The Reboul-Berlioz Collection," p. 14.

9. *Cairns 1*, pp. 120–122, 159–160.

10. The tenor Michael Kelly, Don Basilio and Don Curzio in the première of *Le nozze di Figaro*, recalls that Mozart's favorite number in the opera was the sextet. He does so in a volume of memoirs written many years later. Mozart may well have made such a remark in passing and at some particular moment. But can we therefore say that "we know which Mozart's favorite number was"?

11. *CG* II, p. 274.

12. See *NBE* 26, pp. 174–175.

13. See Michael Rose, *Berlioz Remembered* (London: Faber & Faber, 2001).

14. Neville Cardus, in *Sir Thomas Beecham: A Memoir* (London: Collins, 1961), claims that Beecham was not interested in either politics or religion. But he was. As Edmund Tracey observed in his review of the book, "It takes two to make a conversation. Perhaps Sir Thomas decided that religion and politics were not Mr. Cardus's strongest suits."

15. Ferdinand Hiller, *Künstlerleben* (Cologne: M. Du Mont-Schauberg, 1880), p. 105.

16. V. Donnet and C. Moureaux, "Le Baccalauréat-ès-sciences d'Hector Berlioz," *Marseille médical*, 3 (1969), pp. 1–7.

17. *Memoirs, Premier Voyage en Allemagne*, tenth letter (chapter [LI-10]).

18. *CG* I, p. 417.

19. William Hazlitt, *Notes of a Journey through France and Italy* (London: Printed for Hunt and Clarke, 1826), p. 160.

20. It is said that Frank Walker, whose *The Man Verdi* (New York: Alfred A. Knopf, 1962) is one of the finest studies of any musician, disliked Verdi by the time he finished the book—outraged, perhaps, by Verdi's treatment of the dying conductor Angelo Mariani.

21. *Revue et Gazette musicale* (28 January 1841).

22. Edward Cone, *Music, a View from Delft: Selected Essays*, ed. Robert P. Morgan (Chicago: University of Chicago Press, 1989), p. 217.

23. *CG* VII, p. 102.

24. *Memoirs*, chapter L. But Berlioz refers appreciatively to Claude, Michelangelo, Canova, and Guérin, among others.

25. *Journal des débats* (3 September 1863).

26. *Journal des débats* (19 and 22 May 1860); *À travers chants*, pp. 88, 103.

27. *CG* V, p. 301 (to the Princess Sayn-Wittgenstein).

28. *CG* V, p. 424.

29. See Gounod's preface to Berlioz, *Lettres intimes*, 2nd ed. (Paris: Calmann Lévy, 1882), p. vii.

Contributors

LORD ABERDARE (ALASTAIR BRUCE) brought out *The Musical Madhouse*, the first complete English translation of *Les Grotesques de la musique*, in 2003. An edition in paperback appeared in 2005. He is treasurer of the London-based Berlioz Society, a regular contributor to the *Berlioz Society Bulletin*, and a frequent lecturer on aspects of Berlioz's life and work. Aberdare is a management consultant in London specializing in helping businesses to contribute positively to their communities.

JEAN-PIERRE BARTOLI is author of *L'Harmonie classique et romantique, éléments et évolution* (2001) and coeditor (with Pierre Citron, Cécile Reynaud, and Peter Bloom) of the *Dictionnaire Berlioz* (2003). Author of articles on orientalism and exoticism in French music and on the evolution of the musical language of the classic and romantic periods, he is a founding editor of the journal *Analyse musicale* (now *Musurgia*). Bartoli is Professor of Music and Musicology, and vice-president for research, at l'Université Paris-Sorbonne (Paris IV).

JACQUES BARZUN, author of the *Berlioz and the Romantic Century* (1950; 1956; 1969) and of countless seminal papers on Berlioz, was associated with Columbia University from 1923 to 1975 as student, professor, dean, and provost. Excerpts from his writings—which include nearly fifty books, editions, and translations, on subjects ranging from history, language, and literature, to the academy, sport, and crime—appeared in *A Jacques Barzun Reader*, edited by Michael Murray, in 2002. In 2003, for unmatched contributions to intellectual life in the United States of America, Barzun was presented with the nation's highest civilian award, the Presidential Medal of Freedom.

PETER BLOOM is editor of volumes 7 and 24 of the *New Berlioz Edition* and of three previous collections of essays on Berlioz: *Berlioz Studies* (1992); *The Cambridge Companion to Berlioz* (2000); and *Berlioz: Past, Present, Future* (2003). His *Life of Berlioz* appeared from Cambridge University Press in 1998. Bloom is Grace Jarcho Ross 1933 Professor of Humanities at Smith College, in Northampton, Massachusetts.

GUNTHER BRAAM is editor of *The Portraits of Hector Berlioz* (volume 26 of the *New Berlioz Edition*) and of the first fully annotated German translation of the *Mémoires* (2007). He is coeditor, with Arnold Jacobshagen, of *Hector Berlioz in Deutschland: Texte und Dokumente zur deutschen Berlioz-Rezeption (1829–1843)* (2002). Braam is Professor of Mathematics and Physics at the Pestalozzi-Gymnasium, in Munich.

DAVID CAIRNS, independent scholar and former music critic for the *Spectator*, the *Financial Times*, the *New Statesman*, and the *Sunday Times*, is the distinguished English translator of Berlioz's *Mémoires* and author of the definitive biography of Berlioz: *The Making of an Artist* (1989, 1999) and *Servitude and Greatness* (1999). His latest book, *Mozart and His Operas*, appeared from Allen Lane and the University of California Press in 2006. In 1997 Cairns was appointed Commander of the Most Excellent Order of the British Empire (CBE).

GÉRARD CONDÉ is a composer of chamber music, songs, and operas, including *Les Orages désirés* (on Berlioz's childhood) and *La Chouette enrhumée* (a comic opera for children). He has edited writings by Weber, Gounod, Massenet, and, under the title *Cauchemars et Passions*, a collection of Berlioz's criticism. Condé, a regular contributor to *Le Monde* and *L'Avant-Scène Opéra*, is currently at work on a biography of Charles Gounod that will include a newly numbered and exhaustive list of the complete works.

PEPIJN VAN DOESBURG is a freelance writer on music and a frequent contributor to hberlioz.com. In 2006 his annotated Dutch translation of *Les Soirées de l'orchestre* appeared from Atlas, in Amsterdam, as *Avonden met het orkest*. Van Doesburg is flutist with the Noord Nederlands Orkest, in Groningen, The Netherlands.

JOËL-MARIE FAUQUET is author of, among other books, *César Franck* (1999) and (with Antoine Hennion) *La Grandeur de Bach: L'amour de la musique en France au XIXe siècle* (2000). He directed, edited, and contributed prodigiously to Fayard's *Dictionnaire de la musique en France au XIXe siècle* (2003). Fauquet, who prepared a critical edition of Berlioz's *De l'Instrumentation* (1994) and edited volume 22a of the *New Berlioz Edition* (2005), is Directeur de recherche en musicologie et en histoire sociale de la musique at the Institut de recherche sur le patrimoine musical en France (IRPMF), a division of the Centre national de la recherche scientifique (CNRS), in Paris.

FRANK HEIDLBERGER is author of, among other books, *Carl Maria von Weber und Hector Berlioz: Studien zur französischen Weber-Rezeption* (1994), and editor of *Les Troyens à Carthage: Dossier de presse parisienne* (1995) and of *Hector Berlioz: Schriften—Bekenntnisse eines musikalischen Enthusiasten* (2002). He is a member of the editorial teams preparing new critical editions of the complete works of Weber and Meyerbeer. Heidlberger, editor and annotator of Dagmar Kreher's new German translation of the *Mémoires* (2007), is Professor of Music Theory in the College of Music at the University of North Texas, in Denton, Texas.

HUGH MACDONALD is general editor of the *New Berlioz Edition*, publication of which was completed in 2006. He is author of *Berlioz Orchestral Music* (1969), *Skryabin* (1978), and the Master Musicians *Berlioz* (1982; 1991), and coeditor of volumes V–VIII of Berlioz's *Correspondance générale*. Macdonald, currently at work on a thematic catalogue of the works of Georges Bizet, is Avis H. Blewett Professor of Music at Washington University in St. Louis, Missouri.

JULIAN RUSHTON is author of *The Musical Language of Berlioz* (1983), the Cambridge Music Handbook *Berlioz: Roméo et Juliette* (1994), *The Music of Berlioz* (2001), and the Master Musicians *Mozart* (2006). He is editor of volumes 5, 8, and 12a of the *New Berlioz Edition* and coeditor of *The Cambridge Companion to Elgar* (2004) and of *Elgar Studies* (2007). Rushton, chairman of *Musica Britannica*, is Emeritus Professor of Music at the University of Leeds.

Index

Eastman Studies in Music

These twelve essays bring new breadth and depth to our knowledge of the life and work of the composer of the *Symphonie fantastique*. Hector Berlioz, his career and impact, has been the subject of much of the scholarly achievement of the international panel of contributors assembled here, among them Jacques Barzun, David Cairns, Joël-Marie Fauquet, Hugh Macdonald, and Julian Rushton.

Berlioz: Scenes from the Life and Work demonstrates the continuing fecundity of Berlioz scholarship in the first decade of the twenty-first century. It has profited from the recent completion of long-needed critical editions of Berlioz's music and letters, and from the results of the world-wide celebrations, in and around 2003, of the two-hundredth anniversary of the composer's birth.

Presented in six contrasting and complementary "pairs," the essays treat such matters as Berlioz's "aesthetics" and what it means to write about the meaning of his music; the political implications of his fiction and the affinities of his projects as composer and as critic; what the Germans thought of his work before his travels in Germany and what the English made of him when he visited their capital city. We learn in explicit detail how Berlioz deployed the mezzo-soprano voice, what he seems to have written immediately after encountering Shakespeare's *Romeo and Juliet* (a surprise), and where he benefited from Beethoven in what later became *Roméo et Juliette*.

The volume closes with two reflective essays on Berlioz's literary masterpiece, the *Mémoires*.

"These dozen pieces of vibrant scholarship and analysis, from familiar voices and new ones, splendidly kick off Berlioz's third century. Berlioz here receives his 'due place' (to borrow Jacques Barzun's phrase) as the focus of serious thought and passionate response about topics as varied as the origins of *Roméo et Juliette* and reactions to Berlioz's music during his concert tours of Germany and England."

—D. Kern Holoman, author of *Berlioz* and of *The Société des Concerts du Conservatoire, 1828–1967*

"This volume is entertainingly and expertly written by leading scholars. It sums up recent thinking about Hector Berlioz and his world, and it points the way for future work. Indispensable for those who love Berlioz's music."

—Thomas Forrest Kelly, author of *First Nights: Five Musical Premieres* and of *First Nights at the Opera*

"For all lovers of Berlioz, a splendid book from the leading experts on his life and music: detailed analysis of the music, large scraps of small histories, and an essay from Jacques Barzun on the possibility of the meaning of music."

—Sir Colin Davis